KINDERSZENEN

JAROSŁAW MAREK RYMKIEWICZ

KINDERSZENEN

Translated from the Polish by
CHARLES S. KRASZEWSKI

Introduction by
ART GRABOV

SL/NT
BOOKS

KINDERSZENEN

Translation copyright © 2023 Slant Books. Jarosław Marek Rymkiewicz's Polish text copyright © 2023 Evviva L'arte Foundation. All rights reserved. Except for brief quotations in critical publications or reviews, no part of this book may be reproduced in any manner without prior written permission from the publisher. Write: Permissions, Slant Books P.O. Box 60295, Seattle, WA 98160.

 This book has been published with the support of the ©POLAND Translation Program.

Slant Books
P.O. Box 60295
Seattle, WA 98160

www.slantbooks.org

Cataloguing-in-Publication data:
Names: Rymkiewicz, Jarosław Marek.
Title: Kinderszenen / Jarosław Marek Rymkiewicz.
Description: Seattle, WA: Slant Books, 2023
Identifiers: ISBN 978-1-63982-150-1 (hardcover) | ISBN 978-1-63982-152-5 (paperback) | ISBN 978-1-63982-151-8 (ebook)
Subjects: LCSH: Warsaw (Poland)--History--Uprising, 1944--Personal narratives, Polish | Warsaw (Poland)--History--Uprising, 1944 | World War, 1939-1945--Children--Poland | World War, 1939-1945--Personal narratives, Polish

Contents

Introduction: In Search of a Lost Child | vii
—Art Grabov

From the Author | xvii

My Identity Card | 1

Cats in Gnojno | 10

The Number of Tigers: The Uprising as Methodological Problem | 16

Meine Herren, Wir Sind Keine Mörder | 25

The Hole | 33

The Curtain on Krakowskie Przedmieście: The Uprising as Aesthetic Object | 39

My Notebook | 48

Poland In Europe: If Not by Force, Then by Kindness | 55

Inside the Trap | 62

Life as Russian Roulette | 68

War Head | 72

Adolf Dygasiński and His *Hare* | 79

The Last Skater in the Swiss Valley | 86

The Ammunition Carrier Enters Kiliński St. | 93

The Sense of Murder | 101

The Entrance of the Turtles | 110

What Happened on Wąski Dunaj? | 117

The Life and Death of Ivan Vashenko | 125

The Little Prop-Job Betwen Gołków and Piaseczno | 132

Explosion | 138

The Uprising as an Eruption of Insanity | 144

Crayfish on the Corner of Koszykowa and Śniadecki | 151

Massacre à la Greim | 158

Turkish Romance | 168

The Causes of the Explosion | 176

The Death of the Turtle | 182

Glossary | 189

Introduction
In Search of a Lost Child

Art Grabov

AT FIRST GLANCE, this book presents us with a portrait of the author's childhood. However, it is not a mere record of facts, such as one might use to compose a family album complete with photographs, nor is it a coming-of-age story drawn from emotional memories. It is, without question, the artist's autobiography—the autobiography of an original poet and creator of an exceptional genre of prose, one that unites the historical essay with allegorical parable and drama, at once formally innovative and rooted in tradition. All the same, the artist presents himself to the reader in his immaturity: the child, the protagonist of this narrative, is at first simply a child—and therefore, each one of us.

With time we lose sight of our shared humanity, as it gets obscured by our particular role in society, our mask, which we assume so as to play our own part in the interpersonal drama of life. But as that life draws to a close, as we slowly begin to make our exit from the stage, we begin to feel both the desire for and the capacity to return to our beginnings. In that moment, we rediscover ourselves in a narrative as if we were an "other"—and that other, a fuller person. If we were to agree with this conviction, it would be necessary for us to acknowledge (along with the Romantics, the works of whom Professor Rymkiewicz especially concerned himself) that every person is born an artist. In his case, a writer who lives through various phases of his development: a poet in childhood, a narrator in adolescence, a dramatist in maturity, and finally, a chronicler in his old age. Our personhood contains within itself the embryo of our human essence, our identity fulfilled, which is *homo creator*—both created and creative.

Rymkiewicz studies the manner in which human beings—created in the image and likeness of the creator—are shaped by history, or, in other words, the circumstances generated by our forebears and neighbors, in order to become the forebears of our descendants—the creators of a world for other people. The narrative of the artist's childhood, set against the background of a significant political and historical event, thus becomes, in the eyes of his reader, a statement on the theme of civilization. In this case, it is a civilization of ever-expanding rings: Polish, European, Western, and finally, human.

When the German army entered the city of Warsaw in September of 1939, the author of this book was four years old. He was fated, as a little child, to grow up in a totalitarian state, which treated the local population as slaves, reduced to the level of tools to serve other people, acting as proof of the racial superiority of those "other" people over all the peoples of the earth. Then, in August 1944, when an armed uprising broke out in Warsaw on behalf of that trampled human dignity, he was to look upon it all through the eyes of a nine-year-old boy. And at last, when the Germans were driven out of the Polish capital by the Red Army, the boy suddenly found himself in another totalitarian state—this time one governed by an occupier who subjected the local populace to servitude for another forty-five years, transforming once again the human community into a labor camp of slaves and subjects of unconditional ideological indoctrination.

The story of these events is, therefore, the story of a man formed by history in the poetic phase of his own adolescence and who, like it or not, was to shape the environment in which his own children would mature. At the same time, it is the autobiography of a writer—poet, essayist, dramatist, literary scholar—something we ought to read as a chronicle, an epic, and finally, a drama—both a tragedy and a morality play. In other words, to read it as both lesson and warning.

Introduction

The central figure of this book is, of course, its author—the one who writes of himself as he remembers himself most intimately, or who creates, as narrator, using the material of remembered events, images, and emotions. But the book has other heroes as well—perhaps not protagonists of the drama, but certainly central figures. They include beasts (or subhumans) and Germans (or Übermenschen). In the middle of them all, we find the Child—that original and essential human—Everyman, for whose soul the body and the mind are locked in a struggle. Somewhere in the background, we see the Mother—that caretaker so full of graces. God, however, is absent from this morality play, for his competencies have been taken over by History, which here represents the creator hidden in his work. In this autobiographical story, with its descriptions of small, individual episodes, Rymkiewicz follows the process of transformation of the Child-Soul—and so each of us—into the Narrative Mind.

The stage is set in Warsaw during wartime, but could it not just as well have been set in the salons of the Parisian bourgeoisie a long while before the war in question erupted in Europe? After the manner of Marcel Proust, that French master of prose both intimate and "meta," it seems as if the Polish writer were using his chronicle-like memoir to suggest that we live in a world made up of the worlds we create by narrating them to ourselves, composing these narratives from the tatters of our memories. Proust taught us that each of us is his own novel. Rymkiewicz adds to this that each of us is also the author of novels for others. Both writers analyze their own emotions in detail, as if they gripped them with the delicate pincers of the senses and, through precise language, relished their meaning, in the belief that, in this way, they would be capable of noting down the ciphertext of reality.

But whereas Proust brings his long narrative to its end with the death of the author (who expires in exemplary fashion, bent over his final sentence), Rymkiewicz composes the recorded episodes not only for his own satisfaction but also with the intention of leaving behind a witness to history. The former author is innocent, eagerly lurking for the reader's delight; the latter narrator consciously undertakes

Introduction

the risk of readers' approbation or condemnation, or even more: he assumes the risk of acting as the reader's guide through the city. We are not responsible for what will occur to us, but we must assume responsibility for how we speak of it to those for whom the story will become myth, epic, tragedy. For the author not only reminisces and describes, but he also has the courage to analyze and come to conclusions—delivering verdicts. His book records, researches, and evaluates. Even more—it lays blame.

Jarosław Marek Rymkiewicz was born on 13 July 1935, the son of a Polish writer of German extraction, the author of many (rather weak) historical novels. His mother, on the other hand, who was descended from a German aristocratic family, was a physician. Rymkiewicz liked to say of himself: "I don't have a drop of Polish blood in my veins, not a single fragment of a Polish gene in my cells. Polishness is neither biological nor genetic. It is not a matter of blood, nor even—as can be seen in my case—is it a matter of descent. Polishness is a fierce spiritual force which we do not choose, for we cannot choose anything—it chooses us."

Poland—Polish culture, the Polish spirit, the Polish state, that land wretched at the time and enslaved—most clearly seduced those two Germans. During the German occupation, Jarosław's parents could easily have become so-called Volksdeutch; that is, as people of German descent and most likely speaking German, they might have accepted the citizenship of the Third Reich. Yet this they did not do. Polishness, identification with the victims, turned out to be more attractive to them than Germanness, identification with the "superhuman" conquerors. After the war, the young alumnus of the University of Warsaw, a promising young literary scholar, joined the Communist Party, of which he was to remain an active member until the 1970s. However, with time, the poet and essayist began to understand that his youthful idealism had found for itself an improper form of realization.

From the early 1980s, and so, from the rise of Solidarity—that mass movement of opposition to the Communist régime and Russian dominance in Poland—he found himself drawn to the milieu of the

Introduction

dissident intelligentsia in opposition to the Communist government. In the 1990s, when the group of Solidarity dissidents became polarized into two camps—into the patriotic-conservative group and that of the progressives, whose loyalty was directed towards the European Left—Rymkiewicz unequivocally associated himself with the former. Without interrupting his career as an author and literary historian, he began to be an active publicist, winning for himself both devoted enthusiasts and fierce enemies. At the beginning of the new millennium, he was universally acknowledged as an authority who often shocked others with his Nietzschean attitude towards social problems, remaining one of the brightest stars of the Polish literary firmament until his death in 2022.

As a literary scholar and professor of the Polish Academy of Arts and Sciences (PAN), Rymkiewicz created an original form of historical-fictive narration, of which he made use when writing about the most renowned Polish writers of the Romantic period: Adam Mickiewicz, Juliusz Słowacki, and Aleksander Fredro. It might be said that he was a scholar who had the courage to humanize his métier through creative writing. In his books—based upon scrupulously thorough archival research—the author narrates the biographies of the poets with an unusual fluidity, with an eloquence that reminds the reader of the characteristic style of seventeenth-century authors, who manifested their own, local originality against the background of the trends of European prose. His essays, composed around the biographies of the poets most important for the formation of Polish spirituality, are supplemented by a series of books devoted to the key moments of Polish political history, chiefly from the turn of the eighteenth century. At this time, the Polish-Lithuanian state, known as the Republic of Both Nations, was the largest political territory in Europe. Furthermore, it was an exemplary democracy with Europe's largest number of enfranchised citizens. At the time when France was conquered by its Revolution, the Polish state was literally cut into pieces by its neighbors, with the silent approbation of all of contemporary Europe under the direction of the tolerant minds of the Enlightenment philosophers.

Introduction

To take just one example: in the bold and provocatively composed essay entitled "Wieszanie" [Hanging],[1] the author describes the events related to the first Polish uprising against the authoritative Russian Empire, the uprising led by Tadeusz Kościuszko (later a hero of the American Revolution). Composed of unusually suggestive scenes, the panorama of Warsaw riven by street demonstrations and the tussles of its citizens with the invading army, this book reminds one more of a reportage written by a contemporary war reporter. This narrative, basically a historical text, is interwoven with images of Warsaw from the beginning of the third millennium as well as grotesque scenes seemingly taken from an eighteenth-century Gothic novel. In his description of the ostensibly marginal events taking place in a Central European city, the author speaks of the essence of Europe, of Western civilization, of modern man entangled in the quarrel of mind and heart. At the same time, he creates a reliable historical document, a convincing report of political events, an adventure novel, and a philosophical parable.

When, on the other hand, his interest wanders into the twentieth century, in such books as *Umschlagplatz*[2] (on the liquidation of the Warsaw Ghetto by the Germans), or indeed *Kinderszenen*, the author was to create a literary form which is thoroughly original, uniting a Baroque-style monologue with a philosophical narrative similar to Enlightenment writing, as well as a contemporary Bildungsroman, and so: a work that makes use of forms simultaneously traditional and innovative, typically Polish and deeply European. Similar generic and stylistic hybrids may be found in Rymkiewicz's poetry and dramatic writing. His poems have the resonance of contemporary stylizations of Baroque or Romantic verse, while his dramas are indebted to Calderon, Shakespeare, or Molière. In a word: products of the mind of an erudite and sensitive poet.

Let us return, however, to the story of the child amidst the flames, of the person maturing to manhood in inhuman times. The central

1. For an English version: J.M. Rymkiewicz, *The Hangings*, trans. Mateusz Julecki (Point Pleasant, NJ: Hussar Publishing, 2022).

2. Translated into English as *The Final Station* by Nina Taylor (New York: Farrar, Straus and Giroux, 1994).

Introduction

motive of this composition, divided into short fragments, is a seemingly insignificant episode from the Warsaw Uprising: the explosion of a booby-trapped tank in a crowd of curious citizens gathered around it. In order to understand the sense of this event, we must first remind ourselves of a few facts. Between August and October 1944, units of the Polish Home Army [Armia Krajowa—AK], the most numerous underground military formation in the history of world conflict, was doing battle with the army of the German occupier, which latter army was supported by units from Lithuania, Latvia, and Ukraine. The numerical advantage enjoyed by the Germans was gigantic. And yet the poorly-equipped Polish insurgents bravely held their ground against tanks and air power. Meanwhile, halted on the far shore of the Wisła [Vistula], which river flows through the center of Warsaw, the Soviet Army was content to look upon the slaughter from afar as the Polish forces were being bled to death. Their only reason for wishing to do so was to have the glory of taking back their city by themselves, establishing themselves as the government of their own nation. Hence the reason for the Russian prudence and hesitation. The uprising was quashed, at last, after two months of battling street by street. The Polish insurgents were recognized as regular soldiers and transported to P.O.W. camps; the civilians were herded out of the city, the great majority of whom were also imprisoned in camps. Two hundred thousand Poles had lost their lives. The Germans then flattened the buildings in the city, leaving Warsaw in utter ruin. Four months later, the Red Army entered the city, along with the units of the Communist Polish Army they had formed and who were to assume the government of Poland following the war.

On 14 August 1944—and so, two weeks after the Uprising broke out—the Germans abandoned a little tank in the general area of one of the insurgent barricades. The Varsovians took this event as something of a miraculous spoil of war granted them by fate. A group of Polish soldiers and a small crowd of civilians gathered around the tank. At a certain moment, the vehicle exploded, tearing several dozen people, literally, into shreds. Bloody body parts were hanging from area balconies and shattered windows. The child-hero of the narrative did not

Introduction

witness this event, but, after all, the hero of the account is each and every child, each child-soul of each person who remembers the thing they saw. Rymkiewicz will return to this episode several times in the course of his narrative. He returns to it obsessively, as if he were trying to dig down to the significant core of the scene. Thanks to these compositional returns—and so, on account of the formal structure of the piece—the event swells to the rank of a symbol. But this is not a symbol of the struggle, not a symbol of someone's victory or defeat, but rather, the symbol of pure and groundless cruelty. This is the cruelty of war per se, but—as the author suggests—of a war initiated not by the inhabitants of the Polish city but rather by the occupiers of that city. The child, who is as yet unable to differentiate good from evil, is contrasted here by the author with a German soldier, who has now lost that ability.

It is for this reason that the significance of the events that took place in Warsaw in the summer months of 1944 will be, for Rymkiewicz, universal injustice and even, as Hannah Arendt would say, the "banality of evil." Both sides had the same motivation to fight in this Uprising: vengeance. The Poles were taking revenge on the Germans for the years of terror, slavery, and life under ceaseless terror and the sense of degradation that they had experienced since 1939; the Germans were taking revenge upon the Poles because these "subhumans" had dared to raise their hand against the "supermen" and because these "primitive Slavs" hated the "cultured Aryans" more than they feared them. Rymkiewicz presents hatred as the source of the ineluctable degradation of humanity and as the only manner in which human dignity might be reacquired—simultaneously and reciprocally.

The author builds his story not only upon episodes but also upon concentric circles of space-time. There is the circle of the German occupation of Warsaw, lasting five years and more; there is the circle of the two months of battle carried out chiefly in the center of the city; there is the circle of people gathered around the little armored vehicle, the explosion of which caused the massacre. But there is also the circle of intimacy, the family circle of the small Polish boy, who, in the very eye of the history in which he is surrounded, has to set in order the experience of his childhood in order to become an adult—a writer, a Pole, a European—himself amongst his brethren.

At this earliest stage of his formational journey through life, the little boy is made to experience, above all, the suffering of victims and the cruelty of their tormentors. This takes on different aspects, not only killing—the killing of people by people, the killing of animals by people—but also cruelties that arise in seemingly ordinary phenomena, glanced at through the window every day, even in times of peace: phenomena like crates full of living crayfish at a street market, or the impersonal instructions read in a newspaper of how to raise turtles. In the eyes of that boy, growing up in German-occupied Warsaw, all of this becomes a representation of death, as a matter of course. And yet, paradoxically, the childish imagination is imbued with images which, for adults, had to have been signs of life at the time, for one had to constantly fight for survival each and every day. The quotidian reality of war becomes apparent, therefore, as something inescapably unequivocal: in order to venture out onto the ice in a park skating rink, the boy is going to have to pass through a street roundup; in order to understand the suffering of his parents in the future, he will first have to witness the suffering of household cats.

If such a child simultaneously experiences the touch of a mother's hand and the touch of the eyes of a Gestapo agent or gendarme trained upon him, he will inexorably associate these two touches in one experience, and he will never again be able to separate them. The lessons that this child will derive from his memories—for it is only in this way and in no other that we learn how to live—will be a conviction of the immanent contamination of human nature by the inclination to cause suffering to others. When the boy matures, he will write books or legislate laws, he will become a physician or an instructor. The world he builds for his children will be a world evoked from scenes remembered from his own childhood.

Jarosław Marek Rymkiewicz has written a sad, bitter book, a book that, perhaps, will be difficult to accept for many contemporary readers. But he wrote it as a warning.

From the Author

THE TITLE OF MY BOOK is taken from the splendid cycle of miniatures for the piano by Robert Schumann, the title of which is *Kinderszenen*. Schumann composed his cycle in Leipzig, in the year 1838, at which time he was twenty-eight years old. Schumann's *Kinderszenen* are known, in all probability, even to those who haven't the slightest idea that anyone by the name of Robert Schumann ever existed, who have never heard of German Romanticism or of Clara Wieck. At the very least, they recognize the seventh miniature in the cycle, the wonderful *Dreaming* or *Träumerei*, one of the most famous (and certainly sweetest) works of European music. Whoever hears it once will never forget it, even if he'll never come to like that German sweetness, if it seems to him somewhat sweetly suspicious. Schumann's idea—the musical portraiture of the dreams and events that take place in a child's room—was taken up by numerous later European composers, chief among whom are Piotr Tchaikovsky and Claude Debussy. The cycle of this last-named artist, composed in 1908 and nearly as famous as Schumann's own, was entitled by its author *Children's Corner*. My *Children's Corner* (which is just as good a title for me because even though the war was going on, I lived in just such a corner) or my *Kinderszenen*, are, of course, somewhat different from the works of these great composers. The difference may be found, above all, in the degree of sweetness. According to the dictates of destiny, the *Träumereien* dreamed by a Polish boy in his childhood corner in the forties of the last century were full of blood and terror.

From the Author

This story of mine (like all my stories) is vestigial. It is made up of pieces, fragments, shards, such as are scattered by the force of an explosion. If this narrative has a theme and some sort of hero, that hero is most certainly not the boy that I was then, and the theme is not constructed of his wartime experiences. I will be grateful to my readers for kindly keeping that in mind. The theme and hero of this narrative is, perhaps, the fate that set me (like all of my Polish peers of the same age) at the very edge of life and death but decided that I should survive. Those others, the ones who did not survive, were lain—as the novelist Hanna Malewska relates it—in pieces at the foot of the wall along Kiliński St. Why it turned out like this, who knows? But that's what fate is like—nobody knows what it is or what it does with us. I was a child at the time—seven, eight, nine years old—and understood precious little of what was going on. Even now, I reckon, after the passage of nearly seventy years, I don't understand much more of it.

According to universal custom, I enclose all *noms de guerre* in quotation marks (Captain "Ognisty," Major "Okoń"), which is something I'm not very fond of, because the inverted commas get in the reader's way. And yet it seems the proper thing to do, as it facilitates the differentiation of pseudonym from a person's actual last name. I do make one exception to this general rule, however—also in accord with almost universal usage. I do not write the commander-in-chief's name "Bór" Komorowski, but rather Bór Komorowski.

All citations from the *Journal* and speeches of Hans Frank are given in the translation of their Polish publisher, Stanisław Piotrowski, following the second edition of the *Journal* (1957).

At my request, my publisher has agreed to set all citations from foreign languages (there are only a few, or a few dozen such, in German) in the same typeface as the rest of the book. Usually, in such cases, they're formatted in italics. This is a petty matter, but it was important to me that it be done like this, as it has a connection of sorts with the character of my wartime experiences. These experiences constitute a sort of whole, and the individual elements thereof that might be called "German" were for me, at the time, something obvious and not in the slightest way different from the rest.

In the case of my earlier books, I encouraged the reader to begin reading wherever he or she pleased—from the beginning or the end or from somewhere in between. As for this book, please: read it in order, from start to finish. In that way, the sense of the story will become more readily apparent.

MY IDENTITY CARD

MY OLD, GREEN, PRL[1] identity card (a booklet rather, with a stiff green cover) is forty-one years old, yet it's still in good shape, not bad at all. Some of the rubber stamps have faded somewhat, but the entries are fairly legible if I use a magnifying glass. The PRL, surprisingly, produced decent, long-lasting ink. Perhaps this was in accordance with the demands of the State Security officers and the requirements of the snitches they handled, whose stoolie reports needed to be clear, legible, permanent, and unsmudged. The Militia precinct in my neighborhood Warszawa-Żoliborz produced my ID booklet on 12 May 1967. The photo glued onto the front page shows a young person (one might even go out on a limb somewhat and call him a youngster) wearing a checkered vest and a tweed blazer. The youngster is sporting a buzz cut. As I remember it, the blazer was gray with a little blue in it. The vest had a small, checkered pattern of green and blue with some red to it as well. In the space for "registration of Residence," the first entry informs us that this youngster had been registered as "perm. resd't. 26 V 1966" in Warsaw at 3 Żeromski St., Apt. 21. That was a sad block of flats constructed of concrete slabs and situated on the border of Żoliborz and Bielany. Our flat, which was on the highest floor, was a studio apartment a few dozen meters square with a little kitchen. It was our first Warsaw apartment of our own. From the annotations and rubber stamp, of course, it's clear that this was not my first ID. There had been an earlier one,

---

[1]. PRL: Polska Rzeczpospolita Ludowa ("Polish People's Republic") was the official name of the Polish state following World War II and lasting until 1989, when the country was ruled by the Communist Party, at the behest of Moscow.

produced by the militia in Łódź, which I'd either handed in during some general exchange of IDs (if there had ever been such a thing) or simply lost somewhere. I might also have torn it up and swallowed the pieces. I had such unpleasant destructive tendencies at the time. Much more interesting than that first militia annotation from Żoliborz is the next one. It informs us that on "23.IX.1969," I was registered as a permanent resident at 1 Kiliński St., Apt. 4. And lower down, in the space for "Deregistration," there is another note supplementing that information. On "8 Nov. 1973," some militia lady deregistered me "from perm. res." at 1 Kiliński St. And then, on the subsequent pages, there are various other rubber stamps and entries, the majority of which are most likely interesting to no one but me. On page 9, in the rubric "Annotations of Employment," there are three little seals, all of them stamped there by secretaries of the Personnel Department of the Institute of Literary Research (IBL). The first of these declares that I had been accepted into employment there on "1.XI.65." The second adds that I had been let go on "31.10.85," while the third testifies that I'd been taken back on "1.V.89." And then, on the last four pages, there are big seals and little ones, none of them interesting. The great, red seal that takes up the entirety of p. 11 informs one and all that I possess the right to cross the "border of the PRL" and take myself off "to the People's Republic of Bulgaria," and a few other such geographical inventions of Russian Communism. Two pages later, the little seal of the Institute of Literary Research says that on "1.03.82," I had been presented with "two provision inserts," which is a bit unclear to me, not only grammatically speaking, but also because I don't recall what those sort of inserts were for. Maybe they had something to do with meat or sugar rations and proved that the bearer was entitled to ration cards? But all of that, inserts for meat and eventually sugar, stamps testifying to hard currency bank accounts, the IBL stamps, the People's Republic of Bulgaria, or even the whole PRL with all its militia officers, Security Police agents, secret informers and the excellent inks produced for their convenience—all of this is completely useless now, having no sort of meaning, deprived of even the smallest scintilla of sense, having been

MY IDENTITY CARD

effectively and radically invalidated, introduced to a state of non-existence, reset and annulled, ever since the lady who works at the Borough Office in Milanówek handed over to me a pink plastic card as proof of my being a citizen of the Republic, meanwhile stamping on each page of the PRL ID booklet a large, rectangular seal with just such a radical legend: "annulled." O how pleasant that was. But something that is still valid and shall ever remain so—to the end of one's life—cannot be annulled. For example, those two violet stamps that say that for four years, and even four years and a bit, Ewa and I lived at 1 Kiliński St. And now it seems to me that those two stamps, those four years and some, have changed—in some hidden, secret, silent, invisible manner, so that I knew nothing about it, never even suspected it at the time—my entire life, secretly, hush-hush, without letting me in on it, changing me entirely—forever. Although when those seals were stamped into my PRL ID booklet, I had no idea what they meant, what's hiding beneath them, and what they will mean for me—when a few years later, their hidden meaning will suddenly reveal itself to me, and it penetrates my consciousness, what it means—to live in Warsaw at 1 Kiliński St. What sort of content those words have, what sort of chasm yawns beneath this phrase. But of course, it wasn't like I didn't know, back in September 1969, where it was we were moving to. In that block of flats on Żeromski St., there at the border of Żoliborz and Bielany, it wasn't hard or unpleasant to live on account of the fact that it was unbearably sunlit up there on the highest floor, or that our whole flat measured some fifteen or seventeen meters square. The unpleasantness of that building lay in the fact that it was placed beyond history, was excerpted from history; as a matter of fact, it belonged to no history whatsoever. Should anyone stubbornly insist on setting it in some sort of history, that could only be the history of the PRL—which itself contained a fair admixture of fiction, played out fictively, and was filled with fictional events, which that fictional political creation invented in its own mind—no less fictional—for its own benefit. The entire PRL, with all its apparatus and its entire population (as I thought at the time—today I see things somewhat differently) lay somewhere beyond the history of

Poland, being something excerpted therefrom and belonging somewhere else—some historically empty fragment, a shard of the vacuum, which someday will collapse into its own nothingness to disappear, just as if it had never been. It was a pause in the history of Poland—managed by its Russian occupiers. Or a hole in that history, a hole torn there and overseen by collaborators, that is to say, those who betrayed that history. But, as I say, these days, I have some rather different thoughts in my head about all that. In any event, from the perspective of that fictional block of flats on Żeromski St., its history, its important events, its real fragments, lay somewhere else, farther afield, on Plac Wilsona [Wilson Square][2], in the Bielany Forest, in the neighborhood of the Citadel. Moving into Stare Miasto—the Old Town—I was also (as I sensed at the time) moving into history. I also knew, though not with total clarity, that something had happened there, in that building on Kiliński into which we were to live, and that it had been something terrible. Anyway, this is why the Old Town is so pleasant, so nice to live in. From age on age, so many horrible things have taken place there (hangings, beheadings, killings, and so forth) that strolling over the Rynek [Market Square] or between the two Dunajs [Danube Streets], one is strolling among all these atrocities, kind of taking part in them and kind of not. It is this partial participation (which avoids the worst consequences) which is pleasant. But at the time, all that, all those Old Town atrocities, didn't interest me all that much, as I was translating Calderon's *Life Is a Dream* and thinking whether, once I'd got done with that work—and I was just about to finish it—I should set myself to the translation of St. John of the Cross's *Dark Night of the Soul*. Was the *Dark Night* something that I'd be able to recreate in Polish? That is the great question of my life. At the time, the following options were before me: either St. John of the Cross and his *Dark Night* or Góngora and his sonnets. Now, as far as the Warsaw Uprising was concerned, much more than

---

2. We use Polish place names throughout the book. In the first instance of introducing a name, the English equivalent is given in brackets, thereafter not. There are a few exceptions to this: "Old Town" is one, to preserve a better flow to the English narrative. Streets and locations named for persons—such as Kiliński and Żeromski Sts.—are not translated.

all the various horrible things that had played out in the Old Town and its environs, I was interested in something that touched upon my life more directly, to wit: what had happened in Śródmieście [Central City], near the building in which I lived throughout the entire war—that is, near the corner of Marszałkowska and Koszykowa, not far from the Hala na Koszykach [Koszyka Market] on Pius St., near the Plac Zbawiciela [Savior's Square]. What I wanted to find out (and this I still don't know) was whether the apartment building on Koszykowa, nr. 38, the second one past the corner of Marszałkowska, had been bombed by the Germans during the Uprising, or if it had been destroyed by them after the Uprising. Now, if I had known then what I know now, if we really had known it back then, or if Ewa had known—would we have looked for somewhere else to live, deciding not to move into the place on Kiliński St.? That doesn't seem very probable. The apartment on Kiliński that was allotted to us (this was an apartment in an ownership-cooperative, and we paid no small sum for it, but that's the way it was expressed in the jargon of the day—We're allotting you, Citizen, a flat; You've received, Citizen, a flat) and so that apartment on Kiliński St. was, for many reasons, unusually attractive. First of all, because of its beauty and its convenient location—it was close to everything. Ewa could make her way to the National Theatre on foot. Same with me: on my way to the Staszic Palace, I'd have a nice stroll down Krakowskie Przedmieście [Kraków Suburbs Boulevard]. The building in which it was located had just been finished. Set between other buildings reconstructed after the war—in other words, buildings just twenty years old or so—it was, for those times, splendidly built. It was constructed of brick, which was a great rarity at the time, for almost everything was made of huge concrete slabs. Our flat, on the first floor, was, although not large, very pleasant and pleasantly situated. In the center of our largest room (we had two rooms there and a blind kitchen) stood a large column—one of the building supports. It looked a little as if the building, squeezed in between two other structures, one from the Podwale [Embankment St.] side and the other from Miodowa [Honey St.], sort of plastered onto them, was a kind of bridge hung on that pier. Well, as a matter of fact, it was a bridge in my life—I passed over it on my way to something else, which at the time did not exist in my life. Should I go for pathos here and speak of this exactly as I feel? All right, then. But I won't write out the phrase. You can make your own conjectures. We considered the column in the middle of the room something droll because there was something playful and funny about it—living with such a rotund column in the middle of the room was like living in some sort of little palace. Back then, it was droll, really, and only now do I understand (that is, back then, I didn't give it a thought; I didn't probe it) the destiny and significance of our palace column. The building was hung like a bridge on that support pier, doubtlessly because they didn't want to set the foundations too deep. And why was it that they gave up on deep foundations? Because (in 1969) they didn't want to dig too deeply. And why was it that they didn't want to dig too deeply? Good question. Let me tell you. They didn't want to find out what was lying there—deeper. Right beneath our windows, there was a place on the ground floor of the building which was shortly to come in quite handy for us. This too, after all, was a testimony to the quality of the building because, back then, they generally put up buildings economically, modestly, you might even say skin-flintedly, and such spaces as I'm speaking of here were rather not included in newly-built apartment blocks. It was a little storage space for bicycles and prams. You accessed the stairwell from the rear, the yard, or rather the passage along which, by turning right, you found yourself off Kiliński and Podwale, or by turning left, to the rear of the buildings along Miodowa. At the time, there was a music school located there—there probably still is—exactly to the rear of Miodowa, and when we'd open our windows in spring and summer, we'd hear the pupils practicing on violins, trombones, trumpets, and clarinets. Sometimes we'd also hear drums, which were quite appropriate to the location. You'd see the pupils go through the yard: beautiful little girls and jolly boys carrying their instruments in their black cases. All of this was very pleasant indeed. Now, whoever decides to take up residence in a large city (it doesn't matter what city, in what country, what part of the world) must resign himself to the fact that

MY IDENTITY CARD

he'll be living in a place that's kind of a cemetery. He'll be walking about a cemetery, driving over a cemetery, sleeping in a cemetery. I'm not speaking metaphorically here. In every major city, under the ground, under the streets and pavements, under the supermarkets and the churches, under the buildings and under the basements, there are—literally—anything but metaphorical ruins, cinders, ash, skulls, and bones. Whoever walks about a great city, lives in a great city, is an inhabitant of a city—has to stroll about over all of this. There's no other option. The death of houses, people, and animals are the foundation of the great city. Every great city is built on death. There is, however, a great difference between those two situations, and they are two situations which simply cannot be compared at all, which have absolutely nothing in common with one another: living in a great city built upon death, in close quarters with bones and skulls, is something completely different from living in Warsaw at 1 Kiliński St. Now, had I known that blood had been splashed upon the walls here to the height of the third floor, would I have been able to sit there in my little room translating Calderón? Would I have been able to drift off to sleep thinking about St. John of the Cross? So why were Ewa and I living there? I don't know. Perhaps it was so that those two lovely rooms with the blind kitchen, with the music of horns and clarinets just past our windows, might change our entire lives—secretly, not asking our opinion of the matter, not letting us in on it, keeping mum. On 11 August 1971 (so we'd been living there for nearly two years by then), we woke up earlier than usual, probably even before sunrise—at five, maybe even four o'clock. But it was high time. Sometime around six, we left the apartment and, turning onto Podwale, we ran—that is, I ran, Ewa walked on behind slowly—towards the Plac Zamkowy [Palace Square] because that's where you could grab a taxi. I remember that brilliantly beautiful early August morning very well indeed. Of course, it would be strange and a little inappropriate if I didn't remember it. There wasn't a cloud in the sky above our heads. If anything white was sailing there, it was very far away, on the other side of the Wisła [Vistula River], past the bridges, beyond Praga. The August light flowed down over the roofs, over the walls of the apartment blocks, over the crosses on the churches, over the statue of Kiliński. I was toting a large traveling bag in which we'd packed the things needed for a hospital stay—bathrobe, slippers, a little transistor radio of Lithuanian production, with which you could catch Radio Free Europe. Ewa was dressed in a bright celadon-colored dress that reached down to her ankles, with white sandals on her feet. I seem to remember her wearing sunglasses, for the glare bothered her eyes, but of that I'm not entirely certain. She was toting her large belly in front of her, which contained Wawrzek, who was to be born on that very day. There, where Podwale joins Senatorska and gives onto Plac Zamkowy, I hailed a cab and told the driver that we wanted to go to the hospital on Lindley. And it was exactly (or nearly exactly) on this spot where, two days later and twenty-seven years earlier, on 13 August 1944, two German Tiger Tanks pulled up from Krakowskie Przedmieście and, without driving up to Zygmunt's Column, turned left, toward the insurgents' barricade that cut off access to Podwale from the east. Behind them came another tank. Actually, it wasn't a tank at all, but that's what they called it at the time and sometimes still do. General Tadeusz Bór-Komorowski, who looked down upon it from the second floor of the former Ministry of Justice building (where the Headquarters of the AK [Home Army] were located at the time—moved there, in fact, on that very day, 13 August, from nearby Barokowa St.), recognized in it an armored ammunition carrier. That's what he wrote later, too, in his beautiful book *The Underground Army*. The building of the former Ministry of Justice, in other words, the Raczyński Palace (burnt during the uprising—today a replica stands in its place, which houses the Central Archives of Historical Records), was located on the corner of Kiliński and Długa [Long] Sts., not far from 1 Kiliński St., nearly opposite it, in fact, and Bór-Komorowski was looking on with the eye of a soldier, so it's doubtful that he would be mistaken. If that vehicle wasn't an ammunition carrier, it had to be something quite like one. So, let's accept the nomenclature used by the Commander in Chief to describe the tank trap. The General wanted to holler down for no one to approach that ammunition carrier, but it was too late because the window at which he was standing suddenly ceased to exist. Just like the wall in which the window had been set. I opened the taxi door and somehow got Ewa inside (which was no easy doing). Oh my God, I thought, how beautiful she is with that huge belly of hers in that long bright celadon-colored dress and white sandals. I don't deserve her. Not at all. She was more beautiful than that brilliantly beautiful August day, more beautiful than that white and blue August light above Podwale, above the Cathedral of St. John, above the Wisła.

CATS IN GNOJNO

WHEN DID IT HAPPEN, that history with the cats? Probably in the winter of 1939–40, because it was then that we spent the winter months at my grandmother's manor at Gnojno—which Grandma had renamed Świerczyn a few years before the war. That decision was taken on practical as well as aesthetic grounds. There were a few wooden houses standing in the little forest behind the manor house, and these were let out to summer vacationers from Warsaw. Grandma figured—surely with reason—that her summer guests would not be all that enamored with spending their holidays in a place called Gnojno or "Manureville." The original name, although unpleasant, turned out to be more enduring than its certainly more advantageous rival Świerczyn (from świerk, świerczyna: spruce, sprucewood) thought up by Grandma. I was a little child in the winter of 1939–40; I was four years and a few months old. Exactly the same age as Anielka, Wawrzek's daughter and my grandchild, is now at the midpoint of 2008. The cats in Gnojno constitute my first clear memory—the first whole recollection that more or less imprinted itself upon my childish brain. I reckon that the clarity and permanence of that memory has something to do with the fact that, due to my grandmother's cats, I came into contact with a certain existential phenomenon which up until then had been unknown to me. I came to understand the existence of death. If today, when I am nearly seventy-three years old, the existence of something like that still makes an impression on me, one can just imagine what an impression it made on me when I was four. Just try to explain it to someone who doesn't know, who has no idea that such a thing is even possible, and you'll see what an effect it has on him. I really have no other earlier memories from the pre-war years or the period of the so-called rajza, the September journey that led us to the bridge in Zaleszczyki and back—indeed to Grandma's Gnojno. I can only recall some individual images torn from some greater and unfamiliar whole, and not even whole images at that, but rather tatters of images, tiny pieces of them: the well in Gnojno, yellow balls flying this way and that over the tennis courts, a fragment of Nowogrodzka St. visible from my childhood room, a hand turning the crank of a Pathéphone in the salon along the Nowogrodzka side (in those days, records on the Pathéphone were set in motion by a crank) in order to play my favorite song entitled "The Bargemen"; a bomb flying diagonally past a hotel window (in Brześć, I think), as well as a German, a fat soldier, standing at the entrance ramp to the bridge. That German and that bomb (I see it in its diagonal entirety) are, of course, images from the rajza—I described them in *Rozmowy Polskie* [*Polish Conversations*], and I don't want to repeat them here. I don't know why we went to Gnojno then and remained there for the winter. Maybe because our apartment on Nowogrodzka had been bombed, and it wasn't clear if my grandparents (on my father's side) would agree to our moving in with them to their apartment on Koszykowa St. My parents' decision might also have been influenced by the terrors of war and the yet unknown threats attendant upon it. Gnojno and nearby Kleszewo (the estate of my great-grandparents) and nearby Pułtusk was my mother's home region, and it's possible that she felt at the time that we would be safer there than in Warsaw. Now, on my grandmother's estate, there was an innumerable crowd of cats—a few dozen, maybe even more. There were other animals there as well, of course, which might have constituted an interesting, even attractive phenomenon for a four-year-old boy. I'm sure that I must have had some contact with the horses, cows, and piglets. I have a dim memory of the adults talking about the piglets around the table in the dining room, but I wasn't interested in what they were saying, as they were speaking of technical matters, which I didn't completely understand: to pierce or not to pierce for nose rings. A German was sitting at the table too, with his uniform unbuttoned, and he also took part in the conversations on piercing. But my memory places all the horses, cows, and piglets of Gnojno at a later period, as I rather associate them (that is, my contact with them) with spring or summer. The explanation for this probably lies in the huge snowfalls and bitter cold of that first wartime winter. As all who survived the war remember, it was a very hard, very long, and vexatious winter. Because it was so cold and everything was buried in snow—there were even whole weeks during which the snowdrifts reached the eaves of the slanting roof of my grandmother's manor house—it could have been that I wasn't allowed to go outside. And so Grandma's stables, barns, and styes, with all of their piglets and horses, were out of my reach. The long and bitter winter of 1939–40 might also be the reason why all of Grandma's cats (probably all of them) lived in the manor house. In the countryside, the natural arena of feline existence is, at least as far as I see it, outside—around the courtyard, along the steep banks of the river, in outbuildings, and in the little forest in which the little wooden houses of the vacationers stood. If the cats lived in the manor house that winter, my Grandma had to give permission for that—for how else might it have been allowed? She must have acknowledged that outside, in the courtyard, or somewhere in the little wood or the surrounding areas, it would be too cold for the cats, and they wouldn't survive. This, in turn, would suggest that Grandma was favorably disposed to the cats, cared for their needs, had a soft spot in her heart for them. This presented my grandmother to me in a different light from what I was used to. For I always thought of her (and I don't think I was mistaken) as a cold, severe, and even harsh person—hardhearted, as one says. But if she let the cats in the house in the wintertime, if she didn't just let them freeze to death outside, well, if she did have a hard heart, it was only with respect to people. Hard-hearted towards people, tender towards cats. Maybe there's nothing strange in that, after all. The times were difficult, and there was a lot to suggest that animals are better than people. If you have to love anyone, it's safer to love animals. It's safest to love trees: birches and pines—that's obvious. My memory doesn't record what my grandmother's cats looked like. My penchant for detailed description ought to be united to a penchant for detailed memorization. But in this instance, I can remember nothing. There are those who affirm that everything we've ever experienced is recorded in our memory. Whatever we've seen or gone through is preserved there. It's quite possible. And if it actually is true, then somewhere in my memory, there should be a page, a cell, a synapse, some drop of chemical fluid, in which the physical appearance of the Gnojno cats is recorded and plainly visible (but to whom, to whom?), the features of each one of them, each one of their movements, each of their yowls, each of their screeches, recorded there. But I can't find my way to it; that synapse has gone encysted or been severed or what have you. I only remember that there were lots of cats and that they ran from room to room, and I ran after them, crawled under the beds after them, though I can't imagine why. I guess I wanted to be friends with them. I might also have been chasing them with something else in mind—who knows? Because you simply can't explain, you just can't comprehend why four-year-old children chase after things like that, things that move, that run away. It is (most likely) something encoded in the genes of our species—chase and catch, chase and then squeeze until it yelps, then squeeze again, even more tightly. Then, sometime in early spring, or maybe earlier, the cats began dying. I should probably use the verb zdychać here, which is animal-specific, rather than umierać, which in Polish is reserved for people. But the difference between zdychanie and umieranie is doubtful, at the very least, and when you think about it a little, you suddenly realize that there's no difference at all, really. The result of umieranie is exactly the same as that of zdychanie. The result is, quite simply, that something that was once alive has now ceased to be alive. Life (and why? absolutely no one knows) goes off somewhere, evaporates, dissipates, disappears—that's what comes of zdychanie as well as umieranie. That's all we know through experience, and whoever states otherwise is simply playing false to his experience. So let's stick with that first verb, *umierać*. The cats died. And they died in a way that can only be described as disgusting. There's no other way to put it, and, anyway, there's no need to cover it up—they died repulsively; it was horrid. Convulsions, swollen bellies, vomiting, their fur covered in yellowish slime. Do you want me to describe it exactly, in detail, just as I remember it? It's not difficult to perfectly describe yellowish cat vomit—I can handle that. There was also a yellowish-bloody vomit. But let's give that one a pass. It was a dying-off *en masse*; that is to say, cats were dying day by day until the very last day when the very last one of them died. Every morning someone would come by (probably one of Grandma's servant girls) with a rag to pull out from beneath the beds whatever there was to be pulled out and to wipe up the yellowish vomit. Those yellow and bloody-yellow puddles near our beds, mine and my sister's, that's what I really remember best from all that. It must have been some feline epidemic that attacked the stomach. Of course, one might've called a vet who could have put an end to it and prevented more cats from dying, but I doubt whether back then (in 1939 or at the beginning of 1940) the custom of calling in veterinary aid for animals who brought no one any real profit, who lived only for themselves and one's entertainment, even existed. If one ever called the vet at all, it was for sick cows or horses. Had a vet been summoned to take care of vomiting cats, he'd surely have thought that my Grandma had gone nuts. Or maybe it was because of the war and the advent of the Germans. I have to say that I don't quite understand my grandmother. At the very least, on account of the aesthetics of her beautiful Gnojno. I'm not joking. It was so beautiful there that even now, when I think of that beauty, when I think of the riverside beauty of my childhood, my throat constricts, and tears rush to my eyes. So if she went and named her beautiful Gnojno Świerczyn, how could she allow little children (me and my sister, but there were probably some other children there as well, because the manor was full of people—maybe refugees)—how could she permit little children to look upon that repugnant process of dying? When all the cats had died, the first winter of the German war was coming to a close. Not far from Grandma's manor, the River Narew flowed by—all you had to do was run through a field, and you'd be standing on a high bluff looking down at its black waters (sometimes black, sometimes green). How far was it from the manor to the place where the bluff broke off suddenly and plunged down? A hundred meters, maybe even a little less. So I stood on that bluff and waited until, amidst the white sheets of the ice floes, some of the dead cats would appear—floating in the black or green water in the direction of Kleszewo and farther on, to Pułtusk and Warsaw. I waited in vain because, of course, no one threw the dead cats into the Narew; nobody, not even in those days when every corpse was gotten rid of in haste, and who ever would dream of that. The cats' corpses (or carcasses, if you prefer) were, as one says so repulsively these days, utilized in a different manner. Most likely, they were buried on the sly (so that the kids wouldn't see where and build their little cemeteries), somewhere in the woods behind the manor house, among those wooden cottages that Grandma had built for her summer guests, or maybe they were just tossed on the manure pile, I don't know. But I, standing there on the bluff, imagined it otherwise. My imagination was waiting on an aquatic funeral for the cats, for the Narew to bear them away from Gnojno, and for them to float on, amidst the white sheets of the ice floes, along with their yellow vomit, somewhere far away, that they should disappear beyond the bend, where the river turned towards Pułtusk and the great, black floodplain began.

THE NUMBER OF TIGERS
The Uprising as Methodological Problem

I WROTE THAT ON 13 August, two Tiger tanks rolled up to the barricade that closed off Podwale from the Plac Zamkowy, escorting the armored ammunition carrier or, perhaps, plowing a clear road for it. However, the truth is that the number of Tiger tanks remains undetermined. And to all indications, it will remain so. The version of the event that speaks of two Tiger tanks comes from Antoni Przygoński's book *Powstanie Warszawskie w sierpniu 1944* [*The Warsaw Uprising of August 1944*]. "At 13:30, two armored vehicles of the Tiger class rolled onto the Plac Zamkowy, accompanying a light tank of the Marck I type, which pulled right up in front of the insurgents' barricade, where it was abandoned." Of course, Przygoński based his account on the relations of some of the insurgents (whom, however, in this instance, he neither cited nor identified) as well as the reports that Major "Róg" sent that same day, 13 August, to the commander of the "Northern" Group, Col. "Wachnowski." That the escort was made up of two Tiger tanks seems to point to—however unclearly—the narrative found in the famous book by Stanisław Podlewski, *Przemarsz przez piekło* [*A March Through Hell*]. As is well known, Podlewski drew upon many accounts, hundreds even, but he did not reveal his sources. In the chapter entitled "Black Sunday, 13 August," he wrote: "The barricade and the historical apartment buildings in the Plac Zamkowy were being fired upon by three tanks from the Pancer Viaduct.... After a barrage that lasted an hour, one of the Marck I type tanks—smaller, but much nimbler—drew up to the insurgents' barricade on Podwale, where it stopped at a distance of a few dozen meters. Suddenly, the turret flap opened and out jumped a tanker in a black uniform, who then ran off. . . . The Tigers withdrew, as if unconcerned with the fate of the smaller tank. We also have mention of two Tigers—perhaps this ought to be taken as decisive—in the report that the aforementioned Major Stanisław Błaszczak "Róg," commander of the "Róg" unit, which was defending the Old Town from the side of the Wisła and from the southwest, presented to Col. Karol Ziemski "Wachnowski," informing him of the capture of the tank: "At 13:45, a light tank was burnt with bottles near the barricade on Podwale; a PIAT was sent against two Tigers in the region of the Plac Zamkowy." Perhaps this is indeed decisive, but the two greatest authorities of the battles in the Old Town, Col. Adam Borkiewicz, author of the magisterial monograph *Powstanie Warszawskie 1944. Zarys działań natury wojskowej* [*The Warsaw Uprising of 1944: A Sketch from the Military Perspective*], and Piotr Stachiewicz, author of the similarly detailed—perhaps even overmuch—yet marvelously written *Starówka 1944* [*Old Town 1944*], clearly state that it was not two, but three Tiger tanks. (Of course, they also base their statements on someone's account and reports.) In Borkiewicz's book, the Tigers roll up—not as in Podlewski's book, from the Pancer Viaduct—but from the south, from Krakowskie Przedmieście. "At 18:00 three tanks rolled up on the Plac Zamkowy from Krakowskie Przedmieście, firing upon the barricade at Podwale St., as well as at the neighboring buildings. Soon after that, they withdrew, but the little Marck I tank advanced quickly upon the barricade." Let me first draw attention to the discrepancy in time. Borkiewicz speaks of 18:00, while in Major "Róg's" report 13:45 is mentioned. Przygoński gives us 13:30, and finally, in *Old Town 1944*, three Tiger tanks appear in the indeterminate afternoon hours: "In the afternoon hours, there occurred another attack of three tanks, which came from the direction of the Plac Zamkowy. However, some PIAT rounds dispersed two of them, while one was hit, though not immobilized, and it remained. A little while later, the Germans destroyed the tank's tread with an anti-aircraft round so as to eliminate the possibility of the insurgents capturing it and making use of it. A few moments after this, a little tank of the Marck I type, used for reconnaissance, approached the first of the barricades on Podwale. After a few shots, the driver of the tank leapt out and escaped." The operational officer of the III Unit of the Main Staff Command of the AK, Lt. Col. Felicjan Majorkiewicz, also informs us of three tanks in his memoirs, *Lata chmurne* [*Cloudy Years*]. The whole event is described there rather unclearly, but the fact of three tanks is quite clear. "Soldiers under the command of Maj. `Róg,' the commander of the eastern sector. . .damaged three tanks with Molotov cocktails. The tanks withdrew, except for a little tank of the Marck I type, which was captured after its crew leapt out and ran off." As can be seen, of the three tanks in Stachiewicz's book, one was hit, first by the insurgents, then by the Germans, and that one, with the damaged tread, remained on the Plac Zamkowy. In Majorkiewicz's book, all three were damaged, but all three were able to withdraw. That is, if there really were three Tiger tanks because perhaps only one Tiger appeared on the square at the time. And perhaps it was not a Tiger at all but some other type of tank. Robert Bielecki provides just such a description of the event, based on various accounts, in the book *"Gustaw"—"Harnaś." Dwa powstańcze bataliony* [*"Gustaw"— "Harnaś." Two Insurgent Battalions*]. There we have two tanks rolling up from the direction of Nowy Zajazd, and one of them is that small tank, which was shortly to explode. As to the other tank, the author of the book about the two battalions does not express himself clearly— he judged that it might have been a Tiger, but it could also have been a Panzer, which was a bit smaller than the Tiger. "Suddenly, around 11:00, the observation posts reported that two tanks had begun advancing from Nowy Zajazd in the direction of Plac Zamkowy. The first of these was a regular fighting vehicle. . .the second—very much smaller than the first—had neither cannon nor machine gun." As we can see, on the basis of the accounts available to him, Bielecki solved the matter of the number of tanks differently. But also, the matter of the place where they were noted in his book—and that means in the accounts of the insurgents upon whom he was relying—is different. They were not coming up "from Krakowskie Przedmieście" as in

Borkiewicz, that is, from the south, from the direction of Plac Hoovera [Hoover Square] but "from Nowy Zajazd," that is, from the east, from the Kierbedź Bridge. The time is also different in *Two Insurgent Battalions*—not 18:00, not 13:30, not in "the afternoon hours," but "suddenly...posts reported"—to our one, two, and three Tiger tanks, let us add, really just as a point of order—"an indeterminate number of tanks." For this is how they are spoken of in the book written by Capt. "Ognisty," Lucjan Fajer, the operational officer of the "Godziwa" Battalion, which was fighting in a region neighboring Podwale, Miodowa, Bielańska, and Senatorska Sts. Although Fajer was on Kiliński St. at the moment of the explosion (he was "swept off the stairs on which he was standing" and fell from the third to the ground floor, perhaps of the apartment building at Kiliński 5), he did not see the tanks advancing on the Plac Zamkowy. However, he worked up his version of events, as he put it, from "eyewitness accounts." Now, these "eyewitnesses" who, from the start, observed the maneuvers of the tanks on Plac Zamkowy told him that there were several Tigers that forced their way into Podwale, "plowing through our first barricade" (that is, the one that closed off Podwale from Senatorska—the other, lower barricade on Podwale was near Kapitulna). In this way, they cleared the path for the little Marck I tank (or the armored ammunition carrier), which could then proceed farther, through the breach made in the forced barricade, to the crossroads of Kiliński and Podwale. So, when the first barricade had been breached, the tanks, having accomplished their tasks, "retreated to the Plac Zamkowy," and afterwards they withdrew quickly to Krakowskie Przedmieście. What are we to make of all this? How are we to reconcile all these accounts so that they might form some sort of coherent narrative? Is such a thing even possible? Tiger tanks are a serious issue, but it's already clear from the foregoing that the problem we're faced with deals with something even more serious than Tigers on the Plac Zamkowy, namely: the way in which we are to comprehend the history of the Warsaw Uprising. Because the question now arises (which again is not merely concerned with the explosion on Kiliński St., but rather with a certain problem that one might term methodological): what will we get from it; what advantage will we derive from the certainty—which someday shall appear—concerning the exact number of the Tigers: two, or three, or several, which appeared before the barricade on Podwale? And should it suddenly become perfectly clear whether they rolled up from Nowy Zjazd or from Plac Hoovera—what then? In the wake of these questions, more pop up—is it even necessary for us to know these things? Is access to just such truth—truth so understood—absolutely necessary to us? If there were some stubborn historian, absolutely confident in his abilities, who could finally state that "following the extensive research I've carried out, I know absolutely everything about this issue that needs to be known. . ." (and so, thanks to him, we do too) "that there were two Tigers rolling up from Nowy Zjazd and that one of them, approaching the barricade on Podwale, suffered a direct hit from a PIAT but it was able to retreat (dragging its ruptured tread behind it)." In that case, whoever stated that he saw one Tiger or three Tigers, or two Tigers and one Panzer, would only have seemed to have seen these things, or would have forgotten something, or would be mistaken, as such a historian would then say "as far as the historical truth is concerned, which I present in my account. For historical truth is unique; there cannot be two different historical truths that speak of one and the same event, the same piece of history. No, from this moment forward, all the other narratives must withdraw from the position they occupy, for that belongs rightfully to the truth alone, the truth" (he would say) "that I have confirmed—concerning the two Tigers." And yet one immediately sees that, even if such a stubborn (and imaginary) historian were to declare such a thing (that he has found the objective truth, has come into possession of the objective truth), the question that I have just posed retains its validity: what advantage will we derive from his information? And, immediately again, we perceive something else: namely, that the question touches not merely upon the Tigers and the little tank they were escorting but many other fragments of the history of the Warsaw Uprising as well, even the entire historical account. Where exactly did that Liberator fall to earth, shot down by the Germans on the night of 14–15 August above Miodowa St. (most likely after it had made its drop on Plac Krasińskich [Krasiński Square])? Did it fall onto the carriageway and northern pavement of Miodowa? Or did it perhaps strike the roof of the Pallottine cloister and, only after the roof caught fire and caved in, fall onto the street with its incinerated crew? There are insurgents' accounts that report it falling onto the roof, while others say it fell directly onto the street. There is also a well-known account of the event that has the aircraft coming down elsewhere—near the (prewar) Archive of Historical Records, nearly at the corner of Długa St. and Plac Krasińskich. Another familiar version has the Liberator plowing straight into the Archive of Historical Records building. And yet another oft-repeated account has the airplane crashing onto the roof of a building on Miodowa with one of its wings tumbling onto the street. Monika Żeromska (Stefan's daughter) saw with her own eyes the incinerated remains of the airmen lying next to what was left of their plane on the corner of Miodowa and Plac Krasińskich ("next to it the pilots—black, burnt bodies in what was left of their uniforms"). But someone else again saw with their own eyes how the burnt bodies of the pilots were extracted from the crashed plane on the burning roof of the cloister and transferred from there to the garrison church. And that anti-tank cannon set up in Simons Passage that gave the Germans what for? Was that little cannon captured (in a somewhat miraculous fashion) during the battles around Stawki? But there are others who speak of a cannon taken from the Liberator, and both of these place the weapon in Simons Passage. Or maybe between Simons Passage and the Arsenal. There are still others that claim that the weapon was not an anti-aircraft gun at all but a heavy machine gun removed from the Liberator—to the five-story building on Przejazd St., which was blown into the air on 16 August (along with two poets: Gajcy and Stroiński). As the accounts relate, German or Azer sappers found their way there in one of three ways: through the basements from the Mostowski Palace, through basements from the side of the barricade on Leszno, or from the side of the wall enclosing the ghetto. There are accounts reporting that, while they were setting the explosive charges, they were surprised in the basements by insurgents from the "Nałęcz" unit and engaged in a battle with them. (Stanisław Podlewski relies on such accounts in his *March through Hell*.) But there are others that claim that they got out just as they'd entered, unnoticed, and that nobody was aware of their presence up to the very explosion and collapse of the building. These are just a few fragments from the history of the Uprising in the Old Town, but similar accounts concerning all the areas and neighborhoods of Warsaw, just as contradictory and reciprocally exclusive of one another, can be found in the hundreds and even thousands. The ambitious and stubborn historian will, of course, be able to handle these mutually untenable accounts: he'll massacre them, arriving at last at his historical truth. The problem lies in whether it was worth it (or proper) to conduct such an operation—such a massacre. If something that appears in various versions is reduced to one version—that is, if that which is called historical truth becomes apparent and, from that moment on, by that very token, all versions inconsistent with the determined truth are disavowed—if it will someday become known, finally and unassailably, how many Tiger tanks escorted the little Marck I tank to the barricade on Podwale and from what direction it rolled onto Kiliński, from Nowomiejska or Wąski Dunaj—if it will become known what it was that caused the explosion at the entranceway of the building at Kiliński 1, the direct cause—if all of this is finally determined, once and for all times, and in a manner that admits of no doubt, well then: the dramatic question then arises (not so dramatic, perhaps, for professional historians of the Uprising, but dramatic indeed for our future knowledge of the Uprising), what, therefore (here's the question), is to be the future destiny of all the accounts that do not agree with the accepted version? All those unclean, uncertain versions, which scatter and then regroup like smoke above the insurgent barricades? Must all these versions be cast aside, overlooked, forgotten, after the determination of the most truthfully truthful version? Such a determination would not be unjust, it would indeed be nonsensical, thoughtless. For the truth of the Uprising lies in all these accounts. Their chaotic content: unclean, feverish, dark, and muddled—that is the truth of the Uprising, really, because in thousands of such chaotic, tangled, feverish versions, the life of those who were in Warsaw at the time, who lived through the Uprising, appears, gives notice of itself—in just such a way. We can settle the matter—why not?—that two Tigers rolled up to the barricade on Podwale, that the Liberator that fell on Miodowa flew up from the direction of Żoliborz (it flew over the Plac Krasińskich, after all), and we can also determine that it flew up from the direction of the Kierbedź Bridge (it flew over the bell tower of St. Anna's church)—historical truth might be found in this or that case (or in yet another), but, as I see it, it would be better if two truths were to be found in each of these cases (and in all such similar ones) so that the Liberator flew up from the direction of St. Anna's and from Żoliborz, so that the incinerated airmen lay both on the corner of Miodowa and the Plac Krasińskich and on the burning cloister roof, or that in this question there existed as many truths as existed at the time it all occurred—two, three, or even more—because if we cast away one of these truths (if we arrive at the conclusion that we are able to come into the possession of one and only one truth), then, along with that discarded truth, that truth ignored, we are also discarding and ignoring the entire truth of the insurgents' lives, acknowledging them to be something unimportant, insignificant. And yet there is nothing more important than the truth of a life—no greater truth than that truth, which, even though it be made up of many half-truths—because that is inevitable anyway—of quarter-truths and little fragments and shards of other truths, and also of many truths of the sort that are not truths at all, or maybe truths, but only after a certain fashion. Let me catch my breath. The Warsaw Uprising is an extraordinary historical phenomenon. And thus, it is also an extraordinary methodological phenomenon—such as never before appeared in our history. For such a thing never occurred before. And so, the Uprising demands its own methodology of historical research, peculiar only to itself, and its historians must create just such an extraordinary methodology for it. For the time being, as long as we are possessed of no such methodology (and the Uprising is treated with the same methods used to discuss the Battle of Grunwald), let us hold to the idea that among insurgents' accounts, there are no better or worse ones, ones that present a certain state of things in better or worse fashion, ones that draw us near some sort of truth and ones that lead us farther away. From a methodological point of view, all these accounts are equally good and equally truthful because they all speak of what those who created them actually saw and actually experienced. In other words, they speak of their lives, which is the truth of the Uprising. Life is a many-sided affair of varied aspects, varied "faces"—a spiritual side as well as a material side, a historical aspect and an eternal one, an aesthetic side and an ethical side, an aspect of actuality and one of imaginings. That which is life is what appears from all this, becoming available and approachable to us only because of all these aspects, in all these aspects. We know of life only as much as we know of its various sides, as much as we are able to recognize them and describe them—the rest is just illusion.

MEINE HERREN, WIR SIND KEINE MÖRDER

THE *DIARY OF HANS FRANK* [*Der Tagebuch von Hans Frank*] fell by coincidence into the hands of the Americans in May 1945. Before that, it had been preserved at the University Library in Heidelberg, where the American 7th Army had set up its center for documentation. From there, by a rather roundabout route, it arrived in Nuremberg, where Stanisław Piotrowski, a member of the Polish delegation to the International Tribunal, made an abstract of it. In this way, it became material evidence against Frank at his trial. If not for the *Excerpts from the Diary of Hans Frank* [*Auszüge aus dem Tagebuch von Hans Frank*] presented before the International Tribune in Nuremberg, the General Governor would most likely have escaped with his skin intact. For what was found in the *Diary* provided evidence sufficient to sentence him to death. You might even say that Frank plaited his own noose. For he might have destroyed his *Diary* or hidden it, but he did neither; rather—as he later so strangely boasted—he even handed it over to the Americans himself. As he wrote in his prison notes: "I handed over my wartime journal to them, voluntarily." To inquire as to the whys and wherefores of that decision—was it recklessness or the hanged man's considered decision—is not worth our trouble. In his "Introduction" to the *Diary*, Stanisław Piotrowski, who published it, included (in the 1957 edition) some extraordinarily interesting fragments from a few of Frank's speeches, which the General Governor delivered in the summer of 1942 in Berlin, Vienna, Heidelberg, and Munich. *Der Tagebuch* (being not so much a journal in the classical sense of the term as rather a collection of speeches, protocols, and notes from the sittings and councils of the German rulers of the General Government) is chock-full of exhortations to murder. Of course, there's nothing strange about that. When he was speaking in Warsaw or Kraków before the high command of the SS or the police, such was the nature of the beast, if one might put it that way: Frank had to call for murder—this was associated with his function; it arose from the very office he held. He was, if we might so express it, the chief in charge of the massacre, its commander; he had to measure up to his task—this too inclined him to such bloody exhortations. Such was his life. He couldn't recoil from it—at least, I can see no possibility for withdrawal. Now, if these very bloodthirsty exhortations found in the *Diary* constituted for the Nuremberg Tribunal a hefty argument in favor of sentencing the General Governor to death (as I assume the case to have been), then his 1942 speeches might have been acknowledged by that same Tribunal as something along the order of extenuating circumstances. I don't know whether or not Frank made reference to those speeches during his defense in Nuremberg, but doubtless he might have. Even today, so long after it all, they make one pause and consider just who was that General Governor of ours really. Of course, he was a criminal, a murderer, a thief—a pilfering fingersmith even, who took great pleasure in pillaging Jewish furs and Jewish jewelry. Nor did he hold Polish eggs and apples in contempt, as he sent great quantities of these back to Bavaria from the General Government to nourish his family there—something which was illegal, even according to the German laws of the day. Those addresses from 1942 set even these miserable thefts in a new, somewhat strange light. Indeed, all of Dr. Frank, the most illustrious German jurist of his generation, president of the German Legal Academy, as well as Reichsrechtsführer or Leader of the German Legal System (a title bestowed upon him by Hitler) appears to us in a somewhat different light. In the lecture that Frank delivered on 9 June at the University of Berlin, he spoke of law and freedom. "There has never been such a state as had no law or was set up in opposition to law. Such a thing is inconceivable," Frank said. "As our experience of the history of the world teaches us, the state and the law constitute one whole. . . . You cannot rule a nation by force; a nation's life is inconceivable without law. Force is merely a technical element which can never replace law. As a free nation, the German nation lives by its own law and cannot be bound into a national community by force." Frank moves on from the problem of the state and the law to the problem of freedom: "In just the same way that a nation cannot live without law, it cannot live without freedom. Now, freedom also means the possibility of spiritual development. The goal of our national life is, and always has been, creative individuality. . . . I believe in sacred, eternal law." Frank continues with his defense of sacred and eternal law in the following addresses delivered in June and July in Vienna, Munich, and Heidelberg. In the lecture that took place on 1 July at the Viennese Academy of Sciences, he said that the "ideals of the police state" that destroy the human person cannot become the ideals of National Socialism and cannot replace "ancient Germanic legal concepts." "The law is also a human institution. The sense of humanity has lost some of its value; some people negate it entirely. I am of a different opinion." The lecture he delivered at the University of Munich on 20 July was devoted to the independent judicature and also to the independence of the human person. "The independence of the judge is one of the most ancient Germanic cultural treasures. To stand in its defense is no manifestation of any liberal-democratic, Jewish-parliamentary decadent reactionism or anything of that ilk but a very Germanic characteristic. The existence of the individual in no way impinges upon the authority of the Reich, incarnate in the providential figure of the Führer." In the lecture delivered on the next day, 21 July, in Heidelberg, the General Governor spoke out against the existence of the police state. "The police state should never exist at all. I reject it!"—and also against capital punishment: "Europe wishes to be humane. That means there is no need to always, and for every reason, decree a sentence of death. We wish to be humane. There exists no state that would be harmed by behaving humanely." As can be seen, all of this was—and remains—quite valid. What were Frank's intentions when he came out—and this, in 1942—in defense of "sacred law" and "Germanic legal concepts" (being, as one might surmise, the age-old creation of the Germanic tribal community)—this I cannot say. Perhaps some German historians, who busy themselves with the history of Germanic law and the history of the Third Reich, know something more on that topic. The Polish publisher of the *Diary* was of the opinion (and in this, he was certainly correct) that Frank was engaged in a certain type of political gamesmanship and that the speeches were some element in that game. But what that game, directed against Hitler's closest collaborators, might lead to is hard to say. It doesn't seem possible that Frank might have been counting on getting rid of Himmler and Bormann so that in this way he might find himself right next to the Führer, number two in the Reich. Whatever the case may be, even if it was just a political game (although, as I see it, there is something more to be found in these addresses, something that sheds light upon the whole German personality of those days, if one can put it like that—at one and the same time, we steal Polish eggs and realize the sacred laws of the Germanic tribe, securing our age-old Germanic identity, because the theft of eggs is actually the realization of those sacred laws), so, even if Frank was playing some sort of game, it ended for him—if not fatally, at least not very well. For when Hitler was presented with the strange addresses delivered by the Reichsrechtsführer, he is said to have been overcome with fury. He forbade Frank from public appearances at universities and deprived him of various positions of honor. From then on, he was permitted to appear in public only in his role as General Governor. Bormann and Himmler had an influence on this decision of the Führer's, doubtlessly intriguing so as to clip Frank's wings and limit his influence. In the context of political games, it all ended in August 1942 with Frank submitting his resignation from the post of General Governor, which Hitler, however, did not accept. To those passionate addresses of Frank's from the summer months of 1942 and to his passionate defense of the sacredness of German law, it is worth adding what the *Diary* has to say about all that. This is what we learn there: During an address in Kraków on 30 May 1940, at a meeting devoted to police matters ("Polizei-Sitzung am

Donnerstag, dem 30.Mai 1940. Beginn der Sitzung 10.20"), the General Governor harangued his collaborators on the necessity of "putting an end already to the mob of seditionist politicians of resistance" and "coming to terms with the Polish banditry that we've inherited." He said: "I freely admit that several thousand Poles, above all, from the spiritual and intellectual leadership of Poland, will pay with their lives.... Gentlemen, we are not murderers, not at all. Now, this is a terrible task for the policeman and SS man who, on the basis of this edict, is by office or profession duty-bound to carry out such executions. The signing of hundreds of death sentences here is but a flick of the pen for us. But it is a terrible burden to oblige Germans, honest German soldiers and their comrades, to carry them out.... Every officer of the police and the SS, who has the difficult duty of performing these executions, must be 100% convinced that he is acting as the executor of a sentence established by the law of the German nation." "Meine Herren, wir sind keine Mörder"—how are we to understand that? A murderer is giving murderers an order to murder in expedited fashion ("in beschleunigtem Tempo Schluss zu machen") and declaring to them that they are not murderers at all. Of course, he's a murderer, and yet he's not an idiot after all; this is no cretin, no German moron speaking; on the contrary: this is a thinking man, a man of intellect, educated, a renowned jurist, a specialist in the explication of German law, including its sacredness—so, how are we to comprehend this? We are not murderers—is this just a propaganda slogan that occurred to him, something intended to make murdering easier for murderers, to convince them or encourage them to murder? It would be naive to think so. For, after all, the Polizei-Sitzung was a meeting of the high command of the police and the SS—accomplished experts all; it was a closed meeting, where there was no reason to propagate something that was (I'm thinking of murder here) sufficiently well-propagated. Frank had no reason there to convince or encourage anybody to do anything. In stating that these colleagues of his, SS and policemen, gathered at Wawel, were not murderers all the while they murdered, was nothing but an acknowledgment of a certain factual state of things. "Wir sind keine Mörder" was something well rooted in the German psyche. Frank's SS men and policemen would be murderers if they were murdering in accordance with the laws of a police state. But Frank would not even consider such a thing, knowing that if the Reich was to endure, it could not be based on summary or interim law; no, its laws must be eternal and sacred. But if that murdering was founded on age-old Germanic law (if, to take the matter in hand from a different angle, it was justified by the age-old interests of the German nation), then it wasn't murder; indeed, it had nothing in common with murder at all; it was the implementation of justice. Or, perhaps it would be better to look at it thus—it was the introduction of justice, age-old and founded upon the conviction that Europe (and even the whole world) ought to be governed by the Germans, who were the only ones capable of such a thing. So those who do not agree with this must (oh, horrible necessity!) be exterminated. And so, although murder (on the streets of Warsaw) was an everyday occurrence in the forties—that too, like all other manifestations of age-old law, was something sacred and even festive. For this reason, in that speech that Frank delivered at that May Polizei-Sitzung (and it was an important speech—it must be considered as such), the phrase "wir sind keine Mörder" was attached to the phrase expressing that every SS chief who sentenced a person to death and carried out that execution "must be 100% convinced that he is acting as the executor of a sentence established *by the law of the German nation*" (my emphasis). This wasn't an easy thing to do at all (that murdering, which in its volume lost its murderous character), for those who organized the executions and participated in them took upon themselves a great and heavy duty—bringing into existence the law of the German nation, shaping life according to that law. "Die haute Pflicht." And also, "eine furchtbare Aufgabe." A heavy duty, a horrible task. As can be seen, there was even something pitiable in all this. But those to be pitied—according to Frank—were not those who were killed, but those who did the killing—courageously realizing German national law. It is for this reason that, in this speech, Frank expresses his great concern for the health of the soldiers who were to carry out the executions. As he saw it, only the best and healthiest soldiers would be capable of such a thing. "For this reason, I am very grateful to party comrade Siebert for publishing the instructions, which enjoin upon the organs of the police the duty of taking into consideration the physical condition of the people who are to be entrusted with these executions. Gentlemen, I beg you to respect these instructions as far as possible and in all circumstances." These words might be understood in such a way, too, to suggest that any person who lacks the proper physical predispositions for this task is incapable of it, not only because he might break down and be incapable of carrying it out but also because he is unworthy, he does not have such elevated moral stature as would enable him to bring the law of the nation into existence. In one of the few photographs that record a street execution in Warsaw—actually, the photo was taken after the execution had been carried out—we see four men, prisoners, most likely, tossing the corpses onto the flatbed of a truck. The photograph was taken in the autumn of 1943 (perhaps in secret, from some window, at the risk of the photographer's own life), probably somewhere on Wawelska St., somewhere near Grójecka St.—but there can be no absolute certainty about that. It's hard to make out any details. No faces are clearly visible; one sees only the wretched clothes they wear, short sports coats. One of the men in the cleanup detail is wearing a cap; the rest are bareheaded. The one in the cap is not wearing a coat but is in shirtsleeves. So, if this was taking place in the fall, it was most likely early fall or the end of summer. Four men are lifting a corpse by the arms and legs. As one might well assume, they're about to swing it upwards; in a moment, the limp, broken body will fly up into the air to land a moment later on the flatbed—which we see from the side, something that allows us to judge that, at least in the case of executions, not the tailgate but the side-walls of the truck were lowered. This way, it'd be easier to unload and reload them. The loading here has just begun. No one is yet sprawled on the truck's flatbed. Right next to the four men holding the body, some German officer, probably in a Luftwaffe uniform, is passing by at a sprightly pace—you can tell because he's taking long strides. Then again, his uniform is a bit too light-colored to be Luftwaffe; maybe he's from some other branch of the service. The officer is not looking at the four men who are tossing corpses onto the truck, nor does he glance at the man being tossed. He's looking straight in front of him. He has some papers in his hand. Most likely, he's on his way to deliver them; he's got some purpose, and he gives one the impression (as I understand it) of being somewhat upset, in a hurry; maybe what he's got to do is something urgent; maybe he has to deliver a critical command. It seems as if this scene of tossing corpses didn't interest him at all. He passes by indifferently as if what was taking place right next to him was not worth his notice. Or something that—seen so many times already—no longer holds any interest for him. If we accept Frank's point of view, this fellow from the Luftwaffe, bearing his papers somewhere, was, there on Wawelska St. in the summer or fall of 1943, to be pitied.

THE HOLE

WE WERE DRIVING FROM Gnojno in the direction of the highway that links Pułtusk and Ostrołęka. It wasn't far from Gnojno to the highway (it still isn't)—one kilometer, maybe one and a half. Most likely, now that I think of it, we were leaving Gnojno to return to Warsaw—and if that was indeed the case, if we were headed to Warsaw, passing through Kleszowo and Pułtusk, it would have been the spring of 1940. And rather late spring than early. I remember that the fields were already green. And if indeed it was that spring, then I was just about five years old. But it might also have been that we were leaving Gnojno in another direction and with some other aim in mind. And at some indefinite time—not the spring of 1940, but earlier or later. I don't remember our means of locomotion at all. Was it some wagon from the courtyard—some rustic peasant's hayrack or my Grandma's buckboard? A few people were riding along with me. Besides me, my mother was certainly there, maybe my sister was too, and perhaps our uncle as well. And there was baggage: valises, suitcases—so it probably was a wagon and not the buckboard. I don't remember who was driving; I don't even remember the back of the coachman, but I do remember the black horse who was pulling the wagon (or buckboard) perfectly because he was a good friend of mine—one of many good friends I had there. All of Grandma's horses—even though I wasn't allowed to approach them (so that I wouldn't get kicked)—were my dear friends. I would stand there near the stables and, gazing at the horses, imagine, deeply moved, that they were gazing at me and thinking of me with the same deep emotion, thinking of me, too, as their friend. There, where the old black windmill (or, rather, the prop designed to look like a windmill) stands, near a pleasant garden on the slope, with a restaurant and something like a motel (merely a hundred or so meters divide the location from the highway to Pułtusk, surely no more than that); in 1940, there was neither windmill nor restaurant nor motel—just fields; perhaps there was some cottage or out-building—I don't remember. From there, you could already see the highway and the turn—if you wanted to go to Kleszowo and Pułtusk, you turned left—and whoever was driving the horse urged him on appreciably—he was in a hurry. Now I understand why. There were two German soldiers standing by the road while, a few meters, or a few dozen meters farther on, a woman was lying on her stomach. As far as I can remember, there was nothing threatening about those soldiers, nothing that frightened me at the time or made an unpleasant impression on me—they were probably Wehrmacht, with garrison caps on their heads, wearing long greatcoats; maybe they were leaning on their rifles, maybe they were smoking cigarettes. They would have seemed scarier to me if they had been wearing helmets. In any case, they were no unpleasant gendarmes with the tin on their chests or, even worse, SS men. It was very unpleasant and aggravating (even for a little boy like me)—but I remember this from some later experiences—coming across soldiers from the Luftwaffe—those in their black uniforms. Did those two soldiers have something in common with the woman lying on her stomach not far from them? Were they guarding her so that no one should approach her and take her away? That was probably why they were standing there, but now I can rather make such assumptions; at the time, I didn't really reflect upon what they were doing there, why they were standing there. The woman's head was dangling over the slope of a roadside ditch. Her face, hidden in the weeds, was not visible. Her skirt—a dark blue or black one—was hitched up, and I was able to see (this I remember well, because mysteries such as that, what a woman has beneath her skirt, interested me greatly at the time) her sheer, dark brown stockings with the seam running up the back, her white thighs between the bands of those stockings and her hitched-up skirt and perhaps a bit of her underwear. Was the woman wearing an overcoat or a jacket? This I am unable to recall. But between her shoulder blades, exactly—a little bit below her shoulder blades, at their lower extremity, there was no overcoat or jacket or even a blouse—maybe there were some rags of stuff, silk, or wool—but there, where there ought to have been a jacket or a blouse, there was just a giant, deep hole full of red meat and black blood. This hole had the shape of an inverted cone. The blood—for certain, or now it seems certain to me—was just coagulated or just about to coagulate. It was better not to know by whom, how, or why this large hole had been made in the back of the woman who was then tossed with that hole of hers into the weeds of a roadside ditch—had it been made by those two soldiers in their garrison caps, or maybe some other soldiers from the border guards (for the border between the Reich and the General Government ran not far from Gnojno or maybe Ostland—for the German border guards would sometimes show up at my Grandma's properties or maybe it was gendarmes from Pułtusk, or (as the phrase went back then) boys from the woods. It was for that very reason, so as neither to ask nor to be asked about the cause of that hole and who made it, where the woman came from, that the driver (probably one of Grandma's servant boys) lashed on the horse. Then some time passed—not much, maybe two years, maybe three—three at the most, and once more, I saw that hole in the woman's back, and maybe even the woman herself. In 1942 or 1943 (I was some two or three years older than I was back then in Gnojno), I felt a pain in my abdomen, and it turned out that I needed to have my appendix removed. I underwent the operation in the hospital where my mother worked (in the internal medicine ward)—the Child Jesus Hospital on Nowogrodzka St. Everything went smoothly. A few days after the operation (because of my mother's position there, I was well taken care of and enjoyed good conditions—a private room), I was wheeled into the room where my bandage was to be changed. The previous patient was still being attended to, so the wheelchair in which I was sitting was placed near the door, where I was to wait. I had a fine view of everything; I could see everything perfectly, as the doctors (most likely my mother among them) had moved over to the window where they were discussing something. In front of me, in the middle of the room, there stood a high hospital gurney upholstered in white oilcloth (just like my wheelchair). On this gurney, with her back to me, sat a woman. She was undressed to the waist. I couldn't see her face; I can't say how old she was—she may have been a young girl, but she also may have been a middle-aged woman. Most likely, she had just been brought to the hospital, for she was not wearing a patient's frock or hospital robe— she was sitting on that gurney in a dark skirt, navy blue or black. The woman did not turn around when I was wheeled into the bandaging room, and my chair was set near the gurney; she may not have moved at all. She sat there staring in the direction of the windows, where the doctors were consulting. The room was lit with that white hospital light. Everything was white, brightly lit. In the woman's back, between her shoulder blades, a little below their bottom edge, there was a great bloody hole—very similar to the one I'd seen near Gnojno. I immediately recognized (and later, for many years, even after the war when I was already a teenager, I kept revolving this nonsense in my head) that these two holes, the one from Nowogrodzka and the one from near Gnojno, were not only similar to each other, not only identical, but the very same hole, and that the woman from the Child Jesus Hospital was the same woman who had been lying in the weeds at the roadside ditch. Right near that black windmill, which wasn't there at the time. It was as if—through those nearly identical wounds, their near-identity—someone was giving me some sort of sign, although who knew (as it always is with signs, after all) what sort of sign and why. Now, the size of the hole in the back of that woman in the hospital gives me pause—I can see it clearly, I have it, as one says, right before my eyes—but it seems entirely too large. What I mean is, you probably can't survive with such a huge hole in your back—the person who had such a huge hole gouged into her back ought to die on the spot, and so that woman from the bandaging room in the Child Jesus Hospital ought not to be sitting there like that on the white, wheeled gurney. So I admit the possibility that, with the passage of time, even after the passage of many years, my imagination might have made that hole progressively larger, whereas, in actuality, it was really smaller and not at all as large as it seems to me. It's hard for me now to estimate it justly. Such incursions of the imagination into memory happen quite frequently. The imagination makes something that is small grow large and something large—disturbingly small. When the woman sitting on the hospital gurney upholstered in white oilskin moved, something in her open back moved as well. I don't know what it was—maybe the coagulating blood, maybe the maggots that live in wounds, or maybe it was the woman's lungs that were moving in that hole. I had a great urge to take a closer look at whatever it was moving in there—I had the urge to go right up and place my hand in that bloody hole. And that has remained with me all my life long—that desire to draw near and touch that thing there. Of course, I knew that I couldn't do that; first of all, I couldn't get off the chair, as I still wasn't allowed to walk. Second, because there were adults in the room, my mother among them, and they wouldn't let me do that. I'd certainly pay a high price for a terrible act like that. Now, you shouldn't think of me as some sort of seven- or eight-year-old monster—even if I could have gotten up off that chair and walked at the time, and even if there hadn't been any adults in the bandaging room, I wouldn't have put my fingers into that woman's back, into her bloody wound. Suffering fascinated and attracted me. I wanted to look upon it, but I also knew that you had to respect it—my parents taught me that; certainly, that was an important element of the wartime upbringing of boys my age. At least in our sphere, the social caste that we belonged to. Was that woman at Nowogrodzka a victim of the Germans? At that time, sitting in my wheelchair in the hospital and gazing at that fascinating wound (here I ought to use an even more inappropriate term: admiring that wound of hers, which delighted me), I was certain that this was their doing—they shot that woman in the back with some sort of projectile that makes gigantic holes like that, or they created that wound in some other horrid manner peculiar to them. Now I see it all a little differently. Back in 1942 and 1943, Warsaw was bombed many times by Russian planes, and that woman might have found herself in striking distance of one of their exploding bombs. Of course, it might also have been that the hole in her back had nothing in common with military operations at all but was rather the result of some sort of illness she was suffering from—if there are such illnesses that make holes like that in the human body. Later, many years later, when those two holes, the one from the Child Jesus Hospital and the other from near Gnojno, had coalesced in my mind into one great hole, I recognized them—or I recognized it—as my most important wartime experience. Surely because all my other experiences, metaphorically speaking, fit inside that one experience. A bloody hole—there you have my whole childhood. I can't say that I especially hold this against the Germans, as if I were expecting or demanding something of them in recompense. I only want them to know what they did to me—they destroyed my childhood and completely ruined my eight-year-old imagination. What remains is a pile of rubble, a pile of corpses, a gigantic sump, a gigantic hole filled with black blood.

THE CURTAIN ON KRAKOWSKIE PRZEDMIEŚCIE

The Uprising as Aesthetic Object

EVER SINCE I LEARNED of the curtain on Krakowskie Przedmieście (and I learned of it only very recently, while writing this book, some two or three months ago), I can't get it out of my head. You might say that this curtain (already, as soon as it had been hung there) had a threefold significance—the most important of which was military, and this became, in quite a natural way, in time, after the curtain had vanished, a historical significance, and so it remains today. Now, I would not exaggerate this military significance because it doesn't seem all that great. Perhaps it was even negligible, and for that reason, not much was said about it at the time, and consequently, not much is known. The two remaining meanings—its meaning as symbol and its aesthetic significance—were not even taken into consideration at the time when it was first hung. You might say that they didn't exist or at least not visually, for, at the time, who even thought of such things; there was no time for any of that, nor was there any such desire. The beauty of the Warsaw Uprising (and its symbolic beauty) are such things as became evident only after the passage of many years when the historical events of those days grew distant from us to such an extent that we were able to catch sight of the essence lying beneath their surface—this long-enduring element, which may justly be called eternal. Such is always the case with great historical events, that their essential content, only weakly perceived at first (or entirely invisible), reveals itself to our eyes only many years later. Of course, someone might suggest that in speaking of the symbolic significance of the Battle of Verdun, we commit the ugly sin of neglect or forgetfulness—we don't want to remember what it's like to die in the fumes of weaponized gas; how the mixture of chlorine and phosgene tears apart the lungs; how horrible, and even repulsive a death it is, and what sort of suffering must accompany it. The answer to that is—first, the uncovering of symbolic content needn't necessarily indicate a forgetting of the concrete, detailed appearance of historical events, what was rumbling in the bowels of history, of all those horrifying things, which then made their appearance when the event was actually unfolding. Second—there is no remedy for it; when something truly important happens in history, it's a sure bet that, sooner or later, either we will make a symbol of it in our own heads, or it shall uncover its symbolic stratum to us in its own way, that is, it will reveal, in this or that way, its essential value, its deep, hidden meanings (which require a lot of labor on our part for us to arrive at). All great events that have occurred in our national history have taken on some symbolic value for us with the passage of time; moreover, the very discovery and acceptance of this symbolic stratum, the recognition of their certain value, is what unites us as a whole—in other words, it is what makes Poles of us. We are Poles because we more or less evaluate and experience in the same way Batory at Psków, the Slaughter in Umań, the Battle of Maciejowice, the Storming of the Belvedere, Olszynka Grochowska, the marching out of the First Cadre, and the 1920 Battle of Warsaw. The details of the Umań Massacre (horrible) are little known today, which doesn't change the fact that the event still has a symbolic value—as far as Polish life on the Eastern Marches—the Kresy—is concerned. We may know, more or less, something of these happenings; we may be more or less passionate about their detailed content, more or less moved by them; we may more or less commiserate with the direct participants and understand their intentions in a better or worse way—but it is only the deep significance of the events (if we are able to decipher them) that tells us that we are Poles. But we were talking about the curtain. I know very little about what it looked like, and it seems highly probable to me that (as far as I know) it is impossible to learn much more about it. Still, it is not out of the question that it was described in detail somewhere by someone. There are dozens, even hundreds, of insurrectionist accounts—many of them published, many others lying about in various archives, both public and private, and so it is really quite possible that someone has remembered that curtain, which hung there for a few days, maybe even a dozen or so, and described it. That wouldn't be all that difficult to do. Now, if such an account indeed exists, in which the curtain is described, then, of course, it will someday be discovered and published, and we shall learn many interesting details. For example, its length, which I don't know myself—and whether those who moved about behind it had to crouch down or if they could walk on, totally erect, scorning the threat of the eventual salvo? There is another eventuality: that the curtain was remembered; but later, when it had been taken down, it was forgotten, and no one described it at all. There is also a third eventuality, that the curtain was never described, but now, someone who remembers it will read this wartime piece of mine, at which I am now at work, and decide to reconstruct the appearance of the curtain (and if so, I beg you—please be as detailed in your description as possible). Whoever it might be who might remember the curtain is now well over eighty, even nearing ninety, probably. If the first eventuality is considered—that the curtain is, after all, spoken of in one of the insurrectionists' accounts, that would confirm the probability that, even if it only hung there for a few days, the curtain had to be seen by a few dozen, maybe even a few hundred, insurrectionists. Several hundred Germans also saw it, for sure, for it was they who hung it up in the first place and took advantage of it. So the Germans might have described the curtain too (perhaps they have), but we're not looking for any information about the curtain from the Germans for one very obvious reason: although hung by the Germans and serving the Germans, it was hung in our home, and its present value (symbolic as well as aesthetic) is a value exclusively Polish—it is something that only belongs to us. It is also completely impossible for the Germans to understand the symbolic value of the curtain, which they hung up for us there. Its military value at the time is quite another thing, for at the time it was hanging there, it was worth something only to the Germans—it had an exclusively German value. The several dozen or several hundred insurrectionists who might have seen the curtain might be arranged in such an order—here I'm going to proceed from south to north, and then, in a sort of arc bending toward the east. The curtain couldn't have been visible from the barricade that closed Podwale off from the Plac Zamkowy—that is out of the question. Could it have been visible from the Miodowa St. side? That seems probable to me. In the first days of August, there were two barricades on Miodowa in the vicinity of Krakowskie Przedmieście. One of them blocked off Miodowa from the side of Krakowskie Przedmieście, more or less at the height where now, at Miodowa, the exit or rather the entrance to the W-Z Route is located. The other, set up a little transversely to Miodowa, cut off that little section of Senatorska, which is found between Miodowa and Podwale. From the first of these barricades, that on the W-Z Route, the curtain didn't have to be visible, but it might have been. I'm not completely sure of the height of the buildings along Miodowa at the time—from the Capuchin church (if you climbed the steeple), the curtain would most likely have been visible. It was, however, doubtless visible from the highest floors of the buildings, among which was found the barricade closing off Podwale, and also from the higher floors of the building which blocked off Ślepa [Dead End] St. from the Plac Zamkowy. Do you know where Ślepa St. used to be? It ran more or less parallel to Podwale, more or less there, where today runs the moat that separates Podwale from the Old Town walls. It was called Ślepa—"Blind" St. or "Dead End" St.—for the very reason that it was; it began its course not far from Kapitulna, as high as that, but it didn't reach the Plac Zamkowy, dead-ending right before it reached the Square near that large building of six stories, I'm told, the front windows of which (as I imagine them, but here I could be wrong) were placed just about vis-à-vis the windows of the Palace. Ślepa was, therefore, not so much a street as an alley of sorts. A portion of the windows of the building that closed it off was, thus, oriented toward Krakowskie Przedmieście. From both these windows overlooking Krakowskie and those opening toward the Palace, the curtain must have been perfectly visible. I have in mind here the windows of the topmost floor or floors. It is, therefore, obvious that the curtain was visible to the defenders of the insurrectionist barricades on Piwna [Hazel] and Świętojańska [St. John's] streets and to those insurrectionists whose positions were located in the windows of the buildings forming the northern frontage of the Plac Zamkowy. After a few days' bombardment from the tanks and armored vehicles attacking from the direction of Krakowskie Przedmieście and the direction of Nowy Zjazd, most likely, they were no longer windows but rather just holes in the ruins. The Germans took the southeastern part of the Palace after several attempts between 9 and 11 August, but insurrectionists, too, were still there, at least from time to time, in the west wing (at least for one day, maybe even two or three days). So too, if they were able to lean out of the palace windows (but this I know not), they must have also seen the German curtain. Now we see it as well—now you see (more or less) what sort of curtain it was and where it was hung. The Germans had stretched a steel cable (or maybe two?) between the Bernardines (St Anna's Church) and a building on the other side of Krakowskie Przedmieście, which was known (and still is) as the Rösler Palace or Hurtig's. This was an old, mighty urban palace built by the firm of Rösler & Hurtig in 1785 and remodeled a bit in 1888 when Miodowa was pierced through to Krakowskie. It thus constituted the corner building of Miodowa and Krakowskie—the northern corner, that is, the one closer to Zygmunt's Column. The building had been partially burnt in 1939, and two of its three floors were disassembled. Thus, it became a one-story building. And here my doubts begin. That is, at this point, there begin to appear certain things about which I know absolutely, or nearly, nothing and which my imagination strives to flesh out. In order to stretch such a heavy cable across the street, from which cable the curtain was to be hung, cutting off the entirety of Krakowskie Przedmieście from view (a street that is very broad in this particular place, the space between the corner building on Miodowa and St. Anna's—this is not so much Krakowskie Przedmieście as the former Plac Bernardyński or Bernardine Square), the Germans had to fix some gigantic, strong anchoring hooks in the walls. But what did they look like? And where were they set? If we're talking about the Rösler & Hurtig Palace, most likely (if the upper floors were no longer there), then at the height of the first story. There were, on the first story exactly, two balconies, and the Germans might have stood upon these while they were affixing the hooks or on some fragment thereof. It might also have been that, on the Miodowa St. side, the cable or cables were not fixed in place with the aid of any hooks but were tied to the balustrade of one of the balconies. If there still were any such—at least fragments thereof—if the balconies had not been completely destroyed by artillery fire. The façade of the Rösler & Hurtig Palace, from the side of Krakowskie Predmieście, was so divided that the first balcony, the one nearer Miodowa, was located (if we begin our reckoning at Miodowa) at the third row of windows. The other, significantly farther away, was at the eighth row. There had been ten windows along each story of the façade. That entire little quarter of buildings between Miodowa, Senatorska, the Plac Zamkowy, and Krakowskie Przedmieście, from the Rösler & Hurtig Palace (nr. 79) to the John Palace (nr. 89, also partially consumed by fire in 1939) was in quite a ruinous state around 10 August, and, according to the historians of the Warsaw Uprising, had been taken by the Germans on 11 August, and there they set up their firing positions. And on the opposite side? There, the hook from which that curtain was hung had to be fixed above the main entrance to St. Anna's. Or higher still, between the two columns on the north side, about halfway up the columns' height. All of this is, of course, mere guesswork. Whatever the case may be; however, the soldier who was commanded to fix the anchoring hook had to climb a ladder—and a very tall one at that. So up he clambers, with the hammer gripped between his teeth (the little drilling apparatuses that we would use being unknown at the time), and when at last he finds himself above the church doors, a marksman concealed in the ruins of the building closing off Ślepa St. drills him a little hole right above his nose. The ladder topples, and down the German comes, the hammer falling out of his mouth. What a pleasant sight! But all this—hammer and hook, SS man and the hole above his nose, his climbing the ladder and his fall from the same—take place only in my imagination, as I do not know where the hook on the eastern end of the cable was set. As can be seen, this was some gigantic curtain, such as had never before been hung in Warsaw. All of the Germans of whom we've been speaking were probably soldiers of that infamous brigade of bandits under the command of SS-Obersturmbannführer Oskar Dirlewanger, who attacked the Plac Zamkowy from the Krakowskie Przedmieście side, that is, in the direction of the mouths of Podwale, Piwna, and Świętojańska. After the hooks had been anchored (there might even have been more than just two), Dirlewanger's soldiers hung up their curtain. It was sewn together of eiderdowns, bedsheets, and other old rags. A splendid construction—if you can call a curtain a "construction." You could even say—a splendid Baroque construction, which would certainly have delighted the great artists of the Baroque. It might have inspired a marvelous *veduta*, some phantasmagorical engraving such as Piranesi created. A twentieth-century Veduta di Varsovia. Rugs, bedsheets, eiderdowns, all this had been pillaged, as one might surmise, from Polish homes, from Mariensztat, Bednarska, and Krakowskie, for the Germans had no rugs of their own. And so, in this material sense, it was our own Polish curtain. I'd very much like to see it—all those rugs, bedsheets, wall-hangings fluttering in the breeze, some of them punctured by projectiles, some of them even smoldering or smoking, at least from time to time, but all of this, burning and fluttering, can only be seen now in one's imagination. It can't be seen otherwise. How strange, mysterious, phantasmagoric, a beauty! Singed, smoking eiderdowns, rugs hung across Krakowskie Przedmieście! It's only possible to give unclear and uncertain answers to the questions as to when the curtain was hung and how long it hung there. The purpose of the curtain is quite clear—so that Dirlewanger's SS men could pass between the corner building on Miodowa and St. Anna's Church in relative safety, with the rugs and eiderdowns shielding them from gunfire from the northern frontage of Plac Zamkowy and perhaps even from marksmen positioned on the highest floors of the buildings on Podwale and Ślepa. Because the battles for the mouth of Podwale, the buildings closing off Ślepa from the side of Zygmunt's Column, as well as the mouths of Piwna and Świętojańska, seethed almost to the end of August, the curtain—certainly hung after 11 August, maybe a little later, but certainly following the Germans' taking of the buildings in the quarter between Miodowa, Senatorska, and Krakowskie—could have hung there for two whole weeks, even. But it could also have hung only for a few days. There is also the possibility that the curtain was hung, taken down, and hung again relative to the given military situation, maybe even relative to the weather. When it looked like rain, Dirlewanger's SS men would take the curtain down and go take a nap in St. Anna's, curled up in the perforated, singed eiderdowns. You can still hear the German snores there, among the pews. If we're talking about the road taken by the armored ammunition carrier and the two or three or four Tiger tanks that escorted it, there exist (as we have already noted) two possibilities. It might be that it was rolled up (as Adam Borkiewicz has it in his *Zarys działań wojennych* [*Sketch of Military Operations*]) from Krakowskie Przedmieście—and in such a case, it would have traveled, as may be surmised, somewhere from the direction of Plac Hoovera, Trębecka, the Palace Brühl—but it also might have been (as Stanisław Padlewski asserts in his *March Through Hell*) that it was first seen descending from the Kierbedź Bridge, in which case it can be assumed that it was sent from Praga and that, having passed over the bridge, it made its way onto the Plac Zamkowy either via Navy Zjazd or Mariensztat. The route via Bednarska was none too convenient for armored vehicles, but the Germans had to take advantage of it for quite some time, as the insurrectionists controlled, at least to a certain extent, the mouth of Mariensztat and that of Nowy Zjazd giving out onto the Plac Zamkowy until they were finally driven out of both wings of the Palace completely. As far as the first option is concerned, rolling up Krakowskie from Hoover Square, the armored escort would need to have had the curtain parted for them, unless they were to rip through it. The same would apply if the armored ammunition carrier were to drive up Bednarska. Another eventuality (although a rather improbable one) might also come into play: that the curtain (or a portion thereof) might be drawn apart by SS men hidden in the church of St.

THE CURTAIN ON KRAKOWSKIE PRZEDMIEŚCIE

Anna or in the ruins of the Rösler & Hurtig Palace by manipulating the cables or steel links—say two or three eiderdowns, two or three rugs. According to the second option, if the road led through Nowy Zjazd, the curtain would be avoided—it might be set in motion a bit, fluttering in the blasts of the exhaust pipes. Or in the waves of heat coming from the machines. The version with the old, shell-pierced eiderdowns being parted so that the Tiger tanks (and the little ammunition carrier) might pass through is, of course, much more picturesque. It also certainly has a greater aesthetic and symbolic value. We still don't know what was up with that curtain, when it was hung, and how long it hung there—so we might as well accept this version. I don't mean to frighten you, and it's not even proper for me to do so because I won't live to see it, but there is no such machine in existence that is able to slice horrible thoughts out of one's mind, so this thought can't be cauterized just like that, and since it's shown up, it would be better to think it through to the end (in the event that you do)—perhaps the day will arrive when that curtain will hang again between St. Anna's and the buildings on the corner of Krakowskie and Miodowa. Those shell-pierced rugs will rise again, those dirty bedsheets will flop again in the breeze, the eiderdowns twisting and untwisting, letting some feathers flutter down upon the street; the wings of the curtains of history will part, and you will behold tanks rolling down Krakowskie Przedmieście toward Plac Zamkowy. Or they'll be coming down Mariensztat or Nowy Zjazd from the Kierbedź Bridge—and in such a case, turning in the direction of Podwale, they will brush against the bedsheets, eiderdowns, and rugs, setting them in lazy motion, flapping from the cable. Slowly twisting and untwisting eiderdowns and bedsheets. Like a film in slow motion or a film seen in a dream. Slowly, slowly, dirty-yellow Tiger tanks turning, the slow raising of the cannons, and the slow swaying of the old rugs. And between the Tigers, a little to the rear, still hidden by the rugs, there will be that little tank, that wee little tankie—the armored ammunition carrier.

MY NOTEBOOK

THE AFFAIR OF THE NOTEBOOK took place (as I assume, as I strive to recall it) sometime in autumn, in the last few months of 1943. If this is true, I was eight years old and a few months at the time. It's a silly thing, not particularly interesting and not particularly amusing, and having nothing in common (at least at first glance) with war and wartime events, bombardments and executions, and if it is somehow connected to the war, it would be so mysteriously, deeply, in some manner unseen and certainly uninvestigated. It might also be that this mysterious and profound association is just the work of my imagination, and someone else, to whom this might occur, would acknowledge it as something completely lacking in significance and unassociated with anything at all. But there can be no doubt that many a seven- or eight-year-old child has experienced such things or similar ones, but later they're forgotten, for they're seen to be absurd, senseless. Who even knows whether it's worth the effort to speak of them—or decent, if it might not overstep some allowable limit of decency. If the association of the story with war, including it in the context of the war—is decent. If such proximity (here we have something senseless, and right next door: SS men and Gestapo) doesn't infringe upon the dignity of war, its horrid dignity. I don't even know, at bottom, if I'll be able to relate it in an orderly fashion because it's like this: when I recall it, when my memory, unasked and unsolicited, disgorges it suddenly from its depths (especially in the middle of a sleepless night), something none too good begins to happen with my head—my thoughts get tangled and vanish, and the chaos that arises in them seems like the onset of a fainting fit—it seems to me as if I'm about to keel over, fall off the couch and onto the floor, hitting my head against the screen or the bookshelf. Careful—I say to myself—because that which started when you were seven or eight might now, old man, end badly for you—you'll wind up in the hospital with a nasty gash on your skull. So this might also mean (although sixty-some years have passed since then) that I'm still afraid of what's about to happen—as if I were still eight years old and standing there in the classroom, in the full spotlight of my shame, not knowing whether or not there was a way out of the shame, or if it would ever end. At the beginning of the war, I didn't go to school. I attended those so-called *komplety*, where a dozen or so pupils, or even fewer, would gather in a private apartment, and a teacher would show up who taught everything in succession: Polish, math, history, geography. Such *komplety* were also held in our third-floor apartment on Koszykowa. The building in which we were living was located near Marszałkowska—it was the second building from the corner. I don't remember much from that home schooling except for a few patriotic verses as well as the daughter of the concierge from Śniadecki St., one street over. She was gorgeous, an extraordinarily attractive (erotically speaking) black-haired girl who always sat next to me. She was a little older than I was, but I'm not able to say by how much. On the other hand, I do remember her stockings, which were fascinating. Of course, I wanted to know more about them—how she fastened them there in those depths and what it all looked like there, but I didn't know how to go about obtaining that knowledge. On the drawing room table in front of us lay a book, and we were learning something from it, but that wasn't important; even those patriotic verses didn't seem too important to me, for her knee was touching mine, and later, at night, I dreamt of those two knees pressed together. She was my first love, and these, perhaps, were my first erotic dreams, but—at least so it seems to me now—they were still gentle dreams, innocent. Frightening dreams, full of erotic terror, appear only later on in one's life. After that day's *komplety* were over, I ran downstairs after the black-haired concierge's daughter, and there, on the landing between floors, in the presence of some half-naked negresses—in one corner of each of these landings, right near the large windows giving out onto the courtyard, stood these dark brown figures made of plaster (or perhaps brass), each of which held a torch in one uplifted hand, behind the glass shade of which a bulb was screwed—and so there, in the presence of these mysterious figures, the silent witnesses of my childhood, beneath their naked breasts, I made an attempt to embrace, press against the wall, and maybe even kiss that beautiful friend of mine from Śniadecki St. Beneath these half-naked negresses it also came to blows, that is, if my memory serves me correctly, I tried to punch the concierge's daughter, but all of that, the pressing to the wall and the flying fists, was clumsily carried out, and I felt a great shame at not knowing quite how one does such things. After two or three years of such education, my parents decided to send me off to school. I don't know why, since I was able to be taught at home; perhaps they felt that the discipline of a real school, which was absent from the *komplety* environment, would have a good effect on my character. Most likely, I went straight into the second grade, maybe even the third. The school was close by, on the other side of Marszałkowska. Today, that building on Piękna, which at the time was called Pius St., across from a so-called little PAST [a telephone company building], still contains a school, a school for girls, it seems, training to be nurses. As far as I know, before the war, it was a girl's school named for Emilia Plater; in our home, we would say, "We're off to Missy Plater's." Because both of us went there, my sister and I; she, of course, was three grades ahead of me. This was convenient for my parents insofar as they didn't have to take me to school themselves but could entrust me to the care of my sister, who had to make sure that I didn't fall under any tram on Marszałkowska or wander off on my own to the corner of Róże and Koszykowa, where the Germans from the SD or the SA (in light brown uniforms and shirts, Sam Browns and red-and-white armbands with the black swastika on their arms) had their command post. Those smart uniforms of theirs made an impression on me, but any contact with them might be dangerous, even for an eight-year-old boy, and my mother always imagined the very worst.

Thus there seems to be something none too clear to me in my being sent off to the Plater School on Pius St., something that I'm unable to explain. Anyway, one day, our teacher marched us all out of our classroom and into the large hall, where she formed us up into small groups and had us play ring-around-the-rosy again and again. She also told us that if the Gestapo came by and asked us if we went to school, we were to say that we were all preschoolers. And that's what happened. Several Germans in black uniforms showed up in the hall, along with one fellow in civilian clothes. Our ring-around-the-rosy stopped spinning, and the German in civilian clothes asked me in Polish what I was learning. I replied that this was a preschool and that I was a preschooler. Only once in my life did I ever speak to a Gestapo officer—just then, when I was seven or eight years old. I was dressed in long, thick brown stockings (which I think were called *fil d'Ecosse*, pinned up near my underwear with gaiters) and a navy-blue apron with a girlish, flouncy fringe. Kind of a half-boy, half-girl. And in such stockings and such an apron, I was talking with a Gestapo officer from Szucha Boulevard. Now I sense something of the Brothers Grimm in all this, as if it were a strange fragment, a tiny piece broken off the whole of some horrid fairy tale. And kind of a funny fragment all the same. It seems that my statements weren't all that convincing because, despite the apron, I looked more like a second- or third-grader than a preschooler, but after the Germans departed, I was praised by the teacher—she even patted me on the head. Anyway, I find something strange in all that pretending to be preschoolers. Elementary education (which was called general education at the time), operating under German control in the General Government, wasn't forbidden, so the teaching of children in the lower classes didn't have to be held in secret at the Emilia Plater School on Pius St., I reckon. But maybe things were different in 1943. As everyone knows, the Germans often changed their minds concerning Polish public institutions, which operated at their discretion in the General Government. So now I arrive at the story of my notebook, that is, the story of my shame. I'm sure it occurred sometime after the visit of the Gestapo, since after the events associated with the notebook, the teacher (a person entirely abstract at this remove—I don't remember her name, her clothes, her face, or her figure) certainly wouldn't have patted me on the head. She was rather disgusted with me after the history of the notebook, maybe she was even a little afraid of me (I hope so), as she no longer knew what might be expected of an individual such as myself. Teaching at the school was so organized that each child in the class had only one notebook. Most likely (although I don't quite remember), we also had only one teacher who taught us all the subjects. Whatever the case may be, everything we were to learn and which consequently ought to be written down was to be recorded in that one notebook. It was lined with squares or perhaps in triple lines—I don't remember. So into such a notebook, the appearance of which is foggy to me these days, we took our teacher's dictation and also what she had written down on the blackboard. Such copying and writing weren't difficult for me, as I had known how to read and write for quite some time by then. This art had been inculcated in me—over my protests, that is, despite my screeches—by one of my aunts when I was about five or six. I remember—this is something I could never forget—the way the notebook looked was an unusually important matter at the school on Pius St. In addition, and this was perhaps the most important thing of all this instruction: one had to really set oneself to a careful recording of everything that was dictated or written down on the board, keeping the notebook clean and orderly. Splotches, scribbles, crooked penmanship, diagonal writing, writing up and down or in a circle—all of that was not merely frowned upon, it was forbidden entirely, something inadmissible. I saw how my little friends, boys as well as girls, really bent themselves to the task, taking care that their notebooks were proper and even beautiful. The girls—as is always the case with such awful creatures—did not just take care of their notebooks, they even boasted about them, how lovely they were. They showed their notebooks to one another, and it's even quite possible that a certain rivalry existed in the classroom—which girl had the loveliest notebook, the cleanest. Oh well. I didn't take such care with mine. But that's too vague a statement, because in reality I didn't write down anything in it at all, nor did I copy down anything from the blackboard. I had my own notebook, of course, but it served another purpose. I was fond of the pen nibs known as krzyżówki [crossers]—when such a nib was broken and its ink-split spread wide open by pressing it forcefully against the black, penknife-gouged top of a school desk, you could use it to fish out of the inkwell (inkwells were sunk into a hole in the desktop) all sorts of ink-dregs and sops, which you could then use to make splotches and smear, blur, and blear everything that had previously been blurred and bleared—diagonally, up and down, and in circles, too. I could also use that gap-toothed nib to write, to scribble something down—not what was written on the blackboard, but anything at all, whatever happened to come to my mind. This is what I busied myself with, a little furtively, because I didn't want my classmates to see the fruits of my labors. Why did I do such things instead of copying down letters, words, sentences, and rows of sums, nothing but scrawls and scribbles, smears and splotches? And why was it that what I'd blurred and smeared on one day, I reblurred and resmeared the next? Round and round, roundels were best—I succeeded best at them. And then whatever had been splotched up in a round, I could re-smear crosswise. But I don't know why I did it. I had no reason to behave that way, or there may have been some reason, but it was unknown to me at the time, and it remains so today after the passage of sixty-odd years. Anyway, everything went smoothly until the day when the teacher collected our notebooks, informing us that she would be taking them home to correct them. I'm sure I spent a nervous evening and a bad night, or maybe I just had a head full of chaos, but I can't even remember that chaos—my memory has quite deftly erased all that. The next morning, the teacher entered the classroom and set the pile of notebooks down on her desk. Then, she pulled one of them out of the pile: of course, it was mine. What happened next, I don't remember all that clearly. I know that the teacher lifted my notebook (my shame) up on high and, holding it high over my head, turned page after page, displaying it to the whole class, to all of my friends, boys and girls, including the black-haired daughter of the concierge from Śniadecki St.—all of my horrifying scribbles, scrawl by scrawl. She turned the pages of my notebook slowly, very slowly, as if she wanted every child to have a good look at every single page so that every one of them would get a good look at them and burn them into their memory. O, but if it were all only scribbles and scrawls! Those were smearings, thick pawings, huge splotchings, swine-messy, I'd like to say spitty and snotty too, but I probably didn't spit or blow my nose between the pages. Although, I can't count that out, either. I can't remember anything more of that scene—I don't even remember the big dark eyes of the concierge's daughter from Śniadecki St. staring at me, those eyes wide open in horror (or maybe in awe?). There's no doubt about it: my notebook (and everything scrawled and smeared inside it) was destroyed by the teacher, but I'm not able to say in what manner; did she crumple it into a ball in her hands and toss it in the wastepaper basket, or did she tear it lengthwise and then again across its breadth, after which she laid the quartered sheets down on the desk in front of me, to augment my shame and set me meditating on it, long and hard? One way or the other, annihilation was the result; Miss Teacher had no way out; she had to do that; she had to destroy my shameful work; she had to annihilate that horrible notebook, which shamed not only me but the entire class, all the children, who, despite the fact that such a terrible war was going on, were trying so hard, were so buckled down to the task of learning—that notebook in which was recorded (in a visual way) the first version of the wartime project that was to occupy the entirety of my future life.

POLAND IN EUROPE
If Not by Force, Then by Kindness

WHEN THE GERMANS BEGAN the war and achieved their first successes, occupying the lands of their neighbors, they found themselves faced with a problem in dire need of a solution. There was an obvious problem, both theoretical and practical, namely—what was to be done with those neighbors? The manner in which this problem was dealt with—but, as we can now see with perfect clarity, said problem was insoluble (at the time), and so, the suggested German answers formed in response to it indicate that, during the war years, the Germans were torn between two profound yet incompatible tendencies, one of which can be called the tendency to dominate and the other the tendency to exclusivity. As to these two ontological tendencies, now this one got the upper hand, now that one did, but it seems as if both of them are well-rooted, even from age upon age, in the German psyche. It might be acknowledged (but one really mustn't, as that could give rise to charges of racism) that they are of a tribal nature, such as have had a decisive influence on the fate of the German nation throughout the centuries. One or the other of these tendencies appeared more strongly or clearly at a given time depending upon what was currently to the Germans' advantage—that is, how it was going with Hitler's armies on the fronts of the world war. At the beginning of the war, at that time of great military successes, without a doubt, it was the tendency to exclusivity that predominated. At the time, the Germans thought, perhaps a bit naively (but great naiveté, united to great cruelty, has always been an important characteristic of this tribe, and this must always be kept in mind by those who have dealings with them), and so the Germans, both savage and naïve, acknowledged, at this time, that they should be capable of subjugating all of Europe, and that the time would come when there would be no one else in Europe except them—all of the other nations would disappear for good, which means that they would be effectively exterminated. After all, one must admit that even in the final period of the war, after the Battle of Stalingrad and after the immense bombings of the German cities by the American Superfortresses, when it was clear that the Germans were going to lose the war, that same tendency to existential exclusivity—only we have the right to exist, because only he who is capable of bestowing that right upon himself is capable of possessing it—yes, even then, although with much less frequency, this made itself known. One might see in this a symptom of insanity (the Germans were possessed by the madness of catastrophe), but one might also see in it proof of how profoundly this desire for exclusive existence was rooted in the German psyche (in its dark depths). "When someday, we finally win this war," declared Hans Frank on 14 January 1944, in the conference hall of the NSDAP in Kraków, "I will have nothing against turning all of the Poles and Ukrainians and whatever else is swarming around here into ground meat. You can do with them whatever you like." What a beautiful sentiment. It's worth hearing what it sounds like in German: "Wenn wir den Krieg einmal gewonnen haben, dann kann meinetwegen aus dem Polen und aus dem Ukrainern und dem, was sich hier herumtreibt, Hackfleisch gemacht werden, es kann gemacht werden, was will." Now, if Frank were not a great German jurist but a great German poet, somebody on the order of Novalis or Eichendorff, if he had the soul of a romantic poet, he would have added also that the Germans would then devour said Hackfleisch that they would have made of us and the Ukrainians after the war—smacking his lips the while, like a wild-haired and cross-eyed witch from the Brothers Grimm. But such statements suggesting that, after the war, there would remain only Germans in the General Government (while Poles and other nationalities would vanish, having been processed into Hackfleisch) were, in

1944, something of a rarity, and those who stated such things were rather providing evidence of their alienation from reality, soaring aloft as they were through the pure aethereal regions of German tribal dream. Something like this might even have been pleasing to the Führer, but those SS officers listening to Frank's words at the Kraków NSDAP headquarters would probably have liked to hear something a bit more concrete—is there any real way out of their present, horrible situation, for example. In other speeches given more or less at this same time (but also significantly earlier), Frank lent voice to that other tendency of the German psyche—what I call the tendency to dominate. This second tendency of the Germans is, as I see it, much more interesting and at the same time ominous for their neighbors. It is more interesting to the extent that what is happening in the real sphere of reality is more interesting than that which is being carried out in the fictional sphere of dreams. And more ominous to the extent that what is doable is more threatening and ominous than that which is impossible to realize. The processing of minced meat, or Hackfleisch, of all Poles and Ukrainians, as well as all Czechs and all Slovaks, and in general, of everything that is quite unnecessarily swarming about, herumtreibt, around the Germans, and in consequence, the ordering of Europe in such a way—by its depopulation and emptying, so that it could be inhabited only by the Germans (so that Europe should become the exclusive home of the German nation), all of that was, in the 1940s (and today too), something entirely impossible—quite simply, there was no, nor is there, any such technology capable of effecting it. After all (when he was not soaring about the rarefied atmosphere of dreams), Frank realized well enough that Hackfleisch was a practical impossibility. During his meetings with the SS officers and police at Wawel or Belweder, he would often repeat (the phrase was pleasing to him) that 14 or 16 million—he had all the inhabitants of the General Government in mind here—simply couldn't be mown down with machine guns at their backs. "Wir können schließlich nicht 14,000,000 Polen umbringen. . .in der Form eines gigantischen. . .mitrailleusenartigen Ausrotungsfeldzugen." ("After all, we can't wipe out 14,000,000 Poles. . .by way of some

KINDERSZENEN

gigantic destructive expedition...with machine guns.") But if we're speaking of the inclination to dominate, the matter of instruments takes on, of course, a different aspect. This inclination needn't, after all, make use of technological instruments (machine guns) which, even if such are indispensable to it, can only be employed in a limited way. For it is not technology and tools that are the decisive factors in whether the aims are achieved or not. This second inclination of the German psyche was most clearly articulated by the general governor (though perhaps it might be better, in this case, to say "which," since the general governor was really little more than an instrument himself, a megaphone, something through which something else was speaking, something more powerful, impersonal, or suprapersonal), and so, most clearly, Frank stated the following in the speech he delivered before the German crew at the aircraft factories in Rzeszów (Flugzeutmotorenwerke) on 18 March 1944, that is, two months after his appearance at the Kraków headquarters of the NSDAP, in which he foretold the ground meat. Of course, we mustn't think that by then Frank had given up hope that somewhere, in some far-distant postwar future, the grinding would commence, and the Poles, Ukrainians, and other neighboring peoples should be effectively exterminated—one can only assume that this hope had to be concealed for the time being and cede place to a rather more realistic approach. During his Rzeszów speech (a speech that, it must be emphasized, was directed at Germans, not Poles), Frank gave expression to the conviction that the future German Europe must be a Europe of cooperation—and even if the Germans would be the ones to determine who would be cooperating with whom—this cooperation could not be imagined without the participation of other nations. "Wir können uns," said the general governor, "ein Mitarbeit der fremden Völker in Europa nicht mehr wegdenken." ["A resignation from the idea of the cooperation of foreign nations in Europe is now unthinkable to us."] Amongst those foreign nations who, in that common Europe, would cooperate [eine Mitarbeit] with the Germans, a place ought to be reserved—and this is very important to us, perhaps most important—for the Poles. Frank wasn't too kindly disposed to the Poles; you might even say that he didn't like them, or if he did, that was only in the form of Hackfleisch. While speaking to the Rzeszów Germans, however, he risked (I say he risked because this can't have been all that pleasing to the Führer or to Himmler) something akin to a compliment—for he said that we are, or at the least can be—trustworthy people. "Fundamentally, the Poles are—when one treats them politely and delicately—the most trustworthy labor force in Europe, especially for repetitive, simple tasks." This grand sentence of the general governor's (or, I repeat, of the Germans, since he was but a tribal megaphone) ought to be remembered by us in German too. "Im Grunde genommen sind die Polen, wenn man sie brav und nett behandelt, die Zuverlässigsten Arbeitskräfte in ganz Europa, und zwar gerade für dauernde einfache Arbeit." Of course, one must keep in mind that this was already long after Stalingrad and thus quite near the exhaustion of the German power at the time (although it was still before the Warsaw Uprising). Frank was no idiot; on the contrary, he was a thinking man—evil, intelligent (and an evil intelligence is more intelligent than a good intelligence). So he well understood that the fate of the Third Reich had now been predetermined and that, theoretically at least, some sort of plans had to be made for the future. Still, we need to admit (yes, we must admit it, even though we feel revulsion at the ideas concocted by murderers) that it wasn't an entirely bad plan—as a matter of fact, it was something of a vision of the future, something not dissimilar to prophecy. For it was a vision of the future that would indeed come about, which is being realized before our very eyes. That German prophecy that Poles as "die Zuverlässigsten Arbeitskräfte," a trustworthy workforce, and even (as my German-Polish dictionary tells me) an "unfailingly reliable" [niezawodna] one, will, at last, be of some use to Europe, supporting with their labor that very order that the Germans are to introduce to the continent. And that's not all that I have to say on the topic of the prophecies of our general governor. For likewise, as something along the lines of future prophecy, we ought to understand his speech delivered at Wawel ("im neuen Reigerungssal der Burg," rather, as the use of the name Wawel was forbidden) on 26 October 1943, on the occasion of the fourth anniversary of the foundation of the General Government, three months before his speech dealing with Ukrainian-Polish ground meat. So, in the state hall of the Castle in Krakau, the general governor stated (it might seem a bit surprising) something concerning which people would begin discussing only near the end of the twentieth century, so only a couple dozen years ago, namely—the end of history. At the time, Frank addressed to the Poles a proposition that they leave off their frenzy and quit dreaming already about having their own state, which by German verdict had ceased to exist and would never exist again. "The very idea of any reconstruction of a Polish state is insanity on the part of the Poles." At the time, there was nothing really new in such a statement—that an "independent Polish state" was just some sort of Polish insanity, a madness, der Wahnsinn, as Hitler had stated many times before, and as Frank himself had repeated many times before as well. In this October speech at Wawel, Frank linked the idea of the end of the history of the Polish state with a thought that was new and revolutionary—one might say, making use of our postmodern or post-political way of speaking—and from this thought it emerged that it was not only the Polish state but everything that could be called Polish historicity, the historical existence of Poland and the Poles, which had come to an end and ceased to exist. Again, we ought to come to know this proclamation, in which the end of history is announced, in its delicious, proud German form: "Von dieser historischen Stätte aus möchte ich erklären, daß für den Führer und das deutsche Volk sämtliche historischen Probleme, die mit dem Polentum zusammenhängen, gelöst sind, und daß es uns gar nicht interëßiert, wenn irgendwo in der weiten Welt über vergangene Dinge fantasievoll debattiert wird." ("I hereby announce in this historical place that, for the Führer and the German nation, all historical problems arising from Poland have been settled. We are completely indifferent to any discussions taking place anywhere in the world concerning matters that belong to the past.") Does that which I have called the German tendency to exclusivity not ring through this speech? Rather not. Acknowledging as he did that the history of the Poles was now over and done with (at the very least, that history of the Poles that could be understood as their unique individuality and distinctiveness), Frank did not deprive them of the right to exist. In a certain specific sort of existence. For he had uncovered something that could preserve us from annihilation—or draw out a bit our lingering dying-off. But, obviously, under such a condition: that we agreed to respect the German tendency to domination. "For the Poles," the general governor continued, "only one possibility exists: to offer their labor in service of a Europe under German leadership, for their own good, for the preservation of their way of life, and their cultural distinctiveness." This was the only possibility, "nur die eine Chance." The history of Poland (at least from the German perspective) had come to an end; the Polish state, too, had disappeared, liquidated by the Germans. All that remained was the General Government, that temporary reservation for the Poles. The Poles, deprived of their state and their history, could somehow endure, somehow continue to exist—but only if they determined to enter into the history of Europe and participate in that common, shared history. So, such an entrance into a shared history, of which the chief participants were the Germans, would not mean the complete annihilation of the Poles, who might preserve (surely, only for a certain time) their individuality, their way of life, even something of their culture. All they need do was offer it all up in the service of Europe, "in der Dienst Europas." Was it something of this sort that the general governor wished to offer us? "Einen anderen Weg gibt es für sie nicht," he said. There's simply no other way.

INSIDE THE TRAP

IT'S WORTH HAVING a glance inside the armored ammunition carrier to learn what was seen there, what was found there. The interior of the trap and its—if you can put it this way—outfitting, the type of bait with which it was set. This might tell us something not only about the cleverness of the Germans in this field (that is, their manner of setting traps and attracting their prey) but also about their intentions (or, in other words, what they were motivated by in this particular instance: what their intentions were in sending their mysterious vehicle down Podwale). It's also worth noting at this point that the ancient skill of setting traps and hunting by deception is something peculiar to the human species. It is a certain type of biological baseness, a villainy unknown to other forms of life. Neither cats in relation to mice, nor foxes in relation to chickens, nor hawks in relation to hares, nor tigers in relation to antelopes, nor bacteria in relation to people, employ such means—no, they attack openly, pouncing upon something edible, lunging upon it, swooping down from above, undercutting, chasing, surrounding; they might also lurk in wait for their prey, lie low, creep, steal near, but none of this is the setting of traps—it's not the same thing. Now, please don't misunderstand me—I am not huffing in outrage; there's no reason to. I'm simply stating facts. The essence of the dark interior of the trap is the darkness itself: because it is so dark in there, no one knows what it contains, and that's what's so tempting about it, that's what attracts the potential victim—the darkness is the bait. So let's have a look and see what's inside that dark German trap. When the German driver (a soldier of the armored corps in his black uniform) leapt from the vehicle and raced to the other side of Senatorska, into the ruined John Palace, the soldiers of the "Gustaw" battalion, those who were defending the barricade that closed off Podwale at the place where Senatorska gives onto the Plac Zamkowy, tried at first to shoot the escaping soldier (they missed), and then they put out the fire that they themselves had set by tossing bottles of gasoline on the ammunition carrier. The *Wielka Ilustrowana Encyklopedia Powstania Warszawskiego* [*Great Illustrated Encyclopedia of the Warsaw Uprising*] informs us that the "blazing machine" was doused "with sand and soil." The *Great Encyclopedia* goes on to say this: "The accompanying vehicles that had been covering the little tank then withdrew, and the enemy fire ceased. The insurrectionists took advantage of this lull to inspect the vehicle they'd captured. They found that it contained no weaponry, but their interest was aroused by a contraption resembling a large radio transmitter. The *Great Encyclopedia* does not enlighten us as to the fact whether indeed it was a radio transmitter or just something that looked like one or whether it was closely inspected. In the already-cited book authored by General Bór-Komorowski (*Armia podziemna* [*The Underground Army*]), we find some (rather general) information that tells us that some explosive materials had been secreted inside the armored ammunition carrier, along with a mechanism wherewith it could be set off. The General calls this mechanism a timer. "The Germans had stuffed the armored vehicle with explosive materials set with a timer." This information from Bór's book—the timing mechanism—was to be repeated many times in the future in many other books; it continues to be repeated to this day. "It was filled with explosive material connected to a timer," repeats Stanisław Jankowski, "Agaton," citing Bór almost verbatim in his famous account *Z fałszywym ausweisem w prawdziwej Warszawie* [*With False German Papers in Real Warsaw*]. We might also add here that the officers of the AK Headquarters later arrived at the conclusion, or even the determination (though any such a determination could only be deduced from the effects of the explosion, so these are rather assumptions than determinations, and if determinations, then a little educated guesswork), that there had been about a thousand kilos of explosive material in the vehicle. "We calculated," writes Lieutenant Colonel Felicjan Majorkiewicz, operational officer of the III Division of Headquarters, "that there was about a ton of explosives in there." Very interesting information concerning the interior of the ammunition carrier can also be found in Stanisław Podlewski's book *A March Through Hell*. I remind the reader that, in the composition of his book, Podlewski drew upon many insurrectionist testimonies (collected by himself) but without revealing their authors' names. "Soon thereafter," we read in the *March*, an insurrectionist patrol crawled out onto the foreground of the barricade and, upon reaching the tank, confirmed that it contained no arms. However, some sort of complicated mechanism was found in the interior: "coils of wire and some sort of packed tins." Perhaps we ought to underscore that portion of the sentence that reads, "It contained no arms," as this will soon be needed by us. In another place in the *March*, a few pages on, returning to the interior of the trap, Podlewski adds that the vehicle "had to be stuffed with a great amount of explosive material and outfitted with an automatic timing mechanism." That would agree, more or less, with the information provided by Bór-Komorowski, who speaks of a timer—for such a timer-and-fuse is probably the same thing as the timing mechanism described by Podlewski as regulated by a clock [*automatyczny mechanizm zegarowy*]. And yet it seems that some sort of clock- or timer-mechanism, while it wouldn't exclude that mysterious contraption, which the *Great Encyclopedia of the Warsaw Uprising* describes as something "resembling a radio transmitter," still renders it unnecessary. One might also assume that this contraption that resembled a radio transmitter ("a complicated mechanism, coils of wire") was no radio transmitter at all, but the timing apparatus, which in some manner might be engaged from afar, or maybe not. One also finds mention made of "something like a radio transmitter" in Robert Bielecki's book *"Gustaw"—"Harnaś."* [*Two Insurgent Battalions*]; basing his account on the words of soldiers from the "Gustaw" Battalion, he states (just like Podlewski in his *March Through Hell*) that the ammunition carrier was not outfitted with weapons—in the sense that any such armored vehicle, tank, or mini-tank, might be so armed. "It was ascertained only that the vehicle was not outfitted with weaponry, so perhaps it was used to bring ammunition to the front lines." However, as we learn from Bielecki's book, inside the trap, there were found certain elements of weaponry, but perhaps not such as belonged to the equipage of an armored vehicle. "He opened the hatch of the little tank and slid inside, risking exposure to German fire from the Palace. After the passage of a significant amount of time, he emerged from the cabin, retrieving therefrom two potato-masher grenades." Those German Stielhandgranate mit Brennzunder 39, popularly known as potato mashers (or shaft-grenades, granaty trzonkowe) were hand grenades with wooden pole grips. By pulling down on a string fastened to a porcelain ring that ran through the handle (Abreißschnur), the fuse was engaged, which in turn was found in the metal explosive head. Sometimes instead of a porcelain ring, the string was attached to a little porcelain ball. There were some four seconds between the engagement of the mechanism and its explosion. It seems to us that this is all the information currently at our disposal concerning the German trap, that is, at least as far as what was found (or what might have been found) within it. According to the words of Lieutenant Colonel Stefan Tarnawski (who headed the medical unit of the "Northern" Group of the AK), mention is made of the capture of a "tank filled with TNT," whereas in the report of Captain Lucjan Fajer, "Ognisty," we learn of a "time bomb" inside the tank-trap as well as "600 KG of dynamite," but it seems that in both of these accounts (and in so many others) we find ourselves in the sphere of pure speculation. No one has definitively confirmed the existence of dynamite, TNT, or any bomb, nor was anything of the sort seen there by those who had been inside. And so, it's clear that all that we possess in this regard, that is, information concerning the interior of the vehicle, is very unclear—or we're dealing with something that is very general and weakly corroborated (explosive material with a timer), or with something, the use of which is impossible to specify ("a complicated mechanism, coils of wire"), or with something that has the appearance of being coincidental and of no great significance (two hand grenades with wooden handles). The only concrete things (such as allow one to draw concrete conclusions therefrom) are really those "packed tins" of something from Podlewski's book—in all actuality, only they might bear witness to the fact that there was something in the interior of the vehicle that might explode. Later still, it was adduced (traces of this may be found in the *Great Encyclopedia of the Uprising*) that the explosive material was attached somewhere to the exterior of the ammunition carrier and that the vehicle itself was a specially constructed object intended for the delivery of dynamite or TNT in that very way. But since the review of the German armored equipment drawn up by SS-Obergruppenführer Erich von dem Bach, in his famous *Relation* (written down in 1947), does not indicate that his army had any such vehicles at their disposal during the fighting in Warsaw (whereas he provides us with an exact account of all tanks, mini-tanks, armored vehicles, and armored self-propelled cannons), it seems to me that this is nothing but a desperate attempt at thinking up *something* so as to state something concrete (with the desire of placing that explosive material somewhere, somehow, in some concrete place)—something weakly confirmed or not confirmed at all. But let's get back to the matter at hand. Does anything come of our glance inside the German trap? Certainly. Above all, the fact that the trap wasn't intended to be a trap—there was nothing to be found there in its dark innards that could be considered bait. That we might consider as bait. Sure, there were some things inside there that were necessary for something (coils, apparatus), but their intended use is unclear and cannot be determined without closer study. We must also add that the exterior appearance of the ammunition carrier likewise does not indicate that the Germans had intended it to be a trap. I repeat here that fragment of the sentence from the *March Through Hell*, which we underscored above: "It contained no arms." The other accounts say exactly the same thing. Thus, there was nothing there, inside or out—no little cannon, no machine gun—nothing that might be of use to the insurrectionists in their struggle. There were only those two chanced-upon grenades, with their wooden handles and porcelain rings. What is more, as the *Great Encyclopedia of the Uprising* informs us, the vehicle had no turret. It was a "caterpillar-treaded vehicle without a turret." And that means that there was no place there where any sort of weaponry could be mounted—such as a machine gun or a little turret cannon, anything with which to fire upon the Germans. Of course, a question arises—such as obliges us to look upon the whole event that took place on Kiliński St. on 13 August from a somewhat different perspective. That question is—if that ammunition carrier was not armed, nor could it be (and this was something that might be confirmed at first glance)—how could it be utilized? What sort of advantage might the insurrectionists derive from that mysterious, equivocal booty? What did they need something like that for, something that clearly was not useful? And what was there inside its dark interior that was so tempting? What was the bait that was not there? And if there was no bait there, nothing desirable within or without, then there is nothing, absolutely nothing, to indicate that the Germans had a trap in mind, that the armored ammunition carrier was a trap they thought up. You don't have a trap without any bait; some sort of dark bait must be hidden within the darkness; otherwise, there's no trap. And so, in essence, this German operation was conceived differently; the Germans' intentions were different; their (indubitable) cleverness was directed at something else. And yet that thing which was not intended to be a trap became a trap. That being the case, it doesn't seem possible to provide a sensible answer to the question—why? If something, some object, is by chance employed in a manner inconsistent with its intended use, otherwise than it was supposed to be used, with a different goal in mind, if that object makes use of itself in a different manner than intended, one can only state that that's the way things turned out, that's just what happened, and since an object cannot wish to make use of itself in any way, cannot have any sort of intention, one can only say that thus it was fated to happen. If the armored ammunition carrier was a trap, then it was not a German trap but a trap set by fate—with the dark, unknown bait with which fate set it.

LIFE AS RUSSIAN ROULETTE

AT THE TIME (meaning before the Uprising; also, for a little while after the Uprising), to get to Piaseczno, one took a narrow-gauge railway from the Southern Station in Służew. Just past Piaseczno, the tracks branched. One branch bent slightly in one direction, heading northwest in the direction of Grojec, and the other took a more decided turn in the opposite direction, to the northeast, traveling in the direction of Góra Kalwaria. You traveled through Żabieniec to get to Góra Kalwaria; that was the next station after Piaseczno. The Southern Station, I must add, did not yet bear that name; rather, one spoke of the Służew Station or the Station at Służew. The old name, Szopy—"sheds"—was no longer in use during the war years, I think. For me, my grandfather's house, which he had built in the neighborhood of Szopy, just past Szopy, was (and remains) "the house at Służew." How I came to be in Żabieniec that day, what I was doing there—this I'm no longer able to explain. Most certainly, I never lived there, and so, most likely, I either traveled there from Służew or walked there from Piaseczno. Maybe just once or twice, but I don't know with what goal in mind. I am unable to place this visit or these visits in time—certainly, it was in the summer, in July or August, and so right before the Uprising, or during the Uprising. As for Żabieniec, I remember only a little piece of it—a fragment of tracks, the embankment above the tracks and the forest or rather the woods above the embankment and, further on, in those woods or behind them, some indeterminate bushes, brush, while on the other side of the tracks, a gate, a fence, and a villa beyond the fence—and because I never went back there later, I have nothing to add to that memory of a little piece of Żabieniec. The roof of the villa, not as seen from the road but rather a little from the side, was covered in red tiles. But the roof and the red tiles aren't important; nothing else is important except for the woods, the embankment, and the tracks—they suffice completely. That little piece of earth: the embankment and the tracks, I remember now for one reason only, for it was right there, in Żabieniec, across from that gate beyond which stood the villa with its red tiles, that I launched myself onto the tracks. It was a beautiful leap—in childhood, especially early childhood, the body is light. It ascends easily and flies away, flies over tracks and embankments. Later, it's harder to perform such leaps; they are no longer successful. I remember that the train that rumbled up from the direction of Piaseczno wasn't being pulled by a steam locomotive, a choo-choo as we called it, but rather by a motorized engine that was significantly faster. I also remember that the cars were of two colors, but I'm not able to recall which. White on top and red below? White on top and dark blue below? Yellow on top? There were also cars of one color on this line: green, with open footplates front and rear, but the ones I see now against the background of that gate and that villa with the red-tiled roof are two-toned. But why I decided on that leap from the embankment is no longer clear to me. Perhaps I wanted to get a taste of what death is all about, what it actually is, what a person feels when he's dying. Or when a person's dead—that's even more interesting. Or maybe I decided to jump because I felt it was better not to be than to be. Such a decision made by an eight- or nine-year-old must give a person pause, at least. But it might also have been (and most probably was) something like Russian Roulette: all right, let's see what you're made of—risk it, prove you're not a coward, prove that you're able to die. Let them see that you're not just anybody, that you're capable of a decision like that. Jump, and let's see what happens—if you survive or not. And let's see how they'll look at you after that jump. What you'll be able to read in their eyes. That might have been an important element in my decision. Because I remember that this leap of mine from the embankment and onto the tracks was witnessed by two little girls from Żabieniec. Or they might have been from Piaseczno or Zalesie. Did they leap too, in front of that same train of mine, or in front of another one, the next one, maybe? I don't know. It seems to me now that one of them also jumped, right after me, although this might be a later addition to my memories. But I'm sure that it was they who encouraged me to take that suicidal plunge. They egged me on—bad little girls. They were my age, for sure: eight or nine years old, but here my memory fails me completely, and I remember nothing about them at all, neither their names nor their faces, neither their hair nor the dresses they were wearing. I also don't remember where they came from in my life at the time, where they appeared from, if they were the daughters of some friends or acquaintances of my parents, or some chance-encountered girls from that villa across the way whom I met just then, right before my leap. On the other hand, I remember well enough that it was one of those little girls, either earlier or later, who, in some woods, in some bushes in Piaseczno or Żabieniec (maybe near those very tracks where I jumped), let me do to her what a nine-year-old boy might do to a girl his age, that is, she let me put my hand beneath her dress, between her legs. She even laughed, which took my courage away, and maybe even made me angry because placing one's hand under a dress was a very serious matter for me and—I approached it very soberly. As I saw it, mysteries of the sort of what a girl had under her dress weren't funny in the least, as the very essence of a mystery (of any sort) possesses something which essentially excludes hilarity. I feel no different today—joking with mysteries, even small ones, the smallest, seems something absolutely inadmissible to me. When mysteries become laughing matters—when we laugh at them—they cease to be mysteries and disappear. Only someone who is not attracted to mysteries can allow himself to laugh at them like that, only someone who believes that there are no mysterious things on earth at all, who has no need of mysteries even existing. Memory is egotistic, turned in upon itself; it is concerned with nothing but itself and its own individual needs. It desires to satisfy those needs and is concerned with nothing but that; it remembers nothing more than what it needs. I remember placing my hand underneath the dress of that girl from Żabieniec perfectly. I also remember what I felt at the time I was doing this—something like a weakness or a tightening in the pit of my stomach or around my heart, perhaps in my very bowels. I remember my hand sliding towards its goal (its destiny). The girl, her dress, her knee, her stocking, even that which was higher up, those places, too, in which it all took place, those bushes or that little wood, all of Żabieniec along with its surrounding areas, the one Zalesie and the other—all of that dissolved, vanished, and is perhaps now only to be found in the regions of that war, but if it does exist, it exists only for itself. I hear only that laughter, so out of place as far as I was concerned, for my daring enterprise (so important to me) was made ludicrous by that laughter, in other words, like something that shouldn't be taken seriously. We also laughed, earlier or later, both of us, even all three (we two along with that other little girl) when, after my leap from the embankment, we ran away into the woods and, hidden among the trees, waited with bated breath (probably fairly terrified) for what was going to happen next—whether the adults saw my leap (and maybe that of one of the girls) and if so, how they would react. Our laughter in the woods was a reply to the bawling of the engineer, who stopped the train and got out of the engine (right now, I incline to the position that the car was red and yellow) and, standing on the tracks, gave vent to what he'd just experienced. I'd flown right past his front window, and that must've been quite a shock to him. As far as I remember, I faced no consequences for this deed, which I probably took as an important life lesson—it is possible to throw yourself in front of a speeding train as long as it is done with graceful agility, and it'll be something of a gas, with some bellowing tossed in. The question remains, to which I have no good answer—to which I certainly have no sensible response—why, leaping from the embankment, did I soar onto the other side of the tracks? Why did I not fall onto the tracks? Another way of putting the question, obviously: why am I alive?

WAR HEAD

WHAT EXACTLY DID the general governor, general and minister of the Reich, Doctor Hans Frank, have in mind? How did he see his future, his fate? He knew that all things pointed to the fact that the Hitlerite police state would not be capable of lasting unless it was validated, unless, in its murderous enthusiasms, it found itself some enduring legal basis. Knowing this, he wished to set the Reich (and along with it, all of German Europe) on the firm foundations of righteous Nordic law and righteous Nordic power. This was reasonable and is being realized before our very eyes—its very interesting realization is coming into existence. But what interests me are not so much the opinions articulated by Hans Frank (which are presented in his so-called *Journal* in a manner that leaves no room for doubt) as his beliefs and his presentiments—what did they whisper to him concerning his future? He was not a stupid man; this was no common German beast, no run-of-the-mill German murderer—on the contrary—his pensive face and sad eyes (as well as his gay smile) and his very thinned yet carefully coiffed hair constrain us to see in him, rather, a person who reflected (like every thinking person) on his future, on his destiny (on what was to happen soon enough); he took various eventualities into consideration. He would stand in front of his mirror in the bathroom at Wawel Castle and, combing that thinning shock of hair, grow pensive and think. Was this someone who believed in the grand ideas of his beloved Führer and thus considered that, for their realization, even if it was to take one or perhaps two hundred years, it was worth sacrificing his life—in the name of something so splendid and noble? Both his life here on earth and (eventually) his future life after death? I do not know whether Governor Frank believed in God. Or whether he was a cynical man, cold, even cruel, who achieved a significant amount of power (a power that was all but absolute within the borders of the General Government), who arrived at the conclusion that by making good use of his own talents and the trust of his beloved Führer, he might come into the possession of even more power? And what did he really desire; how did the general governor see his future? Was he counting on the German grenadiers taking Moscow, Leningrad, and Kazan before too long, at which time he would move out of Wawel and into the Kremlin (or perhaps the Winter Palace) and rule from there half of Asia and half of Europe—as the Gauleiter of the whole Greater Ostland, Region Ost IV, Ost V, and even Ost VI? Or was it rather that, thinking only of the use he might be to the Führer and his grand idea, he would bring German order to the cities of Krakau, Warschau, and Lemberg, cleaning them up and civilizing them without a thought to any personal advantage he might obtain thereby? Or maybe this was just some lunatic, a maniac, an insane man obsessed by one thought and one alone—that German civilization must be made available to everyone everywhere, to all of humanity, for humanity never thought up, never created anything greater, anything more civilized than that splendid civilization? Of course, there is no good answer to such questions—it is impossible to conjure forth that mind; we cannot plumb its depths. It is entirely illegible to us. We can't even know whether it would be worth bothering ourselves with such a thing— the mind of a German murderer. The shoeshine boy who sat on his box in front of the ruined Main Station on Aleje Jerozolimskie polishing the boots of SS men, the ricksha cabbie who transported German soldiers from Gajewski's café (corner of Marszałkowa and Koszykowa) to their barracks at Okęcie, the old woman who sold pussy willows at the time near the Sukiennice [Cloth Hall]—they all knew quite well where it was all headed—they knew that the general governor, whoever he was and whatever he imagined, whatever those presentiments of his told him, didn't stand any chance at all, because the decision had already been made (but by whom?): the general governor would be hanged or shot or (in the best possible case) it would all end for him heroically and theatrically, more or less as it did for his pal from the neighborhood, SS-Gruppenführer Reinardt Heydrich— he'd take a few rounds in the stomach or be blown to bits or skewered with pieces of shrapnel from a bomb tossed under his car. But (to make another attempt at penetrating the illegible) Frank too had to know, it couldn't have been otherwise; he at the very least had to have taken it into consideration; he had to see it in his mind's eye: how someone jerks open the door of his car and pulls him out on to the road and aims at his midriff, shoving the barrel of the gun right into his navel, right into the very center of his German essence, or how someone places a noose around his neck; he saw his legs jiggling and dancing in the air when someone's hand pulls the lever, and the trapdoor opens beneath his feet. Whoever wishes to is perfectly capable of imagining it: the adjutants drowsing in the ante-chamber; how they rush in, their tunics undone, releasing the safety on their machine guns, bursting into that bedroom in Wawel Castle after being awakened by the scream of the general governor: he had a nightmare; he dreamt, in the middle of the night, of his own feet, dancing in the empty space where the trapdoor used to be. The *Ilustrowany Kurier Polski* [*Illustrated Polish Courier*], a weekly printed in Kraków in the forties, quite regularly (at least two or three times each month) published photographs of the general governor. This was probably obligatory, just like the photographs documenting the heroic deeds of the German soldiers on all the fronts: Eastern, Western, and African. In these photographs in the *Illustrated Courier* the general governor is most frequently depicted (as was probably obligatory, too) fulfilling his various important gubernatorial duties. And so, in the issue dated 21 March 1943, we see Dr. Frank at the Main Station in Kraków bidding farewell to a transport of laborers heading off to the Reich. The caption below reads: "As the one-millionth laborer setting off on the journey to the Reich, Józef Maciarz, from the Mielecki *powiat*," is presented with a gold watch by the general governor. Dressed in an elegant leather overcoat, Dr. Frank is smiling gaily (he had beautiful teeth), while Józef Maciarz, intimidated, lowers his gaze. In another earlier photo (8 November 1942), the general governor, likewise smiling beautifully, this time in a general's uniform with a Sam Browne belt and other trimmings, converses with the bailiffs and administrators of the villages surrounding Kraków. "Dr. Frank took advantage of the opportunity during his visit to thank everyone for their understanding and willingness to work." The most interesting of the photographs of the general governor printed in the *Illustrated Polish Courier* is that from 1 November 1942. Here the caption reads: "During the third Chess Tournament of the G.G. held in Kraków, Dr. Alekhine, world and European champion, competes against Sämisch, the Berlin champion, whom he defeated. The match was conducted in the presence of Dr. Frank, the General Governor, who is a great admirer of the game of chess." The picture shows the great Alekhine, who at the time was probably about fifty, editor of the chess corner of the *Illustrated Polish Courier*. How Alekhine found himself in the General Government and the city of Krakau at the time, what winds wafted him there, what bizarre idea, what bizarre chess gambit led him to seek a place for himself in the city of Krakau and, what is more, to edit a chess corner in the so-called reptile press—is simply beyond my powers of comprehension. Maybe he was stupid. Or maybe he had no other option, and the last bit of earth beneath his feet that remained him in the world was in Krakau. On the photograph printed in the *Illustrated Courier*, he is facing us directly. We can see Sämisch from the rear, and from this perspective, he is eerily similar to Goebbels—maybe it is Goebbels in the flesh and not Sämisch at all. The match is probably nearing its conclusion since Alekhine (the chessboard is clearly visible) has a one-pawn advantage. But the Russian master is still deep in thought, seeking some good solution, and there, sitting between the two players, Dr. Frank is pondering deeply, too. This time he is in civilian clothes, a suit, hatless, and it is clear that he is going bald—before they hang him, he will be almost totally bald. His head is resting on his palm (his index finger is touching his ear); he is staring at the chessboard, sunk in thought, trying to penetrate the mind of the great Alekhine. It is perfectly clear that Dr. Frank is not merely "a great admirer of the game of chess" but something more—a connoisseur of the game, someone who is capable of comprehending the strategy concocted by the great world master, in what manner he plans on checkmating Sämisch (IV-V place in this tournament; of course, Alekhine defeated them all). So then, how was it, what was churning about in his head? The head of Frank the chess player, fan of Alekhine and other masters? Are we to believe that this chess mind didn't know how the simple game in which he was engaged would end? Of course, he did—and his nightmares certainly brought him much worse imaginings than those legs of his jiggling above the trapdoor, that noose squeezing his throat, and those last convulsive heaves of his. My imagination, my infected imagination (by the German war), clearly beholds the worst of his dreams, but I'm not going to describe them. If he knew how it all was to end, what the end of his life was to be, then why (I repeat again, with that chess player's mind of his), why did he take part in it all; why did he not try to disentangle himself from it all, all that German bestiality? Why, instead of playing chess, did he take on the role of the German Übermensch-modernizer? Was it merely because he loved his Führer and that splendid German culture of his? On the second page of the next to the last November 1942 number of the *Illustrated Polish Courier* (the second and third pages of this weekly were usually reserved for pictures from the battlefield), a photo is printed with the caption "Storm Unit in Stalingrad." There are more such photos presenting the street fighting in Stalingrad printed in the *Illustrated Courier*—all of them interesting. The one that caught my attention bears the additional caption: "As heavy Stuka bombers fly against the partially-ruined Soviet fortress to pave the way for the German infantry attack on the earthworks, a unit of German storm troops awaits the order to advance in the shelter of a wall." In the picture, we see six German grenadiers shielding themselves behind some fragment of a partially demolished wall. One of them even leans a bit beyond it. My eye is especially drawn to a semi-crouching gentleman, middle-aged with glasses, who leans on a rifle—surely some math or physics teacher from Munich or Frankfurt am Main. And there's another one, significantly younger, with a dark beard—something rather rarely met with in Waffen SS units. But maybe these six grenadiers are Wehrmacht soldiers. Their helmets are covered in some sort of fabric or camouflage netting; they carry rifles and automatic weapons and loops of grenades (those long ones with the wooden handles). Anyone in Kraków or Warsaw who bought a copy of this edition of the *Illustrated Courier* and examined this photo of the Battle for Stalingrad could be quite certain (could draw a conclusion bordering on certainty) that, before they even opened the paper to page two, none of these grenadiers were any longer among the living. Five, maybe ten minutes after this photo was taken, the Stukas flew off, their bombardment over; the artillery barrage went silent, and the six grenadiers left the shelter of the wall. "Vorwärts!" They ran forward, lobbing grenades. And then a Soviet machine gun, deeply buried somewhere in the ruins of Stalingrad, spoke up. What was going through the mind of that middle-aged gentleman who, resting on his rifle, had been holding binoculars in his other hand, through which moments before he had been observing the Soviet defensive positions? What was in the mind of Dr. Frank when he awoke in the middle of the night with a scream from that nightmare in which his feet were dancing and jerking over the space where the trapdoor was no longer? Whatever they were thinking about, they had to do what they were doing—there was no other way out because there was no way out at all. History has to move on somehow, has to head in some direction, though that direction be unknown—perhaps that direction is known to her alone. So they had to move on toward their destiny or (if you prefer to imagine it this way) they had to walk alongside their destiny, in its company, as neighbors, fellow travelers, of their own fate. The grenadiers had to emerge from behind the wall out into the open spaces of the ruins of Stalingrad, and Dr. Frank had to exit his cell in the company of his American guards and head toward the gallows—in the direction of those legs of his performing their funny jig over the open square in the floor. And even what that beloved Führer of theirs had in mind was of no great significance at that moment (nor is it now). Whatever they had, whatever they should have had in their minds—the Führer, Frank, and the German grenadiers (as well as all other murderers)—couldn't change a thing. The important thing was (and remains) only what She had in her completely different head—that War Head, as it were. The Greeks called her Moira, that is, Predestination. And she was mightier than all their mighty gods taken together. They didn't know what she really was—nor do we.

ADOLF DYGASIŃSKI AND HIS *HARE*

JUST THINK, I SAID to Ewa, whoever reads the digital versions of these wartime pieces of mine continuously—that is, in the order in which I'm writing them—just think: this must mean something, that nearly all of my wartime recollections concern animals of some sort, animals I met up with over the course of my life and with whom fate somehow linked me—cats, turtles, crayfishes, and horses—whereas I hardly remember a single human being. I don't remember a single one of the servant lads at my grandmother's estate, whereas I remember perfectly well the horse I'm sitting on while someone leads us around the granary, between the stable, the barns, and the carriage house. I don't even remember the hand that held me on the horse's back, but I do remember the light yellow horse's mane and the white stripe between his eyes. It's almost as if the eyes of that very horse and no other are still looking at me, here in front of me, real close, huge and moist, beneath those sandy bangs, and they've been looking at me, examining my life for a full sixty years and more. This must mean something.—And as soon as I said that, I thought, immediately (as any educated person would) that these wartime pieces of mine here have something in common with Adolf Dygasiński, that is, with his ideas as a writer. When was the last time I read Dygasiński? A long, long time ago. But even before I became familiar with *Zając* [*The Hare*] and *Gody życia* [*Mating Life*] (which has to have been when I was in high school, maybe even a little later when I was studying Polish literature at university) and before I became acquainted with the most important works of the Polish Romantics. Now I feel it had to have been an educational mistake—someone overlooked something, or maybe I was to blame because it should have been the other way round, which would have protected me from many unnecessary delusions, and even troubles (both spiritual and in my daily life). On Sunday mornings in that wartime period, my mother would read aloud to me from *Ojciec zadżumionych* [*The Father of the Plague-Stricken*] and *Anhelli*—O, ominous selections! I would sit at the foot of her bed in my long white nightshirt reaching my ankles (it had a little stiff collar embroidered with violet and red thread) and great tears (tears as big as peas, as the saying goes) would fall on the lacy bedclothes, which probably remembered her wedding night. The death of Ellenai! Don't pretend that you didn't weep when you listened to that! I wept with fear and joy—at being a Pole. Whoever has read *Anhelli* in early childhood has been placed into the hands of some higher power by fate: such a person shall become a Polish patriot, not to say more forthrightly—a nationalist. It shouldn't be understood that I bear a grudge against my mother. But it might have been better if, on those bittersweet Sunday mornings, she had read me *The Hare*! I would also, of course, have sobbed tears as large as peas, but for a completely different reason, and, what is more important, I would have looked upon the problematics of life from a somewhat broader perspective, entered somewhat more deeply into its mysteries, and my particular, splendid, and terrible Polish fate, wonderful and full of horror, would have been set against the background of some other mysterious destinies (or destiny would have so set me there)—against the background of the fate of the beasts of forest and field. It's worth noting here that *Anhelli* and *The Father of the Plague-Stricken* are very complex works and probably a little too difficult for eight- or nine-year-olds, for, because of their imagery and language, they refer to other, earlier literary works unknown to eight- and nine-year-olds. Dygasiński, on the other hand, had a great talent for the construction of fables that were (and surely still are) attractive to everyone—the story of *The Hare* will interest any child who sees in the adventures of the earless hare something akin to his own situation, and the adult who will be a little entertained and a little saddened by the adventures of the earless hare (and those who are hunting him) will find in the fable some interesting information that touches upon the mysteries of life that fascinate him. Had I come to know *The Hare* when I was eight or nine, I would have learned from that work (at the very moment such knowledge would have come in handy) many things which I later came to know anyway, but much later and probably too late—when, at the age of about twenty or perhaps a tad older, in the second half of the 1950s, I read *Die Welt als Wille und Vorstellung*. This was not to be found in Polish; I did not read German at the time, but I found an old Russian translation from Tsarist days, and in this manner, in Russian, I became familiar with Schopenhauer. It's good to become familiar with the fundamental Schopenhauerean truths early in one's youth, perhaps even in childhood, when one first attempts to locate and establish one's place in life and when for the first time there appear (still very murkily articulated) questions of belonging and identity—that is, such questions whereby we attempt to learn what this life of ours is, what sort of thing it may be. Of course, when you read Schopenhauer as a punk, to say nothing of when one is a kid, such a thing is simply impossible—intermediaries are needed. Dygasiński and his "hare" can be just such intermediaries. What would I have learned had my mother behaved a bit more reasonably (of course, I am also grateful to her for *The Father of the Plague-Stricken* and *Anhelli*) and, toward the end of the war, read *The Hare* to me aloud? Well, let me try to list the fundamental bits of wisdom that one might derive from a familiarity with Dygasiński's little book. First, I would have learned of the existence of a great community, of which all that lives forms a part—including me. The narrator of *The Hare* is consciously developed (though only in certain portions of the narrative) as part-human, part-hare. So we have two co-narrators, man and hare, or (perhaps it would be better to grasp it thus) one narrator—man-hare or hare-man. "His freedom is such as is not bound by any border or limit. Cornfield, meadow, forest, field, garden, orchard—the whole world lies open before him. As long as his legs are in good shape, he can go anywhere and find a way of life everywhere.

Ah, the wheat, the rye, the barley, the peas, radishes, clovers, cabbages, turnips, lettuce, parsley, mushrooms, berries! Sweet and tart and bitter, aromas, oils. Something to sink one's teeth into morning, noon, and night." So the hare is like a man, and man like a hare. A complete identity, just as life is identical to itself and nothing exists beyond it—beyond that community of all living things. Second, from such Sunday morning readings, I'd also have learned that this community possesses a common area of existence—one in which all living beings must somehow fit. In *The Hare*, this common area is known as Morzelany. "Morzelany, a village with good soil, has the appearance of a bowl filled with the most varied victuals, to which people, four-legged creatures, birds, and even lower animals sit down. How many creatures make use of life on this plain covered by the azure vault of the heavens, lit up in the daytime by the sun and at night by the torches of the stars and the moon, the silent witnesses of the life-adventures of animals constrained at this time only to settle matters of hunger and love!" In this place, which is open to all, each and every one must find and ensure his own place—a fatherland for himself and for his kind—which is no easy task. This place, den, or little burrow—or, in the case of the hare, warren—is conquered with strength, fear, cleverness, and—that which one extracts from the depths of life, what urges all to endure in life—what Dygasiński calls "the energy of despair." One might also call it the energy of life, which allows us to come to know our world and later to take up our place therein. "He was familiar with each clod of earth here, each bed of flowers; he knew where the broad roads lead to and where from and came to learn how to avoid them via small paths when necessary." Third, I would have learned that, although the common area of life is one and the same for all living beings and that all beings have the same right to it—an unrelenting war of everyone with all the rest is being continually waged there. Neither that one common area of life, nor that one common generation of all life, hare-manity, nor belonging to the hare-man community, but that war, indeed, is the one law, the one necessity, the one power that has united and will unite forever and ever all living beings. "The great war, the game, is on—and it is as universal, as immortal, as gravity. These must win, and those must lose. And yet everyone is striving to outplay his competitor, to take what belongs to him, and in this necessity, even the weaker ones have a chance of success: flight, escape, is also a stealthy way of lurking for the life of him who pursues, who will die of hunger, lose his life, if his prey escapes." Fourth, I would have learned from *The Hare* that, in this great war that is being waged in the community's common area, that is, in life, it is not always the strongest one who wins, or the most clever, the wisest, the one who in some way is better—but the one who is lucky, the one upon whom chance or fate smiles—"that blind fate, that chance, thanks to which, sometimes, one safely eludes the snare." As for fate and blind chance, I would have learned that there exists something about which one knows neither what it is nor of what it consists because fate is fate, blind chance blind chance, and nothing more can be said on the subject. "Tetera—an impoverished nobleman, a notorious poacher, could drill a bullet through the center of an ace of diamonds. But his house is a living hell, and whenever his spiritual balance is disrupted, he can't hit the side of a barn. Good fortune for the hare! . . . In the backwoods of Morzelany, there also lives the clever fox Kita, who is so quiet when he walks or crawls that nothing can be heard. But when, by pure chance, he treads upon a dry twig or leaf, the hare races away, spooked." I would also have learned, fifthly and finally, that whomever fate or blind chance favors not must lose, for life is cruel, and there is no mercy. "The storks arrived as well—too soon as it turned out—and one of them, very hungry, kept searching and searching the fields for food. At last, he came across a little bunny, a newborn, curled up in the reeds, and, it seems, taking it for a frog-like creature, he struck it from above with his powerful, hard beak, right between the ears. The poor thing, stunned by the blow, leapt up and hopped away like a frog, with the huge stork following on its stilts, striking and striking at its head with that beak. It fell onto its back in a puddle, twitching its legs and squealing mournfully. . . . The stork picked the rabbit up in its beak as if with pincers, behind the ears, and flew off somewhat in order to consume the fruit of its search in peace. Bleak is the life of a hare!" As one can see, the author of *The Hare* had some pity for his heroes (at least, if I can put it in this way, stylistically speaking), but similar scenes (scenes of human suffering as well—searing with iron taken fresh from the fire) he describes with great relish, which of course proves that he too, although pitying, had no pity. After all, he said this himself, directly— "There is no place for pity here, that emotion which is just now taking root in the human world, alongside hypocrisy." Now, this sounds almost like a direct citation from Nietzsche—they were of the same generation, after all; the author of *The Hare* was born in 1839, so he was five years older than the philosopher. Is there any higher power over such a world ordered as that described in *The Hare*? Some higher necessity? Dygasiński, I think, says—*I don't know.* "The lights of heaven gazed down pitilessly—there was something tiger-like in their glittering. Time passed on the clock of eternity, and, for the one caught in the snare, each moment was endlessly long." Perhaps this is a metaphor of something looking down upon us all from on high— some cruel necessity. But perhaps it is nothing more than the fragment of a description of a winter night seen through the eyes of a hare caught in a wire snare, awaiting the arrival of the executioner's club. The destiny of Adolf Dygasiński himself is interesting. Although some hundred years ago, around 1900, he was a well-respected writer, today, he has been completely forgotten. He's not taught in the schools; I suppose that neither *The Hare* nor *Mating Life* is subjected to analysis in seminars on Polish literature at the universities. The students (and most likely the professors, too) consider *The Hare* to be one long yawn—a bunch of nineteenth-century rubbish. I took my citations from an edition that appeared a few years ago in a series of books with the less-than-attractive title *Less-Known Classics*. If someone's a less-known classic, that means he's not relevant—just a dusty museum exhibit. And whatever he had to say—no one cares anymore. And yet, all that we've just said is unusually topical. We're not moved, not pierced to the core, by that tiger-like sparkle of eyes from above? So, what happened? I imagine that Dygasiński's posthumous decline occurred because he set himself up against something that was taboo in Poland, almost sacred. His little book (*The Hare* is a hundred or so pages long) can be understood as a book that mocks Polish Romantic thought through and through—and all Polish Romantic poetry. It mocks Mickiewicz, Słowacki, Krasiński, all soaring of the soul, all useless enthusiasm, mystical doctrinairism, cosmic invention, eschatological fantasy, religious ecstasy. It mocks *Król-Duch* [*King-Spirit*], *Anhelli, Zdania i uwagi* [*Sentences and Comments*]. It tells us that there is nothing else than life, this life, just as it is: with all its repulsiveness, its wild beauty, and its horrifying energy—nothing more than that. Perhaps we ought to take it thus: *The Hare* cancels out *King-Spirit, Sentences and Comments, Anhelli,* and all other such works. With *The Hare*, Dygasiński annihilates all their contents, tosses them into the realm of non-existence, sets them in the void. Or that just came about—by blind chance. Because all he wanted to do was to describe the hard life of a jackrabbit. And the similarly hard—and, what is more, stupid—life of the people who hunt him down. Shall we ever again return to *The Hare?* I certainly hope so. I recommend it. For it contains great truths that we ought to know. One such great truth—that we are here, only here and nowhere else. What Dygasiński has to say (and what he said so simply and so beautifully) is not—as can be seen—difficult, complicated, or intricate—it is only as difficult and intricate as life itself. You don't have to be an adult at all in order to understand that, although such ordered knowledge on the topic of life as we find in *The Hare* can also come in handy for adults—but it can be understood as well by the mind of a child; it seems completely accessible to the mind of an eight- or nine-year-old. If, instead of *Anhelli,* my mother had read aloud to me from *The Hare* on those wartime Sunday mornings, I probably would have understood the German war better, comprehended more of it. *Anhelli* didn't explain that war—Słowacki and Mickiewicz were no help at all with that.

THE LAST SKATER
IN THE SWISS VALLEY

AT THE CORNER OF Szopena [Chopin] St. and the Aleje Ujazdowskie (or Siegesstrasse), in the Dolina Szwajcarska [Swiss Valley] area, there used to be an elegant café. My mother would meet her friends there, and from time to time, she would take us with her—sometimes me, sometimes my sister, sometimes both of us. Most likely, she wanted to show off her beautiful, smart children. I liked those short trips from Koszykowa to Swiss Valley, most probably because in the region of the Valley, which was not far from the Gestapo headquarters on Szucha, one came across SS men in their classy uniforms and caps with the death's head. When I caught sight of the SS men (my mother would hold me tightly by the hand and even pull me forward so that I wouldn't turn around or even stop there to gawk), I would imagine myself an SS man strolling down the Aleje Ujazdowsie in a cap with a death's head badge. Those death's head caps were beautiful (fascinating, too, as they aroused fear), and those future plans of mine were pleasant to dwell on. I'm not able to locate in time those walks to the café in the Valley, but I reckon that we must have been going there, my mother, me, and my sister, in the first years of the war. Later, perhaps in the second half of 1942, the Swiss Valley, along with Szopena and the Aleje Ujazdowskie, were attached to the German residential district. The German quarter, I believe, encompassed all of the Aleje Ujazdowskie from Szucha to the Plac Trzech Krzyży [Square of the Three Crosses], and such being the case, that elegant café most likely ceased to function. If it continued to be open, it was still inaccessible to Poles, being a café reserved for SS men and other Germans—*nur für Deutsche*. At least, that's what I think these days. Most likely, the café in the Swiss Valley was closed during the winter, although there might have been a winter pavilion there (I don't remember), but that had nothing to do with our walks from Koszykowa—we continued to go to the Valley because in the summer white (maybe green?) tables and chairs were put out, and in winter water was pumped in and a skating rink was set up. In those days, artificial ice rinks were unknown, so the rink was open only on those days when the temperature was below freezing. I have very faint memories of all this—now I see only a fragment of green balustrade, against which I'm leaning, as well as numerous skaters going round and round; I can also hear an orchestra playing for the skaters (although I can't see it—so it had to be located somewhere on a platform above the rink), and these faint memories of mine (if this was the winter of 1941–42, I was six, almost seven years old already, and I should remember something more, at least a larger portion of the balustrade or a slice of the orchestra)—I explain the faintness of these memories of mine in this way—all of my attention at the time was focused on my own suffering—on it alone. This suffering won't allow me to remember anything but that little fragment of green balustrade. The suffering, on the other hand, was great, terribly so, because it was associated with feelings of humiliation and rejection, and I remember it perfectly. And this is how one remembers one's own past—we remember our horrid injuries, our dreadful humiliations and abasements, and things that are much more interesting—orchestras and the rest of that open balustrade, as well as the winter pavilion—disappear somewhere. I'll explain in a moment from where those sufferings of mine arose. Now, those winter strolls to the Swiss Valley were only for my sister (my elder by three years). They were organized for her benefit only, for her pleasure. I was taken along— well, that's it, I really don't know why, perhaps only as company, maybe only so that I'd get some exercise and wouldn't be sitting home all the while doing nothing except submerging myself in my gloomy meditations. And that was my problem—for that very reason, my sufferings erased from my memory the entirety of the green balustrade, leaving in its place only a little portion of it. The problem arose from this: that my sister was permitted to ice skate, and I—no. It wasn't because I didn't know how to ice skate (I didn't, but that's another matter entirely), but because I had neither the blades nor the proper boots for them. Back then (unlike now), blades weren't permanently fixed to the soles of uppers, rather, they were affixed to them with thongs and a screw inserted into an aiglet sunk into the heel. Why my sister had skates and could ice skate and I didn't have ice skates and couldn't, I'm unable to explain. Perhaps it was a sort of punishment from Mama and Dad—my sister was good and sweet; she did her chores gladly, keeping the canary fed and changing the water in his cage, and I had—as was said at the time—a bad character; I was stubborn and rebellious. My mother, who loved me very much (despite my rebelliousness), might also have reckoned that, at just six or so years old and being a completely irresponsible little person, letting me out on the ice rink could end badly for me, with a broken leg or maybe something even worse. That seems quite probable. Whatever the case may have been, deprived of blades and love, humiliated and rejected, I would stand by that bit of green balustrade and, listening to that invisible orchestra playing the "Mounds of Manchuria" waltz, I would watch my sister as she skated out onto the ice where, smiling sweetly, she circled the rink in the company of the other skaters. She skated round, she Dutch-rolled, she performed some complicated pirouettes, and I. . .could watch her. She spun round, and I was supposed to admire her. She circled the rink, her elbows pumping rhythmically to the rear, now one, now the other. Or she spread wide her arms like an airplane, tilting back her head. Probably pretending to be Sonja Henie. It was unbearable. I was choked by my despair and ferocity. I wanted skates. I wanted to waltz and pirouette on the ice; I wanted to pump my elbows to the rear, just like my sister. I remember hurling myself at my mother, who was standing next to me at that bit of green balustrade, screaming something (probably something like "I want to skate!" although it could just as easily have been some weepy howling). I jumped and skipped, trying to reach her better, pounding my fists into the furry fox collar of her winter coat. The savage manifestations of my anger couldn't, of course, have resulted in anything positive (for me): first, because my mother was an impulsive person, even a violent one, and immediately, without a moment's hesitation, she executed the sentence she passed on me, I mean, immediately, right there in front of all the Dutch-rolling skaters—I was spanked or I had my ear twisted; and second, because my little fists didn't strike as much as they sank into the soft interior of her fox fur collar. Ah, the fox furs of my mother! I'm not entirely certain, but I believe my mother owned several such fox collars, at the same time even, sewn from little animals kitted out with glass eyes and fake noses—because I remember an almost black fur collar with white stripes as well as a light brown fur and a dark brown fur too. But maybe it was that my mother wore that black fur with the white stripes before the war and the light brown fur during the war. Or maybe vice versa. My grandmother also wore fox furs, so I suppose this was a generally accepted fashion. While stroking the furry little paws that crossed over my mother's bosom (I very much enjoyed doing that, though the little paws ended in sharp little claws, on which you could cut yourself if you weren't careful), I would meditate upon the fate of those little animals and imagine various vulpine adventures—the pursuit and the escape, which preceded their arrival in our apartment on Koszykowa, but I don't think I would have much considered what the gaze of those glass eyes, staring straight into mine, or the movement of that artificial nose, signified. The idea that life is one great massacre, that its essence, its hidden strength (its inner motor) is slaughter—that life slaughters life, that the glass eyes, artificial noses, and soft paws on my mother's bosom are the sign of that massacre—that it is She, Slaughter, who gazes at us, coldly and indifferently, through those glass eyes. It would rather not have occurred to me at the time because children do not think in such categories; that's not a thought meant for children, a thought approachable by a child's reason; it is a thought so difficult to digest that even adults avoid dwelling on it. An old man, sure, an old man like me at present, knows well enough that life is one great massacre, that everything that lives will be massacred (and massacres, in turn). But let's get back to my sister Dutch-rolling sixty-seven years ago in the Swiss Valley. The unseen orchestra has set aside their bows, the skaters have glided off the rink, and my sister appears at the green balustrade—taking note of my tears (tears of ferocity and humiliation) slipping down my cheeks gone ruddy with the cold; she stretches out her hand (in a green, fuzzy glove) to stroke my cheek, wishing, I suppose, to give me to understand that I've got everything ahead of me, that the time will come when I too will venture out onto the ice. I would have gladly bit through that green glove of hers, but I was afraid of my mother. That evening, back in our flat on Koszykowa following the excursion to the Swiss Valley, my feelings of insult and injury reached their apogee. Now, this was no longer a sense of being wronged—it was anger, fury, hatred that filled my brain, my whole body even; perhaps you could say that they filled my entire being (if such a concept were known to me back then), and I was transformed into an accumulation of hatred directed at the world that refused to buy me skates and did not permit me to fly around the rink on them. I lay there in the darkness, with the eiderdown pulled up to my nose, and considered how I might take out my revenge—on my mother, my father, and my sister, on everyone who ever wounded me, who, in denying me ice skates and forbidding me ice skating so humiliated and abased me. But how could anyone such as I revenge himself on anyone? As completely helpless as I was, without any influence on what was going on in the world? How can you wreak revenge upon the entire world if you're only six or seven years old, nipping at the heels of a world that doesn't notice you, basically, that never gives you a second thought? I could only take out my revenge in my imagination. No other avenue was open to me. In this sphere (that is, the imagination), I had some powerful allies—the Germans. And so (blubbering, snot-nosed, most likely sobbing under the covers), I imagined myself standing at the green balustrade in the Swiss Valley, watching my sister pirouette at center ice, when—from both sides, from Szopena and the Aleje Ujazdowskie, from Mokotowska and Szucha—some vans pull up. Out of these some terrible German gendarmes emerge, with shields on their chests, armed with machine guns. These gendarmes, in their scary helmets, surround the rink at Swiss Valley, and immediately (if I hadn't been so afraid of waking my mother, perhaps I would have imitated the raucous shouts of those gendarmes under the covers), they herd into the vans everyone who had been skating there, as well as all those who had been watching her—my sister!—pirouette and Dutch-roll. The loaded vans then drive off (or vanish in some other way), the gendarmes are annihilated along with their vans, the invisible orchestra (invisible now because also packed off into those vans) once more begins to play and then, out onto the rink skates he whom the gendarmes had not packed up, whom for obvious reasons they had passed over—that one and only skater remaining in the Swiss Valley—me. And who has the skates now, all of you being trundled away in those vans to—you know where? I circle the rink, skating ever faster, ever faster, as if I were racing against someone, but against whom? If I'm the only one there? My elbows (just as before, the elbows of my sister) are flying backward, now one, now the other. My pirouettes at center ice there in the Swiss Valley—can you see them? I also had another, much more drastic (as I now recognize it to be) version of these imaginings of mine. In this version, instead of loading the skaters and spectators into their vans, the gendarmes extract heavy machine guns from their vans, which they set up on both sides of Swiss Valley—from Szopena and from the Aleje Ujazdowskie. And when the German machine guns have spread the ice with the bodies of all those who had been skating there, as well as all of those who had been looking on—children, young people, and adults, men and women, for there is no mercy to be found anywhere nor will there ever be any mercy for anyone—I, the only one left alive there, the last one standing, obedient to the call of the invisible orchestra (since the visible one was also slaughtered), obedient to the strains of the "Mounds of Manchuria" waltz, glide out onto the ice—on ice skates!—on ice skates!—and as I drowsed, half asleep, between sleep and waking, between dream and terror, between dread and happiness, I circled, pirouetted, and Dutch-rolled amongst the corpses carpeting the ice, avoiding, or sailing right through, the pools and streams of blood. While I was falling asleep, did I have any pangs of conscience? Was I ashamed of these vengeful figments of my imagination? This I don't remember.

THE AMMUNITION CARRIER ENTERS KILIŃSKI ST.

SEVERAL VERSIONS EXIST as to the route taken by the armored ammunition carrier as it made its way from the corner of Senatorska and Podwale to where Kiliński St. separates from Podwale in the direction of Długa. According to the reports of the soldiers of Battalion "Gustaw," as related by Ryszard Bielecki (in the book *"Gustaw"—"Harnaś"*), who were defending the barricade that closed off Podwale from the Plac Zamkowy, two soldiers showed up there around 16:00 with the order to take the vehicle deeper into the Old Town. General Bór Komorowski went over to the window of the Raczyński Palace and saw the ammunition carrier "at high noon." Also, the account of Hanna Malewska, a novelist who knows very well what history means and how one ought to treat it, and thus a person completely trustworthy (especially in these matters), tells us that the ammunition carrier—which she describes as a "low tractor"—arrived in the Old Town around noon. "It was noon, all quiet from the side of the Germans, when suddenly, cries and cheers erupted on Podwale. . . . Children and women were gathering around a tank, or perhaps a low tractor, which clearly had just been captured—four smiling soldiers were driving it down the street." The two soldiers, who appeared at the barricade on Podwale at 16:00 in order to take the ammunition carrier away from there to Kiliński St., seem, therefore, to be rather dubious, along with that hour of theirs. Just as dubious, if not more so, seems the order that the two soldiers were carrying out—according to Bielecki, this was a written order, although it's unknown what officer gave it to them. What is more, we don't know anything about its contents—we neither know whither nor with what aim in mind those two soldiers were intending to take that ammunition carrier away from the barricade. And so, the assumption that none of this actually occurred, that there was no such order, seems well-founded. Whether there was such an order or not doesn't seem to have bothered the soldiers of the "Gustaw" battalion overmuch (battalion officers were also in the neighborhood), and they agreed to hand over the vehicle. The barricade was taken apart (most likely, just a small portion thereof), and those two, whether they were ordered to or not, got into the ammunition carrier, inspected its interior, and drove off along Podwale in the direction of Kapitulna. The names of those two, or perhaps even three soldiers (because there may have been three) are known—although not for certain—as well as the pseudonym of one of them. Captain Lucjan Fajer ("Ognisty"), deputy commander and operational officer of the "Gozdawa" battalion, claimed that there were several soldiers and that they were of his battalion—"chiefly from the motorized 'Orlęta' Company." Amongst those few soldiers from "Orlęta" Company, Captain Fajer (in his book *Żołnierze Starówki* [*Soldiers of the Old Town*]) mentions three. "They sat down at the wheel triumphantly and drove the captured vehicle along to universal cheering. These men were Rifleman Czymbo (Zygmunt Salwa), Rifleman Henryk Paczkowski, Rifleman Szczawiński, and others, and thus they arrived at Kiliński St." Riflemen Salwa, Paczkowski, Szczawiński. But it's not known for sure if it was they who climbed into the vehicle, for there exist other versions of the story (this fragment of it). According to one of these, along Podwale in the direction of Kapitulna there drove off, not two or three soldiers from "Orlęta," but two soldiers from the motorized division of the Headquarters of the Warsaw Region, in the ranks of which fought the so-called "Ryszard" Platoon, led by Lieutenant Jerzy Bondarowski ("Ryszard"). In this very platoon, two poets fought: Tadeusz Gajcy and Zdzisław Stroiński. But they didn't die that day; they were to fall later—this was 13 August, around noon, and so they still had three days of life left. Whatever the case may have been, Salwa, Paczkowski, and

THE AMMUNITION CARRIER ENTERS KILIŃSKI ST.

Szczawiński, along with maybe someone else as well, drove off in their ammunition carrier, heading toward death. Since we don't know any other names, we can accept this version. The route they chose, on the other hand, is very unclear, for among the various versions that speak of the event, there exist such as either cannot be reconciled with one another or which it would be extremely difficult to reconcile. Perhaps they can be reconciled somewhat if we accept that the ammunition carrier trundled about the streets of the Old Town for quite some time, going from place to place, to revisit the places where it had been earlier, in search of the location where it should finally come to rest, right there in front of the door of the building on Kiliński St. From Lucjan Fajer's book we can deduce ("And so they arrived at Kiliński St.") that the vehicle traveled down Podwale in the direction of Kapitulna, and at a quick pace, halting nowhere along its route nor making any detours until it arrived at Kiliński. But that seems improbable to me. A very complex—extraordinarily complicated—route is presented by Ryszard Bielecki on the basis of various insurrectionist accounts. "The little tank drove along Podwale to Kapitulna St. where it turned right into Piekarska. Before Zapiecek, it drove out onto the Rynek Starego Miasta [Old Town Market Square]. From that moment on, the progress of the armored vehicle took on the character of a triumphal defilade. . . . The little tank left the Rynek via Nowomiejska. It drove on to Freta, and here it turned left. The journey took quite a while, for a few barricades had to be taken down along the way." As might be imagined, having turned left from Freta St., the ammunition carrier went (that is to say, would have gone, because it's unknown whether it did or not) along Długa St. in the direction of the main entrance to the Raczyński Palace. But this version too seems not at all probable to me. But of course everything here is possible. Still, it is explicitly contradicted by the report upon which Stanisław Podlewski bases his account of this phantasmagorical trip through the streets of the Old Town in his *March Through Hell*. "With a rattle of its caterpillar treads, the tank entered the narrow streets of the Old Town. Everyone was seized with a frenzy of euphoria. It traveled along Podwale to Wąski Dunaj. The boys caught sight of Fr. Tadeusz [Rostworowski] and greeted him with joy. The priest advised them to head along Wąski Dunaj to the Old Market Square. . . . This sounded good to the driver, who fired off a few celebratory rounds from his machine pistol and then turned into Wąski Dunaj." Let us add to all this one version more of the vehicle's journey, one which clearly contradicts the one in *A March through Hell*. It is found in Antoni Przygoński's *Powstanie Warszawskie w sierpniu 1944* [*The Warsaw Uprising in August 1944*]. In it (basing his understanding on some accounts, the sources of which he doesn't reveal) the author states that yes, the ammunition carrier traveled down Wąski Dunaj, but in the opposite direction to that suggested by Podlewski's book. For it wasn't "going down Wąski Dunaj toward the Rynek Starego Miasta" as Fr. Tomasz Rostworowski advised, but rather turned "into Wąski Dunaj in the direction of Kiliński St."—and this means (at least, one can assume it to mean) that it turned into Wąski Dunaj from the Rynek or from Piwna. Now, if the ammunition carrier turned from Wąski Dunaj into Kiliński, or, on the contrary, from Podwale into Wąski Dunaj, and for that very reason: to enter the Rynek, well then, it couldn't have entered the square from Piekarska and Zapiecek. Nor, having turned into Wąski Dunaj, could it have turned from Podwale directly onto Kiliński from the direction of Plac Zamkowy (as it would appear from Captain "Ognisty's" book)? All of this is terribly unclear; streets become mixed up and join up, cross through one another in some order other than that of reality. As if this excursion were taking place only in a dream. As I said, it may have been a roundabout drive, turning back, turning round again and again and driving around things, like barricades, turning away from them, driving around them. A dark circling of one's own death. And yet the intentions of the one, two, or three operators of the ammunition carrier, to direct the vehicle into Kiliński and end up at the apartment block at number 1, remain completely unexplained. Why did they do it? What was their intention in so doing, and where did they intend to go on later from there? If they did intend on going on from there at all. No sensible deduction has yet been formulated on this matter, and it seems that the formulation of

THE AMMUNITION CARRIER ENTERS KILIŃSKI ST.

such an explanation at this point in time is and shall remain entirely impossible. The only guess offered in answer to this question—that of Robert Bielecki in the above-mentioned book on the two battalions "Gustaw" and "Harnaś"—suggests that, as he drove along Podwale from the direction of Nowomiejska (or as he drove along Nowomiejska and later Freta and Długa), the driver intended to convey the war booty up to the entranceway or into the courtyard of the Raczyński Palace, where the AK Headquarters was located that day. Drawing upon accounts known to him from the soldiers of Battalion "Wigry," Bielecki writes: "Civilians. . .were asking who captured the tank, and where. The driver and his insurrectionist comrades explained that they received the order to deliver it into the courtyard of the Ministry of Justice." This assumption—that there may have been some order to "deliver it into the courtyard" is senseless and must be rejected on two grounds. First of all, in order for them to drive up to the entranceway or into the courtyard of the Raczyński Palace itself, they'd certainly need the permission of some high-placed officer at Headquarters, maybe even the permission of Bór Komorowski himself. And nothing indicates that the soldier who was driving the ammunition carrier, or those who were directing him, ever received such permission, tried to get it, or even asked anyone about it. The Armia Krajowa, the Home Army, was a real army, not some mob in which any soldier could do whatever he pleased (and, moreover, in wartime conditions, a stone's throw from the front). Bór Komorowski only learned of the existence of the ammunition carrier a few moments before the explosion when he was standing at the window of the Raczyński Palace and saw the vehicle turning into Kiliński. Certainly, no one asked him earlier if it was his wish to have the armored vehicle brought into the courtyard of his headquarters. What is more, the short account of Lt. Col. Felicjan Majorkiewicz, the operational officer of the III Staff Unit of Headquarters (which may be found in his book *Lata chmurne, lata dumne* [*Cloudy Years, Proud Years*] seems to point to the fact that nothing was known at Headquarters (that is, the Raczyński Palace) about the ammunition carrier before the explosion—no one there was even informed of the existence of such a vehicle, nor of the fact that the Germans had abandoned it or set it up in front of the barricade on the Plac Zamkowy. Second, on Podwale, right at number 23, to the rear of the Raczyński Palace, there was a large barricade which (supposedly) had been partially taken down at the very moment when the ammunition carrier made its appearance, and for that very reason, so that the vehicle, having turned onto Podwale from Nowomiejska, could then turn from Podwale onto Kiliński. The point is that if those who were driving the ammunition carrier wanted to enter the courtyard or drive up before the entrance to the Raczyński Palace, the dismantling of the barricade on Podwale as well as the turn into Kiliński (so as, later, eventually, to proceed along Kiliński in the direction of Długa and turn right, that is, in the direction of Freta) was not only entirely unnecessary, but also completely nonsensical, because you could arrive at the courtyard of the Raczyński Palace from the rear—from Podwale, and that was the only road leading there at the time. As we learn from the account of Lt. Col. Majorkiewicz, the entrance from Długa was blocked off at the time. It wasn't being used for security reasons— "one used the entrance from Podwale." Why then should the barricade on Podwale be dismantled, and why should the ammunition carrier turn (as at least it attempted, intended to do, since it didn't completely turn, it turned just a bit and stopped, immediately) from Podwale into Kiliński, if the notion of turning from Kiliński onto Długa only to enter the Raczyński Palace from Długa was completely senseless? Well, third, the account of Lt. Col. Majorkiewicz explains to us that the operator of the ammunition carrier intended, of course, to exit onto the intersection of Podwale and Kiliński (and it was most likely that, to enable its exit, the barricade to the rear of the Raczyński Palace was partially dismantled), but it was intended to drive out onto the intersection, not so as, having turned right from Podwale, to travel down Kiliński in the direction of Długa, but rather, having turned left, to go down Podwale in the direction of the Plac Zamkowy. O God. Why did he, why did they, want to go in the direction of the Plac Zamkowy if, having just driven around (as it seems) a sizeable chunk of the Old Town, they had been coming from there in the first place? Why at someone's order, or ordered by no one, had they just taken the ammunition carrier away from the barricade on Plac Zamkowy? But this is what Lt. Col. Majorkiewicz explicitly writes, and there is no reason not to believe him because he (catching sight of the ammunition carrier and not really knowing, not really understanding, what was going on) had no reason to present the scene otherwise than as he saw it—from his perspective, standing there, where he stood. So he was standing on the corner of Kiliński and Podwale, on the Raczyński Palace side, with the intention of going further down Podwale in the direction of the rear entrance to the palace. "Three young lads from the 'Gustaw' battalion, in scout uniforms, were standing on the little tank, and the one in the middle was proudly grasping a staff from which was unfurled a red and white flag. The driver of the little tank, after making his way through the outer barricade on Podwale, triumphantly drove past the place where I was standing, to the applause of the crowd gathered there, before heading in the direction of the Plac Zamkowy." So that was the intention of the lads from "Orlęta" Company, or the Motorized Division of the Regional Command; that's what they wanted—to drive towards the Plac Zamkowy. It seems as if this was a senseless thing to do (if they had just arrived from there), that is, this was an aimless drive, but for that soldier, who was driving the vehicle, or for those soldiers, who were driving it, that forcing of the barricade on Podwale, that entrance into Kiliński, that turn in the direction of the Plac Zamkowy, all of this had to have some sort of meaning. All of this was, had to be, intentional. Well, no. There "had to be" some reason for driving onto Kiliński, and then again, there didn't have to be any at all. Many such things happen in life; many such situations occur, which have no sense or meaning whatsoever and yet, despite it all, fit into that life perfectly and even occupy very significant places, even very important ones. Perhaps some gorgeous girl lived at Kiliński 1, or somewhere a little farther on, down Podwale near Kapitulna— some gorgeous nurse or beautiful cook from the battalion kitchen— and the driver wanted to show off his armored vehicle to her? But this is a stupid, even improper supposition to be making. I withdraw it immediately. So where then was he heading, that soldier, who got into the vehicle on Podwale near Plac Zamkowy and drove off on a roundabout route to the corner of Kiliński and Podwale, no farther, because he'd run out of time? Was he simply driving where his eyes led him? As fate determined? Happy-go-lucky? As fate determines, soldier boy, as fate determines. He drove onto Kiliński, he wanted to turn in the direction of Plac Zamkowy as he pulled up in front of the entranceway to the building at Kiliński 1. That's as much as we can say on the subject, and we'll never learn anything more about it. According to General Bór Komorowski (who, I repeat, was observing what was going on from a short distance, for he was standing at the windows of the Raczyński Palace), the driver of the armored ammunition carrier, having turned into Kiliński from Podwale, executed some strange maneuver—he stopped the vehicle, but in such a way as to block the roadway. The General didn't deduce anything from this fact, but now, when you think about it, the assumption seems justified that the incomprehensible maneuver might have been executed for two reasons: first, because the driver no longer had control (or if any, only partial control) over the vehicle, and he drew it to a halt however, wherever, the machine itself allowed him to; second, the driver pointed the vehicle in the direction of the Plac Zamkowy but didn't know where he was supposed to go or where he wanted to go, and he pulled to a halt to think it over—and the place he chose was haphazardly chosen—by pure coincidence. As Bór Komorowski was to write, "this was a German vehicle with a Polish flag affixed to its front. The crew was made up of Polish soldiers. The driver cleared the barricade capably, to the accompaniment of cheers of a crowd of women and children; he turned about and came to a halt perpendicular to the roadway, at the edge of the pavement." And it was at that very moment.

THE SENSE OF MURDER

THE MOST INTERESTING TYPE of murder, if one may be permitted to use such a term, somewhat violating its sense, to speak of a certain specific type, which not only clearly differentiates itself from others but also clearly stands out among them—and so, the most interesting type of murder, at least to me, that we come across when reading accounts of the Warsaw Uprising, is the murder of old people. All other types of German murder can be acknowledged as more or less sensible (although at times only with difficulty). To put it more clearly, it's possible to find an answer—even if it be an unclear one, a general one, one that is not entirely satisfactory, to the question— why, in August and September, did the Germans in Warsaw murder women, children, wounded soldiers, and wounded or ill civilians? My interest here is not, as is so frequently the case in our postwar literature, to cause any unnecessary outrage because that sort of outrage and subsequent condemnation of the Germans (or condemnation of Hitler or Himmler, since one of them once gave the order for the murders to be perpetrated—a condemnation, like all others, from some moral or moralizing point of view) is futile in this sense, that it impedes our grasp of the essence of things, and so it's enough to say in a calm voice that, from the German perspective, the killing of Polish women and children can be seen as something sensible and even justified. The Germans killed Polish women and children, as well as wounded soldiers and wounded civilians, because their aim, which they didn't disguise, was the extermination of the Polish people. Their intent in exterminating the Poles seems, in turn, justified by this, that the Germans wanted to get rid of their neighbors (most likely, these included other neighbors of theirs too, besides the Poles) so as to obtain for themselves the most living space possible, that is that which today might seem a little unclear, but which in their philosophical terminology (if one can term it such) was known at the time as Lebensraum. The fewer Polish children, the more Lebensraum for German children. Such was the sense, quite clear, if perhaps a little unpleasant for us, of that murdering. Now, this does not mean that such a sense of murdering (its overarching sense) was recognized by those who directly carried out the job, who personally busied themselves with the murderous tasks, going from building to building, from Podwale to Kiliński, from Kiliński to Długa, from Długa to Freta, from Freta to Świętojerska [St. George's St.] shooting, throwing grenades, soaking with gasoline, burning. They—the soldier-murderers murdered for a different reason; their murdering had a different (somewhat different) sense. But we're not going to busy ourselves with that right now. The important sense here is a higher one, the one that was known to the commanders, the leaders of the massacre, the ones who gave the orders. All right, then. But why murder the old folks? What sort of sense did that have, the murdering of people in their seventies or eighties? Those about whom there was no doubt that they'd be calmly dying on their own soon enough, leaving behind in that way one more sliver of the Lebensraum that the Germans were after. Such murdering seems completely senseless now. But if the Germans took on this unpleasant task (and the murdering of old people is something rather unpleasant, not only for the murdered but for the murderers too), I guess they found some sense in it after all. To put it differently—I suppose they knew what they were doing. This, to me, is very interesting—what sort of sense could such murdering have?—for personal reasons, of course, even very personal ones. I'll be turning seventy-four myself in a few months' time, so I'm of an age now at which (if they started murdering around here again, that is, if something along the lines of the Warsaw Uprising came about again) I would be murdered by the Germans, not, now, as a child, not as an insurrectionist, not as a wounded AK soldier, but as an old man. Mine would not be a soldier's death—that is, a death possessed of the clearest sense, the easiest death to understand, the sort that is plain for all to see—no, I can't count on such a death, simply because I'm no longer fit to be an insurrectionist—maybe I'd still be able to shoot at the Germans, but—to throw a grenade with precision? To climb up over burnt-out staircases, keeping watch at night among the ruins, or leaping down from a barricade for a mad dash at a tank, bottle in hand? Well, at my age, in my physical condition, already fairly limited, these things are rather impossible. Of course, sixty-four years ago, in August 1944, if I were in Warsaw, if I were living at the time in the Old Town or at Wola, I would have been murdered, or (at least) I would have stood a good chance of being murdered—indeed, a very good chance as a nine-year-old boy, and that would have been completely comprehensible to me, then and now, because, by murdering me, the Germans would be broadening that Lebensraum of theirs a bit. So my death would have had a certain sense, for me and for them, which might in no way be questioned. But I'd like to know for what reason I'd be murdered (and there is no doubt that I would be) if the Uprising were to break out right now—that is, if the Germans came back here again, and, trying to push them back out, we called forth another Warsaw Uprising. The Germans aren't such people as to provide me with an answer to my question—why would they murder an old man like me? Perhaps it is that they don't want to busy themselves with this problem at the moment; perhaps they feel that this is no longer any concern of theirs; perhaps their imaginations are none too agile. O, you philosophical German minds—do you know why you murdered old folks sixty-four years ago? They don't know. So I have to search out the answer by myself. In the little street, or rather alleyway, that runs right alongside the Church of the Visitation of the Blessed Virgin Mary, linking Kościelna [Church St.] with the Rynek Nowego Miasta [New Town Market Square] and Wójtowska St., an old folks' home was located, before and during the war. This little street, which still exists today, is known as Przyrynek, and the home in question was located at number 4. During the war, Przyrynek, like all the other streets thereabout, wasn't the object of much German attention, and thus it retained its Polish name, whereas nearby Bonifratska St. was renamed Klosterstrasse. When the Uprising broke out, Przyrynek suddenly blossomed in significance. As Juliusz Kulesza writes in a recently published book on insurrectionary deeds on the streets of the Old Town (*Powstańcza Starówka* [*Insurrectionary Old Town*]), "the narrow and heretofore neglected street. . .suddenly became an important artery of communications with the New Town." This important role fell to Przyrynek because it was through this little street that the straightest and safest route to the "first line of defense" ran, that is, to the State Manufactory of Securities. In the first days of August, when the AK soldiers had taken this building, the residents of Przyrynek rose to the occasion—as we learn from Juliusz Kulesza—for they "took part in the storming of the building, joining the attacking soldiers, axe and crowbar in hand." Among those who stormed the building, armed with crowbars and axes, there may well have been some inhabitants of the old folks' home (of course, this is mere speculation on my part). I myself am an old man, and there's not much I can do in such a situation except to look on with admiration, applauding the deeds of the residents of Przyrynek, my peers, storming the building, axe in hand. Now, the matter of that building at number 4 is none too clear. Juliusz Kulesza writes of "the nursing home at 4 Przyrynek St.," while in his book *The Warsaw Uprising of August 1944*, Antoni Przygoński writes that "two shelters for elderly women were located at 4 Przyrynek St." But this discrepancy isn't all that important. According to Kulesza's account, the battles for the Church of the Visitation were over by 30 August. The insurgents withdrew at dawn on that day "behind the Kościelna St. lines" and thus to the New Town Market Square, at which time the Germans entered Przyrynek and took the residents of the refuge in hand. How many there were is unknown. According to Przygoński, "there were about four hundred of them," but a certain number of the residents of the old folks' home had died during the fighting and the bombardment and another group of them were driven off by the Germans to be murdered elsewhere. Kulesza brings his account to an end with the account of Fr. Czesław Baran, a historian of the Franciscan Order. "The aged men and women from the nursing home at Przyrynek 2 were herded out in front of the Church of the Visitation of the Most Blessed Virgin. The Germans hurled grenades at them, doused them with gasoline, and set them on fire. As for those ill persons who remained in the nursing home, these were finished off and cremated by the Germans. We saw no one remain alive from the three asylums on Przyrynek. All we saw were the bones of the cremated." Now, many years later, when the tears have dried, looking on from a distance of sixty-four years, calmly and attentively, ruminating on those old men and women standing in front of the smoking ruins of the Church of the Visitation of the Most Blessed Virgin Mary, waiting, hand in hand, for the Germans to execute their task, to throw those grenades already (and they, the Germans, standing in the middle of Przyrynek, smile at those old people of theirs and lift their grenades, arming them with a quick tug at the porcelain rings dangling near the wooden handles—all of this happening in slow motion, as if in a dream, slowly, slowly, no need to hurry, you Germans), now, therefore, when the tears have ceased to flow, we can think the matter over calmly—did the August and September murders of old women and men have, at the time, from the German point of view (even if that point of view is that of a madman) any sense? Could they have had any sense? And how are we to make sense of that sense now? I speak here of the German point of view because the sense of these killings, if there is any to be found, can only be found from the German point of view; only then, when we consider the matter from their side—through the eyes of the murderers, for it is only for them, and for no one else, that murdering could have any sense at that time. I've pondered long on this matter, but even at first glance, it can be seen that, from the German point of view, the murdering of old people could (eventually) have a triple significance. First, the old folks, ill and none too spry, were troublesome; their very existence constituted a problem; their very presence on the field of battle required that some action be taken in their regard. They had to be gotten rid of somehow, and every attempt at getting rid of old people must take into consideration a few logistical difficulties, perhaps (from the German point of view) stupid and unnecessary ones. Old people have to be fed; they'd have to be transported somewhere, under escort, and then housed somewhere—in some temporary concentration camps. Maybe it'd just be easier and simpler to murder them, liquidating the whole problem with the aid of a few hand grenades and a couple of gallons of gasoline. Was that the sense behind the murdering of old people in Warsaw in August and September? Were they murdered because they were troublesome, because they complicated things unnecessarily? Maybe yes, maybe no. Of course, the old people were problematic, but, after all, you didn't need to roll up any trucks, lift the old folks in on stretchers, and drive them off to concentration camps. Because they didn't really present any threat to the German plans, military or political. All you had to do was enter that house on Przyrynek St., tell (or rather growl at) everybody, "Alles raus!" and order the old folks to beat it, get out of there, go off somewhere, carrying their own stretchers, walking away on their crutches. Let them go off to the Puszcza Kampinoska [Kampinoska Wilds] or somewhere else, wherever the road leads them. In short—tell them to disappear. Without a doubt, the old folks would have obeyed that order. But I also admit the possibility that, wanting to get rid of the problem, the Germans chose the simplest solution, the first thing that occurred to them, and the killing of the old people had only that sort of sense—they just wanted the problem of the old people taken care of. So that one more problem ceased to exist. Second, the murders on Przyrynek (and also wherever else the problem of old people with mobility issues arose) could have a sense that we might call political or, better yet—ideological. Because it so happened that (and here I have in mind the Uprising as a whole, its fundamental idea, constantly considering the same from the German point of view)—it so happened that Polish subhumans were rebelling against German Supermen, coming out against them armed, in which case the Supermen had to address this issue, as monstrous, unheard-of, and outrageous as it was—and this had to be something radical. They had to call those half-humans to order, to punish them, to take revenge upon them (for that unheard-of brazenness). In this case, the sense of the killings, and what is more, the killing of all half-humans without exception or respect to age—men, women, children, the aged—would clearly be understandable because it would be revenge. In this revenge, we would find a lesson to be taught: never rebel against the Germans, because the Germans are stronger than you, and the penalty they impose upon those who do rebel is severe: everyone will be murdered without exception. It is plain to see that such a point of view and such a sense to the murdering was, at the time, accessible only to certain higher-ranking officers of the SS and the Wehrmacht, those who had certain ideas in their heads, who thought in ideological terms and reflected upon ideological issues. (Here a question arises, which I am unable to answer: at the time, in the heat of battle, in the blizzard of murder, was anyone capable of reflecting on ideological issues?) On the other hand, it doesn't seem likely that simple German soldiers were capable of conceiving such a rationale for the murder of Polish oldsters and Polish children and women; I'm speaking of such soldiers as were known in Warsaw at the time as Kalmuks, Vlasovites, or Ukrainians; Azers from the "Azerbaijani" regiment, not the SS men/criminals from Oskar Dirlewanger's brigade. Even the simple, honest Wehrmacht soldiers, who also murdered after all, probably had no access to such a rationale for murdering. It seems to me that, by imposing such a sense upon the murder of old folks (understanding it as revenge and a lesson to be learned), we are on the right path, that is, we are recognizing the German intentions quite properly—the intentions of a nation for which the very thought of their neighbors not wishing to subject themselves to their rule is simply unbearable. Thirdly, at last, the murder of old people, wounded and ill people, from the German (but in this case, not only the German) point of view might arise from a desire to establish or introduce some sort of order—or from the desire to reestablish an order, which due to historical events had been disrupted. In the old folks' homes on Przyrzynek St. and Zakroczymska St., in the AK basement hospitals on Długa, Podwale, and Kiliński, in churches and cloisters transformed into hospitals, there seethed a mass of some sort of beings, some of them unable to move about on their own, some of them damaged and incomplete (lacking arms and legs)—and something had to be done with them all—that means, it all had to be cleaned up somehow. One might say even more here: the whole Uprising caused such immense chaos, and even, as its very essence was an immense chaos, that chaos was a challenge for all who opposed chaos (the noble German soldiers), a spur to them to introduce order to it all. The shooting, the dousing with gasoline and the cremation, the burying under rubble, the annihilation of those incomplete beings from the basement, and all those unnecessary, crippled things (there you have it—the old people!), all of this could lead (at least, as a prelude of sorts) to the ordering, that is, the liquidation of all that the German mind (though in this case, not necessarily, not exclusively the German mind) cannot stand, cannot tolerate, cannot bear—chaos. There can be no doubt about it that the Germans, entering Old Town at dawn on 2 September, along with their plans for the introduction of German order to the place (speaking of those who actually entered, I have them all in mind, from Adolf Hitler to the lowliest SS private), pictured that order to themselves and even had to picture it to themselves in very different ways. Adolf Hitler and Heinrich Himmler had one vision of the final order in mind; SS-Obersturmbannführer Oskar Dirlewanger had another; SS-Obergruppenführer Erich von dem Bach, who was in command of the whole Warsaw operation, had still another, and still other visions of the liquidation of chaos had to be in the minds of the rank-and-file SS men or in the heads (heads which didn't quite comprehend it all) of the Kalmuks who brought order to some small area—in one of the basement rooms, or in one of the hospital wards, where they were to introduce order through the extermination of a few or a few dozen mysteriously roiling, hideous beings. Whatever the case may be, killing was necessary in order that chaos might give way to order, and in this way, the overarching (even supra-historical or ahistorical) sense of the murdering became apparent, including and even above all the murdering of old people. Have we exhausted all of the possibilities of the existence and appearance of the sense of murdering? Of course not—perhaps there exist others (and each of us

THE SENSE OF MURDER

senses, or at least would like to sense, that there exists) still some higher rationale for murder—some mysterious and incomprehensible sense, one not even open to Heinrich Himmler's comprehension, nor to that of von dem Bach nor to Oskar Dirlewanger's, nor to the Kalmuks nor the Azar soldiers from the "Azerbaijani" regiment, nor to me—in general, to no one. I'm talking about the sort of rationale that (incomprehensible because of its sublimity) will never be deciphered—on the topic of which nothing can be said by anyone. But maybe it's also the case that the murdering was senseless, that it had no sense, or, to put it in a different way, it means nothing. At the time, as it is easy to see, everything that existed or happened in this world was, at least for us, entirely lacking in sense. The Warsaw Uprising was the greatest event in the history of the Poles—never in all of our history had there ever been (nor, most probably, shall there ever be) an event greater than that. And from this greatest event in our history, different great lessons emerge, too—whole decades, centuries even, will be needed to come to know them all, to think them through and understand them well.

THE ENTRANCE OF THE TURTLES

STEFAN KRASIŃSKI'S ARTICLE "Turtles: Armored Vertebrate Reptiles" appeared in the twenty-fourth issue of the *Illustrated Polish Courier* on 13 June 1943. Stefan Krasiński is without a doubt a nom de plume—all of the articles in the *Illustrated Polish Courier* were written under pseudonyms, which is certainly reasonable, considering the fact that publishing one's works in the "rags" or "reptile press" of the General Government could certainly result in some unpleasant consequences: one might have one's head shaved (as happened to the whores—of both sexes—who were living with Germans), or, in extreme cases, one might be shot. From the masthead of the *Illustrated Polish Courier*, we learn that this periodical was published in a city named Krakau. This interesting little tidbit is probably to be explained by the fact that the name Kraków had been forbidden, at least in print. The same was true of Warszawa—the checking account of the periodical in question was located in the city of Warschau. Allowable, on the other hand (for reasons unfathomable to me) was the name Piłsudski, for the address of the *Courier's* editorial offices is given in this form: Krakau, Redakcja: ul. Piłsudskiego 19, tel. 213–93. Why don't you ring that number up? Maybe somebody will answer— some devotee of a common Europe arranged under German hegemony. The workings of the censorship at the time, be that German or Germano-Polish censorship, are worthy of note for other reasons as well. (I don't know whether any historian or philologist among us has taken this in hand yet). The word Polska [Poland] was entirely

THE ENTRANCE OF THE TURTLES

forbidden if we can judge on the basis of the *Illustrated Polish Courier*. I have not come across that name in any of the numbers I've looked through (which is about half of the total print run). Even landscape photos published in this weekly are captioned, more or less, like this: "The beauties of the General Government countryside. Old willows in Krasnystaw." The unclear existence of Poland (or perhaps the unclear existence of the Poles) was, however, uncovered to one's eyes in adjectival form. There certainly must have been some propagandistic reason behind this, even if difficult to fathom today. Perhaps it was that Poland had been forbidden on account of its being radically, finally, and forever liquidated, and thus any reference to its existence, even if it were a hidden existence, was, from the perspective of the Germans, something impermissible (as it threatened the German order introduced at the time to our common Europe); however, there was no way of pretending (for practical purposes, indeed) that there was no such thing as a Polish language, Polish peasants, or Polish laborers. These had to exist, so that Volksdeutsch and Reichsdeutsch could exist in distinction to them. And also, so that Germans might actually exist, some sort of Poles also had to exist, because the Germans needed to be better than somebody; there can be no existence of any super-race, logically, without the concurrent existence of half-humans. But let's return to the turtles, because that's what we're talking about here, not Poland. The article in the Cracovian *Illustrated Courier* concerning armored vertebrate reptiles is, on account of my (existential) interest, invaluable. For at the time, it was that turtles, even being my best-remembered memory of the war (I even incline to the opinion that those turtles are the best-remembered memory of my entire life), well, those turtles are a memory that I had been completely unable to firmly fix in time. Both of the turtles, a large one and a small one—the small one was black; it had black paws, a black shell and a black head, but there was also a slight admixture of yellow to that black, as on its shell it had some little yellow stripes; the larger one was grayish-green, that was the color of both its skin and its shell, although it was really his rough skin that was emphatically grayish-green, whereas his shell was a little lighter in color: grayish-yellowish green—I remember both turtles very well. You might say that, when I think of them, they regain their full existence in my memory. The clarity of this memory suggests that these turtles appeared in my wartime life rather late—when I was seven, eight, maybe nine years old. If it had been otherwise, that is, if it had occurred when I was a small boy, the entrance of the turtles (into my life), I rather wouldn't be able to remember them so perfectly. It also seems to me (although my knowledge in this matter is not so great) that a small, five- or six-year-old child is not possessed of so developed an emotional life (so developed a capability of concentrating and directing his emotions) for him to be able to enter into any clear and enduring emotional contact with another being—such as that of a little turtle entering his life. It is very important when, at some age, we enter into close contact with another life, another form of life, when we become aware of the fact (when it hits us) that life has many different forms, an infinite number of them in fact, so that (in its essence) life is formless. The manner in which we come to know other forms of life certainly depends on when, at what age, we do so. Stefan Krasiński's article in the *Illustrated Polish Courier*, the very fact of its publication, at that very time, causes all of my doubts to disappear and allows me finally to establish when the turtles appeared in my life. So this was in April or May 1943. Of course, merely by becoming the owner of a turtle, this did not mean that I needed to, nor could I, possess any knowledge on the topic of turtles. It's difficult in any case to demand of a child who gets a turtle as a present any knowledge concerning a turtle's way of life and customs. The article in the *Courier* was written with adults in mind, that is, all parents who acquired turtles at the time in order to give them to their children. This was a widespread phenomenon at the time, considering the number of turtles that were then in Poland (that is, the General Government); it doesn't seem possible, yet it is a well-founded supposition that thousands, if not tens of thousands of them, made their appearance at the time. Maybe I'm exaggerating, but it seemed as if turtles were taking up permanent residence in Poland—to multiply on the banks of rivers and the shores of lakes, to camp out in thickets and among the nettles, to become Masovian natives, creatures of true Slavic extraction. So one might say that the article in the *Illustrated Courier* was right on time and carefully read in many Polish homes (although the reading of such rags was sharply condemned for patriotic reasons). Stefan Krasiński's knowledge on the topic seems remarkably deep to me. It seems that in composing his article, he had recourse to many an encyclopedia, and perhaps even some textbooks in zoology. As we read in the *Illustrated Courier*, "Turtles (chelonia) have their bodies enclosed in a bony shell made up of two portions: front and back, or shield and buckler, which are fused strongly together at the edges. Within this bony armor, which is incredibly hard and resistant, the turtle can hide the greater portion of its head and its tail and pull in its front and hind legs somewhat (depending on the species: some can pull them in entirely) through the holes created in the shells for that very reason. . . . A turtle has lidded eyes; its ears are not externally visible; the skin on the movable parts of its body is covered in scales. All turtles have two pairs of legs, which differentiate them significantly in shape from other species. Turtles move about very slowly on land but swim and dive in the water with great ease." Having explained what turtles are and what they look like, the author of the article moves on to a detailed description of their five families and thirty subgroups. "The reptiles in question are divided into five families, to wit: 1) sea turtles, 2) soft-shell turtles, 3) amphibians, 4) mud turtles, and 5) tortoises." We don't need to worry over much about the soft-shells and amphibians, nor is Stefan Krasiński's knowledge of sea turtles necessary to us at all. Completely sufficient is what we learn in the article concerning land turtles; the author himself wrote his article, above all, and even entirely, to inform us about them. "The land turtle, to which species belongs the 'Greek turtle,' which is currently so popular in Kraków, has a vaulted shell into which its head and feet can be completely hidden, elephantine feet with large soles, short claws, and almost completely unmoving digits. It thrives in humid, warm climates with much vegetation and feeds on plants and insects, for the eradication of which it is popular to keep them in gardens." Further, the author, that collaborator and perhaps even Volksdeutsch "Krasiński," presents (with true German cruelty) the easiest way to murder and prepare a turtle. "The manner of killing a turtle for gastronomic purposes is to pierce its neck with a long, sharp instrument at the place where the skull is attached to the neck. After a moment, the reptile expires due to the piercing of the aorta and cerebral nerve. Thereupon the skin that attaches its rear legs, front legs, and neck to the shell is sliced away, which permits one to extract the creature therefrom." As if in contrast to these cruel instructions, the collaborator brings his article to a close by directing an ardent appeal to youngsters and children not to torment the turtles in their captivity because the abuse of animals is inhuman. "It is important to note that all tormenting of turtles kept captive at home, playing around with them and conducting various experiments on them, as sometimes are undertaken by light-minded children, is inhuman and deserving of punishment. Like all living creatures, the turtle is capable of adapting to living conditions imposed upon him, but his captivity must be compensated by good treatment; he must never be abused even in what might seem to be the most innocent amusements such as turtles, being sluggish and slow by nature, do not tolerate." I can assure the author of these words (who, of course, is no longer to be found among the living—of course, if he were a Brazilian sea turtle or a Mexican amphibian turtle, that would be a different matter altogether), I can assure him, I repeat, that I never tortured nor abused my turtles; I respected their sluggish nature and, although I was a careless boy, I did not indulge in any sort of "experiments" upon them. Nor did I ever attempt to kill any turtle by slitting through his cerebral nerve with a long sharp needle. This may be explained by the fact that I was not a German boy but a Polish boy: in other words, I was on the side of good, not evil. As can be seen, the article from the *Illustrated Courier* provides us with several interesting and concrete scraps of information. First, we learn, as I have already stated, that turtles had made their appearance in the General Government in the spring of 1943, certainly sometime in April or May. Second, the article confirms that the turtles traveled to us from Greece and were known as Greek turtles. Third, we learn (this was probably unknown at the time in

Warsaw) that the turtles had made their appearance in Kraków and that there too they were sold on the streets. This is very interesting news, but I surmise that now, after so many years, the details of this operation cannot be determined (that is, in what manner a large transport of turtles, which must have been at least one full freight car, traveled from the Warsaw East train station and arrived at the Main Station in Kraków), but it was done with such sleight of hand that it did not arouse the suspicions of German railroad men or gendarmes. Poles are extremely clever people, and the Germans, even though they be a super-race, ought never to underestimate that fact. The fourth noteworthy news item is that which states that "every living creature" is able to adapt itself in time to conditions of captivity, and this must be compensated for, rewarded by "good treatment." It seems as if this statement were not so much directed at the street peddlers, who busied themselves with the sale of turtles, nor at the children, who became their owners, nor at the parents who bestowed the turtles on their children as gifts, as to some other addressee. To whom was this heroic collaborator of the *Illustrated Courier* addressing this message? We can only guess. Most probably, it was directed at all the SS men, SS Brigadeführers, and SS Gruppenführers of his acquaintance, maybe even to the General Governor himself—Reichsminister Hans Frank. To them, he addressed, delicately, by allusion, the message that, if someone is kept in "captivity at home," he ought to be compensated, rewarded for this by "good treatment," and that no "experiments of various types" may be carried out upon him, for such would be "inhuman" and "deserving of punishment." Such a position, that one ought not to behave in an inhuman manner towards one's slaves, that they must be adapted to their slavish existence but never tormented, was nothing exceptional in the war years. We learn from the heroic Count Claus von Stauffenberg—the very same man who carried out the unsuccessful assassination attempt on the life of Hitler on 20 July 1944—about how slaves ought to be treated for the good of Germany. I cite his words here as given by Zdzisław Krasnodębski who first (first in Poland, that is; the Germans certainly were aware of this beforehand) showed us what sort of superhuman thoughts that German knight had in his superhuman head. "They are an unimaginable rabble," the Count wrote of the inhabitants of the General Government, "a whole bunch of Jews and just as many half-breeds. People like that will only be obedient to the knout. Thousands of prisoners of war will be exploited for agricultural purposes. In Germany, they will surely be useful, diligent, obedient, and humble." One has the right to assume that, as to the question of Polish slaves, Count von Stauffenberg was of only a somewhat similar opinion to that of the author of the article on armored vertebrate lizards. Slaves ought to be treated strictly: if you use the stick on them, they will be obedient, but certainly, the Count was opposed to executions and torture. Now, as to our collaborator, his efforts, of course, were all in vain, for neither Frank nor his people read the *Illustrated Polish Courier*, I reckon, and even if they did, still they would take no advantage from the good advice offered by this expert in turtle-centered custom. The fragment touching upon the treatment of creatures kept in captivity, however, spurs us to think of the person who wrote the article, even if he were a collaborator or Volksdeutsch, with some sympathy. Some Gestapo supervisor at the *Illustrated Courier* might have taken an interest in his allusions, and so he was taking a risk in appealing for a halt to "experiments of various types" or (as we might understand these words) public executions and gassings. I'll have something more to say about those two turtles, the black one and the gray-yellow-green one, later.

WHAT HAPPENED ON WĄSKI DUNAJ?

WAS THE WARSAW UPRISING a failure? That's what we (people of my generation) were taught to think—that it was a horrific failure, a monstrous catastrophe, a historical collapse, perhaps even the end of history, or at least the prefiguration thereof. That's what the Communists taught, which is no surprise at all because it was in their interest to spread the idea that the Poles had suffered a terrible defeat, one from which they'd never be able to rise again; this was right in line with their plans for the spiritual extermination of Polishness. But then the moment arrived when everyone (or almost everyone) acknowledged that the Uprising was a great national catastrophe. Not only a great one, but the greatest of all, because nothing of the sort had ever occurred before in Polish history. Thousands of dead and the city in ruins—and all for nothing. This conviction (though now a little hidden behind the drapes of glory, which at last have been spread over those bodies and those ruins) continues to this day. But was it a defeat, really? I searched for images of defeat (which are not difficult to find at all), and here they are: chosen from among many similar accounts—fragments of testimony presented in 1946 before the Commission for the Investigation of German War Crimes. Such testimonies (archived somewhere) number in the dozens or the hundreds, and they speak of what was going on in places very close to my heart—that means, in the vicinity of the Raczyński Palace on 7 Długa St., as well as on Kiliński, Podwale, and Wąski Dunaj, when on 2 September, after the withdrawal of the AK units to Center

City (via the famous sewer leading from the Plac Krasińskich to the corner of Warecka and Nowy Świat [New World St.]), the Germans entered the Old Town. These fragments come, respectively, from the testimonies of Helena Kłosowicz, "Monika," a former nurse in the "Chrobry I" Battalion, Halina Wiśniewska, who near the end of August was in charge of two insurrectionist hospitals—the one located in the Raczyński Palace and the other at the terminus of Podwale (in the Café at the Crooked Lantern), and Edward Kowalski, who was a physician in the Hospital of St. John of God at Bonifratska and later at the hospital at Długa 7. That this trio survived is, of course, a miracle in its own right because just about everyone in these hospitals perished. I cite their accounts as they are presented in the 1962 volume entitled *Zbrodnie okupanta hitlerowskiego na ludności cywilnej w czasie Powstania Warszawskiego w 1944 roku* [*Crimes of the Hitlerite Occupiers Committed on the Civilian Population During the Warsaw Uprising of 1944*], which consists of many similar accounts. It is worth noting that, in 1962, it was forbidden to speak of "Germans" in this context, which term was replaced by "Hitlerite occupiers," while these, in turn, disappeared a little later, transformed into "Nazis." This was the beginning of the German falsification of history, to which task quite a few Poles, thoughtlessly and eagerly, set their hand. Despite the fact that I was a child at the time, I can also come forward as a witness, for I remember perfectly that during the war and after, there were no Nazis—that they didn't exist, no one had heard of them. There were only Germans. Had these testimonies been printed when they were first recorded, that is, in 1946 or 1947, the title of the book would be, obviously, *German War Crimes Committed on the Civilian Population During the Warsaw Uprising*. Perhaps I am anachronistic, but that title seems more precise to me, closer to the truth.

"In the courtyard, I noticed, standing at the wall—to the left of the entranceway as you enter from the direction of Kiliński St.—the medical personnel in their white aprons. There were four men and about fourteen or fifteen women. In the center of the courtyard stood about forty or fifty of the more lightly wounded. Some wounded were lying in the main entranceway, on the Długa St. side, on stretchers.

In the entranceway stood a group of SS men who began shooting the wounded standing in the courtyard and lying on the stretchers with their rifles and pistols. At the same time, I heard shots ring out from the first floor and the ground floor. Among the wounded on the stretchers was Col. Tarło, pseudonym Bobik, a cousin of the chief medical officer of the Kedyw [Kierownictwo Dywersji, Directorate of Diversion]. As they were firing at the wounded standing in the courtyard, I saw the SS men pour bottles of gasoline on the wounded who fell after being shot, after which they lit them afire. I also watched as an SS man approached Bobik who had not been shot. He splashed gas on him and set him afire—burning him alive. 'Monika, save them!' Bobik screamed to me. Wishing to save my commanding officer, I pushed away some SS men, who began firing at me, ran blindly upstairs to Ward Nr 7 on the first floor, and screamed, 'Whoever is able to, run!' I ran over to the stretcher on which my commanding officer was lying. I'd like to point out that all the wounded were lying on stretchers on the floor. Behind me, a nurse ran in, the wife of one of the wounded, in her white apron, and she also tried to rescue her husband. Her name was Janina Różalska. We set to work: I tried to lift my commanding officer and Janina her husband. At that moment, an SS man who spoke Polish, whom I recognized, came in and watched what we were doing. Różalski, unable to get up, said to him in German, 'Go on, shoot me,' and the Gestapo man did. At that moment, Różalska ran up to the SS man and said something to him, after which he shot her dead, too.

"From Kiliński St., through the ruins, along Podwale, with the group of medical personnel from the hospital and a portion of the wounded under their care, about fifty persons in number, we made our way to the Plac Zamkowy via Podwale, under the escort of SS men. After I'd left, I didn't see anyone else emerge from our hospital. Twice, the SS men who were escorting us halted us as we proceeded down Podwale, the first time was in front of a destroyed tank. One of the SS men got up on the tank and said to us in Polish: 'You always were pious people, so say your prayers because these are your final moments.' The second time was at the wall of some ruined building, where a Ukrainian walked among us, dividing us up into groups of five and taking away all the valuables we had on us. I was robbed by an SS man who said in German: 'You shameless Polish mug, you!' He stripped the wristwatch from my hand. . . . We were led out to the corner of Marienstat and Plac Zamkowy, and here the Gestapo men shot to death the more wounded in our group. There could have been about thirty wounded with us and some twenty medical personnel. How many were shot then, I had no way of knowing, as my concentration was riveted on the person of my wounded commanding officer. The executions lasted half an hour. The corpses were immediately burned.

"At nine o'clock on the morning of 2 September, SS soldiers under the command of an officer entered the hospital on Długa St. and ordered all of the wounded in the other sanitary points of the hospital to be gathered. . . . The command was given to lead out the more lightly wounded and the personnel in the direction of the Plac Zamkowy. At the same time, I saw one of the SS men begin to put to death the seriously wounded patients who were lying on stretchers and on the ground in both the entranceway and on the ground floor. He walked up to each in turn and shot them one after another with an automatic weapon. That Hauptmann, who had visited the hospital in the morning hours, showed up again and began causing a ruckus. He shouted that it was all taking too long. It was then that I began to hear echoes of shouting from the other wards where the wounded were lying. If my memory serves me correctly, it was at this time that the Germans set fire to the hospital, pouring flammable liquid over the staircases and throwing bunches of hand grenades into the shelters where wounded insurrectionists were also lying along with women and children. After a group of lightly wounded patients and medics had left the hospital, the Germans immediately set about shooting to death all of those who couldn't walk much. I, along with another nurse whose name I don't remember, made our way to the hospital at the Café at the Crooked Lantern on Podwale. There I found neither medics nor mobile wounded, but there were a lot of drunken SS men. We took one of the more wounded men on our shoulders, wishing to take him to the Plac Zamkowy. Every few steps along Podwale, we came across the bodies of Polish soldiers lying on the ground: these were men from among the lightly wounded group who had been executed. Not far from Kiliński St., we were stopped by an SS man. He demanded that we hand over the wounded man we were carrying. When we refused, he roughly pushed away my friend and, from a distance of no more than two paces, shot the wounded man, who had been leaning his full weight upon me. The shot was fatal. After cursing us out, the German told us to move on.

"We were formed up into a marching group. We moved along in such a formation, sensing what the fate of the wounded who remained behind on Długa would be. We able-bodied ones were carrying or supporting the wounded, believing that in this way, perhaps, we might have a chance to save them. I was carrying a wounded girl in my arms, gazing at our macabre parade. I saw people completely exhausted, with bandaged heads and limbs, hobbling along, dragging themselves forward in spasms of pain, their faces half-drained of blood by fear. They dragged on their limbs encased in plaster, limbs bound to splints, with the last strength that remained them. As a physician, I marveled at them, unable to understand how people so wounded could be in any condition to move at all. The Germans struck them and kicked them, wanting to speed up the pace of our macabre march. We went along Podwale in the direction of the Plac Zamkowy. They halted us at Wąski Dunaj St. An SS man harangued us there, calling us swine and bandits and so forth. His ugly speech ended with his selecting several dozen of the seriously wounded and separating them from us. They simply tore from our hands all the wounded who couldn't move sprightly enough under their own power. The SS man took them into Wąski Dunaj. We heard a series of gunshots. None of us were in any doubt as to what those shots meant. [In] 1945, I saw ashes on Wąski Dunaj St."

It seems to me that we've forgiven the Germans too quickly and too easily. There are such things in history that are never forgiven—because there is no reason to. The Church hierarchs and the prime ministers of successive Polish governments should never forget this.

In order to forgive, you need permission, not from God, for God has nothing to do with this, but from the Poles. And such permission no one has given to anyone, nor ever should they. Imagine for a moment the presence of God there, at that time, on Wąski Dunaj St. But we were supposed to be talking about something else—was it a failure? These images from Podwale, Kaliński, and Wąski Dunaj tell us just so much—that it was a failure, a catastrophe, some ominous foretelling of the end. A prediction that said that the Poles will never struggle to their feet from this, that there will be no more Poles anymore because they're not able to see to it that Poland should continue to exist. A failure, and such a failure as cannot be compared to any other, such a one as the Poles had never yet undergone—the greatest one of all up until then. And that was how it was understood later, and it was also said that it was not only the Germans who were to blame, who were responsible for it, but that they were too, those who took the decision to start the Uprising in the first place. But now more than a full half-century has passed since then, and it has turned out that the frightful prediction from Wąski Dunaj did not come true, that the historical prophecy turned out to be mistaken. Why? Because the Uprising was a victory. The proof of this, evident for all to see, is right here, next door, all around us, and all of us who are living here now, also, are proof positive. Proof is this independent Poland. It was for this very reason that the AK Headquarters and the Government Delegation for Poland took the decision for the outbreak of the Uprising—to achieve this and no other result. Exactly this result. This was the one and only reason, the one and only goal—there was no other, nor could there be any other. Whoever thinks otherwise, i.e. that the Uprising ended in catastrophe because it capitulated, because on the night of 2–3 October, the delegates of Headquarters signed in Ożarów the pact of cessation of hostilities with von dem Bach, is slicing up history into little portions (a couple of weeks, a couple of months, a couple of years) and giving expression to the conviction that these little slices have nothing in common with one another; they are not linked to one another in any way. It must be said that, following the Uprising, that's how one thought—that the end of this little slice of history is the end of everything. There were even poets who thought like this, although better ought to be expected of poets—at least (in agreement with the grand traditions of Polish poetry) some sense touching upon the future, near and far. Following the capitulation of the Uprising, describing Warsaw as a paling specter, Kazimierz Wierzyński wrote, "Nothing but ruins and defeat." But history cannot be sliced up into little portions, independent of one another; that is a completely illegitimate procedure and a completely senseless one. You simply can't isolate a single event (it doesn't matter if it's small or large, important or trivial), plucking it out from among other events, earlier and later, and say—oh, here it began, here it ended, and there, where it began you can find its causes, and there where it ended, you have its effects. History unfolds in a different manner; its events are linked together in a different way, and it's not necessarily the case that they unfold in a chronological fashion from what occurred immediately before them, conditioning in their own turn what happens immediately in their wake. A certain event, something that happened once, can have an immediate effect (and usually does have some immediate effect), but it can also have an effect of some sort several years or several decades later. Some event, something that just (right here, before our very own eyes, under our very hands, during our lifetime, at this very moment) happens, might have its direct cause just next door (and usually it does have such a direct cause), but it can also have, and usually does, even must have, some more distant causes, deeper, far away—distant by months, years, decades. If we consider history in this way, that is, as a chronological chain of events, events that order themselves harmoniously, creating a sufficiently explicable picture of the whole, how many isolated images of facts assume a permanent place in history—but are unable to explain one another reciprocally, understand one another reciprocally. The Warsaw Uprising had its (horrid) immediate effects, but it also had its (splendid) results, which were not apparent at once but only became so after the passage of a certain amount of time. One of these effects, the most important one, is the independence enjoyed by the Poles today. And we can be certain that the legends of the Uprising, the blood then spilled, the sacrifices then offered, all of the suffering of the time, and all of the glory of those days, will continue to function all throughout our history, and in our national history they will have their distant results. And this means that they will be the cause of many more results, such as we are unable even to imagine at present—unimaginable events, which, if we live to see them, will surprise us all. If we can agree that the Warsaw Uprising was the greatest event in the history of Poland, if we at least agree that it was one of the greatest historical events that ever happened among us, that entered into Polish history, our national fate, one such event among others that touches (by the grace of fate) all Polish generations past and future, then it would be complete nonsense to suggest that this event came to an end in the first days of October 1944 or in the several months afterward, when all of Poland found itself under Russian occupation. Just as it is with the baptism of Poland—which is also such an event that continues to have its important results because it continues to be renewed, mysteriously, and we continue to renew it—whether someone happens to like it or not, because our individual likes and dislikes, beliefs and convictions, have very little significance in such matters, if any at all. Only a person completely incapable of understanding anything of Polish history, who doesn't understand it at all and is incapable of deciphering its mysterious, deeply hidden sense (or who does not believe in the existence of such a thing) might write that "the Warsaw battle was worth nothing, ended up a fiasco." And the person who wrote that did so a dozen or so years after the Uprising, when it was already clear to see that it was this very Uprising, with all its legends, that was to decide the future of the Poles.

THE LIFE AND DEATH OF IVAN VASHENKO

THE SHORT LIFE OF infantryman Ivan Ivanovich Vashenko, which ended in his death (how else could it end?), can be seen as something of a perfect anatomical specimen on a petri dish. We gaze at it through our microscope, see what it looks like, how it behaves, how it moves about, and in so doing, we get some perfect information concerning not only that particular specimen but also an infinite number of similar material phenomena (and perhaps spiritual as well, no matter—it's all a question of terminology). The clear information it provides us with tells us that the lives and deaths of phenomena emerging from life (and departing therefrom) cannot be explained because there is no sense to them; the emergence itself cannot be the meaning of that which emerges; or the other way around: they have no meaning because they cannot be explained. Inexplicable, deprived of meaning, providing no answer to the question posed: why? emerging from the emergence, they appear and disappear—that's as much as you can reliably say of them. And in just such a way did the specimen in our petri dish, Ivan Ivanovich Vashenko, appear and disappear. You might say—emerging from the vacuum and vanishing back into it, but such an interpretation would be arbitrary and inadmissible; it would be an interpretation such as cannot be justified by our microscopic observations of movement and behavior, which do not arise in any way therefrom, which therefore have no justification—beyond our fantasy or the imagination of the observer at the microscope, beyond his mind. What we can observe, that perfect complex of movements and behaviors, takes place between 2 August and 2 September—in the year 1944, of course. It is this very period that is covered in the *Dziennik Waszenko Iwana Iwanowicza* [*Diary of Ivan Ivanovich Vashenko*] (thus runs the title of the notes taken by said infantryman). And so everything takes place in the space of one month. The small bit of information dealing with events earlier than those occurring between 2 August and 2 September can either be deduced from the *Journal* or is recorded therein. Ivan Ivanovich Vashenko came from the village of Kociewicze, in the Czasznikowski area of the Vitebsk region. He had certainly been a Red Army soldier (but here we enter the region of suppositions, although well-founded ones); he landed in German captivity, in a German hunger camp for Russian POWs, where, motivated by hunger (this is also just a hypothesis), he found a good way out of his misfortune—by joining the ranks of RONA—the Russkaya Osvoboditelnaya Narodnaya Armiya [Russian National Liberation Army], which was recruiting at the camp. In this way (but here again, when I say "in this way," I am making a deduction), he became a soldier of RONA, that fearsome formation commanded by the infamous SS-Brigadenführer Mieczysław Kamiński. It is well-known who Kamiński's soldiers were and what they did. In Warsaw at the time, they were known (rather imprecisely) as "Ukrainians" or "Kalmuks." Sometime around 3 September—or precisely on 3 September—Vashenko's *Journal* fell into the hands of the insurrectionists from the "Kampinos" group, active in the Kampinoska Wilds under the command of Maj. Alfons Kotowski, "Okoń." It was immediately translated from the Russian into Polish—most likely, it was assumed that it might contain some information useful to the AK Intelligence Service—but there was none such to be found. Later, the Russian original was lost in unknown circumstances (and perhaps was never found again) but the translation was preserved in the "Kampinos" group's archives and later, along with them, at the Institute of National Remembrance (the one erected right after the war). Finally, in 1947, it was published in *Dzieje najnowsze* [*Most Recent History*], a quarterly published by the then-IPN (although only four issues ever saw the light of day). The extent to which the life and death of Ivan Vashenko is lacking in significance of any sort that might be linked to the simple emergence of that life and its vanishing in death is testified to by the manner in which I came into contact with him. After having placed an issue of *Dzieje najnowsze* down on my desk in the Institute of Literary Research (I wanted to read SS-Obergruppenführer Erich von dem Bach's account of the Warsaw Uprising contained therein), I noticed that a portion of the leaves in the issue had never been slit (in over sixty years!). So off I went to the librarian at the counter to ask for a paper knife. And in this way, I came to know the hidden (literally, turned-in-upon-itself) life of Ivan Vashenko and his death (also turned-in-upon-itself) or, to put it another way, "turned-in-upon-its-own-senselessness." Between the pages of a book, uncut pages—but this sounds a bit too poetic, too metaphorical. Yet that's exactly what it's like: all of us, not just Ivan Ivanovich Vashenko, are in this situation. On 2 August, all unmarried men in the RONA regiment in which Vashenko served (and which at the time was stationed in Silesia) were gathered together and told that they were being sent to Warsaw, where they were to "stifle an uprising of the Poles." The next day, 3 August, in the evening, Vashenko found himself in Ochota, most likely somewhere in the general area of Grójecka and Wawelska Sts. (Vashenko was unfamiliar with the names of the streets in Warsaw and does not mention them in his *Journal*.) Later, Vashenko fought (if murder can be called fighting) somewhere in the city center on Nowogrodzka and Wspólna near the Child Jesus Hospital; later still, his regiment or some portion thereof was sent near Old Town. From the information provided in the *Journal*, you can get the fuzzy sense that after 20 August, some RONA battalions or companies were stationed at Stawki and on Inflancka. Such at least is suggested by the notes to the *Journal* worked up by Col. Adam Borkiewicz, the author of the renowned monograph *Powstanie Warszawskie 1944. Zarys działań natury wojskowej* [*The Warsaw Uprising 1944. A Sketch of Events of a Military Nature*]. If Vashenko found himself there, one might assume that he took part in the fight for the Mostowski Palace and the Simons Passage. In the Mostowski Palace, there was hand-to-hand combat, but not with bayonet or knife—the situation there was that the Poles and Germans (and perhaps Russians from the RONA units) lobbed grenades back and forth when coming across one another. But there is hardly any mention of fighting in the *Journal*. On the other hand, quite a bit of other interesting information can be found there. Vashenko devotes a lot of space to the attitude of the Germans to their Russian allies from Kamiński's Brigade because this is a topic that bears directly upon him. After the ROMA units were brought up to Ochota, the Germans tossed them into the fray and gave them no further mind. The Russians had to take care of themselves. "I get up at five from my bed made of two overcoats [...] and off we go in search of food, house to house. I find some eggs, which me and the boys fry up and eat." It was the same story with water, which the Germans also didn't provide. "Not much water in the city, except for that found stored up by the inhabitants in various vessels. It's none too safe to drink that water, but we drink it anyway, as there is no other." Several places in the *Journal* testify to the fact that Vashenko didn't like killing and probably didn't want to do it. He even posed the question that we might set before his life and death— why? "We enter the city, the soldiers look for people, the company commander shoots them dead—what for? What do those—women and children—have to do with this?" Among the reasons why Vashenko didn't want to kill (there may be more than a few), two are clearly formulated in the *Journal*. First, the author of the *Journal* couldn't bear Germans, and the thought that the murders were carried out in Ochota on German command did not give him any pleasure. "We're fighting for the benefit of the Germans, who are preying upon the Russian people, on behalf of Germans who have done millions of Russians to death by starvation in concentration camps and POW camps." Second, Vashenko admired the Poles, their love of freedom, their courage, and their determination. "As I have already noted, the Poles are the one nation that values freedom the most, who love only their own government and their own national state. A people who love and respect their nation are a nation in the full sense of the word." The author of the *Journal* drew a (very reasonable) conclusion from this evaluation, that killing the Poles is a fruitless endeavor, because there is no way of overcoming people who love freedom. This foresight of a solider in the ranks of the savage RONA formation, stating that the Poles will never be conquered, certainly testifies to his intelligence. "The Poles love the freedom of their Fatherland and stand shoulder to shoulder in its defense. We are helpless against them; the SS are helpless against them; the Germans with their heavy weaponry, tanks, and air forces—helpless." All of this does not mean, of course, that Vashenko, who liked the Poles and did not like to kill, didn't do any killing. On the contrary, one can state without a doubt that he did—that, finding himself in a situation where killing was going on, he couldn't not kill, too. Nowhere in the *Journal* do we find this expressly stated. The author took great care to avoid such things. But a close reading of the text leaves one in no doubt. Right after his questioning of the reasons why women and children had to be killed, we have a phrase indicative of where exactly Vashenko's unit was located. "We're getting ready to spend the night in a hospital." That would be the Maria Curie-Skłodowska Radium Institute he's referring to, which was found on a little street, or rather square abutting on Wawelska St. Kamiński's soldiers spent the night of 4–5 August there (as we learn from Vashenko's notes), and on the morning of 5 August there commenced the horrendous (horrendously bestial and bloody) six-day storming of one of the most famous insurrectionary redoubts by the RONA units—that found on the other side of Wawelska, at Wawelska 60 / Mianowski 15. After this complex of buildings had been taken, which happened on 11 August, the RONA "Kalmuks" murdered dozens of people there—all civilians, as the insurrectionists defending the redoubt were able to exfiltrate to the city center via the sewer system. Other events taking place at Mianowski 15 cannot be recounted in polite company. There is no information on this topic in the *Journal* but (as Adam Borkiewicz sees it) the fragment in which Vashenko describes the search for food and water speaks of it. "We receive the order to move up to a building in which there are thirty Poles with automatic weapons. They say that we are to take that building by storm—inevitable death for many young soldiers, who only wish to live. . . . After entering the building we search for water and food. We find some, but only a little; I find nothing." The massacre continued, and whoever found himself inside the building had to take part in it. Even if all he was after was a little food and water. On 28 August, the company of Lieutenant Ivanin (such was the name of Vashenko's commanding officer, the one who shot up the women and children at Ochota) was sent to the Kampinoska Wilds. Vashenko probably got a little mixed up with his geography, as he thought that he was fighting in the Augustowska Wilds. "Tomorrow, we're off to the Augustowska Wilds, where they say that all of the insurrectionists from Warsaw have regrouped." The last entries in the *Journal* are dated 30 August, 1 and 2 September. "We're being fired on. A dead RONA soldier is lying in the middle of the road. Shot in the head. Someone stripped him of boots and trousers. Further on, we come across dead Poles." In those days, Ivanin's company was fighting near a place known as Truskaw. As the commentary of Adam Borkiewicz informs us, the units of Major "Okoń" emerged on the edge of the Kampinoska Wilds on the night of 2–3 September, circled round Truskaw from the south, and attacked it from the direction of Laski and Izabelin, "completely taking by surprise the two battalions belonging to a regiment of Kamiński's brigade which had been quartered there, completely shattering them. The commanding officer and over one hundred soldiers were killed and just as many wounded." Ivan Ivanovich Vashenko was among that first hundred. Of course, nothing is known about the circumstances of his death, nor do we know where he was buried. The fact that the *Journal* has survived tells us that his pockets were gone through by Major "Okoń's" soldiers before he was buried. Most likely, he lies somewhere near Truskaw—it seems very improbable to me that the corpses of RONA soldiers were ever exhumed after the war, that there was any desire at the time to dig up "Kalmuks" and arrange a second burial for them—unnecessary trouble. They're somewhere beneath a fifty-year-old stand of trees in the Kampinoska Wilds, completely forgotten and completely unnecessary—then as now. Now, it's not that my intention here is to memorialize them—not at all. They're just something that emerged before vanishing once again. And still the question why? remains unanswered. Let's say that he's awaiting the resurrection there in that forest grave of his. I wonder if he'll learn why he killed and why he was killed. Will there be anyone present who will be able to explain it to him?

THE LITTLE PROP-JOB BETWEN GOŁKÓW AND PIASECZNO

IN THE EARLY FALL, after the Uprising, we were living in Piaseczno. This was no safe place to be, as from time to time the Germans organized raids, breaking into homes and taking away all the men whose Kennkarte proved them to be Warsaw residents. They were sent off in transports in an unknown direction, which boded no good. And so my father decided that we should move away to some smaller place, where perhaps the Germans wouldn't be interested in us. He chose nearby Gołków, where he rented a small attic room in a house located near the narrow-gauge railway station. Considering it from the perspective of the railway, or in other words, from my perspective, for you might say that at the time I was a big fan of the narrow-gauge railways around Warsaw, and I knew a lot about them—and so, from the narrow-gauge railway perspective, Gołków was the next station on from Piaseczno in the direction of Grojec. But it seems to me that in the early fall of 1944, the train from the Warsaw South station to Grojec wasn't running. So we loaded our baggage onto a small two-wheeled cart to which my father hitched himself, and with him pulling and me and my sister pushing from the rear, in this manner, we set off on our last wartime journey, to Gołków. It was a well-considered decision because my Uncle Tomek (on my father's side, as he was married to my father's sister), who had been living with us in Piaseczno after leaving Warsaw and didn't want to come along with us to Gołków, was arrested a few days after our departure and

THE LITTLE PROP-JOB BETWEN GOŁKÓW AND PIASECZNO

transported by the Germans to the camp in Stutthof, from which he never returned. In the warm summer evenings before the Uprising, I would wait at the gate of my grandfather's house at Służew for Uncle Tomek's return. I knew when he was near even before I caught sight of him because you could hear him singing grandly all the way from the Warsaw South station (my grandfather's house was just about right at the tracks). Uncle Tomek had a big, beautiful voice (maybe he even considered becoming a singer—before the war, he had been a violinist in the Warsaw Philharmonic Orchestra). He began that grand song of his as soon as he was past the Warsaw South station because he knew that his faithful and only auditor—namely, me—was waiting on him impatiently. Of course, Uncle Tomek's song was also heard by the German gendarmes who patrolled the area of the Warsaw South station after curfew, but it must be said that they had one (and only one) good character trait—they didn't bother anyone returning home drunk with a song on his lips. After supper, Uncle Tomek would sit me down beside him and, to do me a small pleasure, reprise his song. My grandfather—and Auntie Lilka, Uncle Tomek's wife —for sure were none too pleased with that song. Later, when I'd grown up, I tried to find the origins of the song but never succeeded, and now, I probably never will find out who wrote the words. They went like this: "When Barbara died / Bartek gave her a ride / To the very graveside. / Then Bartek did shout / 'Barbara, out!' / And Barbara climbed down / In the hole in the ground. / When she lay down inside / With rocks he filled her in / 'Barbara: here's your dinner! / Bon appetite! / Barbara, bite.'" My grandfather—my father's father—was a strict man and certainly wasn't pleased at his son-in-law, Uncle Tomek, demoralizing a child with such stupid songs. But I adored that song—it was the grand song of my childhood. And because I loved my Uncle Tomek, whom those German bastards killed (killing him, it must be made perfectly clear, for no reason at all; he did nothing to them), I'll say even more: this is the grand song of my life. But let's get back to Gołków. A month or two later, when all the golden swine stitched into the buttons of my sister's navy blue blazer had been sold (back then, you called a long sweater that buttoned down the front a "blazer"), the problems began, as we'd nothing left to live on. Of course, there was no way of our getting back to our flat on Koszykowa, where there were some things that we might have sold (anyway, the building on Koszykowa had most likely already been burnt to the ground by the Germans), and my father had no sort of trade he could make money at. My mother earned a bit by treating the inhabitants of Gołków when they needed a doctor, but that probably wasn't enough to keep us afloat. So my father decided to take up a retail business on a small scale. I'm sure he had no great talent for that sort of thing, and his stupid intellectual-elitist disdain led him to overlook trade in any sort of item that might actually turn a profit, that is, gold or meat or firewood, but only items worthy of a Warsaw intellectual: writing implements. He rented (or maybe he bought) a wooden booth at the Gołków market square and set up shop. When he went home for dinner, the notebooks, nibs, and erasers were hawked by his nine-year-old son. Next to his stand was another, similar one, where you could buy postage stamps. As much as my pocket money would allow, I bought stamps there with Hitler's image. That was a big, multi-colored series, and I wanted to have Hitler in all possible hues. But it must be said that the market for such implements of the intelligentsia as erasers or stamps issued by the General Government with Hitler's image was not a large one. Only when my grandmother arrived with half a piglet, having been expelled from her estate on the Narew by the Germans, were we saved from starvation. But that was later. One day—this was still in the fall of 1944—I went to Piaseczno with my father, who wanted to buy some writing supplies or other from the warehouse there. I was to help transport these notebooks or inkwells back to Gołków. We walked alongside the railroad tracks, indeed, down the center of the tracks themselves. It was a beautiful, sunny day. I remember the young birch trees that grew somewhere near the tracks, their golden leaves and branches caught motionless, and through them the autumn light filtering—the young birches around Warsaw are unutterably beautiful—for me, they are the most beautiful trees in all the world. On this side of the Wisła, the Germans were still holding on, but the Russians had control of the skies. Nearly every night, having something to bomb, they hung their splendid chandeliers about the dark skies. I liked these Russian air raids very much, for it really was a beautiful sight—from our attic, you could see all of nighttime Gołków and the surrounding region all lit up in a whitish, somewhat corpsey light. It was something of a posthumous perspective, so to speak, and as I looked on from the attic, it seemed to me that I was already in the great beyond, having been transported there along with the entire region. There were no more German planes to be seen. In the air, the Russians did as they pleased. So we went along the tracks in the direction of Piaseczno, and suddenly, this Soviet biplane appeared overhead—one of those prop-jobs they called *kukurizhniki*—"corn-crackers," also known to the Allies as "mules." It had red stars on its wings. There was nobody around except for my father, me, and the two Russians in that plane. There had to be two of them because one was doing the flying and another the shooting. They flew low, so low that I got a good look at the slant-eyed pilot, and even though he was wearing a leather helmet, I'm sure that I'd be able to recognize him even today. His face was Asiatic, brownish, and quite tanned. To my left, in the direction of Warsaw, there was a plowed field and beyond it—those autumn birches, actually. To the right, in front of us, but far enough away, distant by some hundred or two hundred meters, little birches too, and past them, villas with gardens, probably the outskirts of Piaseczno. The first attack came from behind, that is, from the direction of Gołków. A series from the machine gun kicked up the dust along the tracks, splintering ties, right at my feet. I've never, before or after in my whole life, been so terrified. Even when I was drowning in the Narew—but I was drowning earlier, in 1941, I reckon—I wasn't so afraid. Even when I leapt from the embankment in Żabieniec near Piaseczno, right in front of the locomotive. We began running in the direction of those villas and their gardens. My father was pulling me along by the hand, but he didn't juke to the right immediately (I have no idea why not); we kept running right along the tracks. The Soviets in the prop-job gave us a little respite—in order to attack from the direction of Piaseczno, they had to fly off a bit and make a turn. The second series fell diagonally to the tracks, right in front of us. If we had been running just a bit faster, we would've fallen right in among those rounds. Later, of course, I returned to that many times in thought, and all that thinking, from which nothing (good) could ever result, led at last to my having nightmares about it—they're flying, rushing after me, somebody, something, I don't know what it is, and I'm running, and there's nowhere to hide. Years later, when I read that novel by Camus, I came to realize that I had experienced something very similar to what he describes there—something analogical—the emergence of alienation. I'm no expert in French prose; I have no idea, therefore, what the biographers of that author have to say. But I am certain that Camus did not conjure that event out of thin air, on some Algerian beach lit up by the bright Mediterranean sun—someone had to tell him about it because such things cannot be invented. Later, I changed my opinion on the subject, coming to acknowledge that the two men in the biplane couldn't have had anything in common with the protagonist of Camus's novel; they didn't have to be strangers, alienated like him, because their intentions were completely different. It could have been (and most likely it was) that they had some free time to kill before returning to the landing strip to the rear of the front, and they wanted to fool around a bit—they wanted to squeeze off a few rounds and see how a middle-aged gentleman walking along with a boy were going to skedaddle, chased by machine gun rounds. It might also be that they took us for Germans. They were convinced that the Reich, Hitler's state, began at the western bank of the Wisła, and so that gentleman and boy were Germans they need to kill. The *kukuruzhnik* attacked us a third time, this time along the path beyond the tracks, but by this point, we were already at the villas where Piaseczno begins. Some woman, who had been watching the whole thing play out, opened a gate for us. I sat on the floor, with my back against the wooden wall, and wept—from fright, of course. The woman's dog, a black Alsatian Shepherd (I didn't like Alsatian Shepherds, because the Germans used to walk them along Pius and Koszykowa) sniffed at my ear. And that's the whole story. Only moderately interesting, for what's interesting in the fact of two

THE LITTLE PROP-JOB BETWEN GOŁKÓW AND PIASECZNO

Russians (or two Asiatics) in a biplane wanting to kill a middle-aged gentleman and a boy walking alongside him, not killing them, and then flying away? And yet, in the moderately interesting story, there is (at least for me) something compelling. Not that those Russians or Asiatics wanted to kill me and my father—just like that, for no express reason—as if they were protagonists in some novel by Camus, emerging (or rather flying out) therefrom. Maybe they wanted to kill us, and maybe not. Maybe they only wanted to have some fun. It doesn't matter. Maybe they wanted to frighten the little boy, to see how he'd run for his life. No, the only interesting thing here is the fact that, at the time, I wasn't surprised in the least that somebody wanted to kill me for no reason. They frightened me, sure, and then some. But that didn't shock me. I accepted their intention without surprise. Or, to put it another way, I accepted it as something natural and obvious that fit within the natural order of things, the order of the world, that it was no disruption of that order at all. There was no reason for them to kill my Uncle Tomek, so why should there be any for them to kill me? What's strange about that? Even later, when I considered the event from afar, I felt no wonder at it, that someone would want to kill a nine-year-old boy walking along with a middle-aged gentleman for no reason at all. Nor does it surprise me today. The war was on the wane, I was nine years old, I was perfectly adapted to life in the civilization which was beginning—it was my home. I had no other.

EXPLOSION

STEFAN ŻEROMSKI'S DAUGHTER, the painter Monika Żeromska:

"I'm in the courtyard, near the entranceway. Suddenly, something hits me in the side, and I am sent flying along the flagstones, unable to stop. It was some nightmarish blast of air that struck me and pushed me several meters on. . . . The Germans had sent up a Goliath, a little tank, filled with explosive material. Right when the tank was surrounded by a crowd of people—including children and women who had emerged from the buildings nearby, on Kiliński St., a narrow passage crowded with tall apartment buildings—the explosion occurred. All that was left of a crowd of many hundreds of people was a bloody pulp. Bodies were hurled afar; tattered human flesh hung from overhead wires, balconies, roofs. All of us are shaken to the core by this crime."

General Tadeusz Bór Komorowski:

"The driver passed deftly through the barricade, to the cheers of a crowd of women and children. He turned around and came to a halt perpendicular to the road, near the curb. At that very moment, I was blinded by a flash: a pillar of fire, shrouded in layers of smoke and dust. At the same time came the roar of the explosion. The blast of air hurled me away from the window and onto the floor near the opposite wall. Completely deafened, I rose to my feet in order to go back over to the window or, rather, to the hole in the wall where the window had been. The smoke and dust settled slowly, revealing to my eyes the horrid effects of the explosion. There wasn't a trace remaining of the soldiers who had made up the crew of the vehicle. Round about lay the torn bodies of dozens of people—there were many children among them. People's corpses had been thrown onto the roofs of the nearby buildings. Heads, arms, legs—torn apart, lay in pools of blood among the ruins of the walls of the two corner buildings. All of the door and window frames of the building in which our headquarters was located were torn away, and cracks appeared in several places in the walls of the ground floor and the first floor."

Lieutenant Colonel Felicjan Majorkiewicz:

"I went into the entranceway of the former Ministry of Justice building. I had no sooner opened the door to Division III at Headquarters when I heard the sudden roar of a powerful explosion. Dust, powder, fragments of plaster, and glass lay at my feet. Dust gritted in my teeth. I ran out into the street. The smoke slowly lifted, and suddenly I saw the bloodied remains of people. . . . The entire carriageway of Kiliński St. was paved with the bodies of the massacred. The explosion had been so powerful, so violent, that some bodies had been thrown onto balconies, trees, low roofs, and even into some rooms. The bodies lay so thickly upon the road that it was with some difficulty that I made my way to the commander of 'North' group without treading upon them. . . . Immediately after the explosion, units were organized to collect the bodies, untangling them from the bloody heaps, arranging them, and then transferring them to the grassy plots near the walls of the former Ministry of Justice building, from the Kiliński St. side, so that they could be buried that evening. When returning from Col. 'Wachnowski' along Kiliński, and then Podwale, I saw that the barricades had been returned to their former state, and the road had even been hosed down with water."

Hanna Malewska, writer:

"Children and women surround the tank, or, rather, the small tractor, which had obviously just been captured. Four smiling soldiers are driving it along the street. A little boy waving a flag is at the head of the parade. Heads lean out of windows—cheers, calls fill the air. The tank reaches the corner. Then, suddenly—but even in memory, it doesn't seem real: that explosion, that shock. You know that it happened, and yet it is nearly impossible to evoke it again in your own mind—how can you share it with anyone else? Panes of glass shattered, the shards flying perpendicular to the ground like salvos of stilettos. An upper wall collapsed. Whoever survived is still unaware, can't understand it… What was that? And then he still doesn't want to believe it. But it's impossible not to. The tank had been set up as a trap by the Germans, stuffed with a ton of explosive material that had exploded—just as women and children were closely packed around it. There, at the foot of the wall—the little legs of children, going blue, lying next to one another like limbs torn off dolls. Unbelievable, how much blood."

Helena Gliwic, student, nurse, and cook in the "Gustaw" battalion:

"A lot of boys and girls ran out of our building and surrounded the tank. Others went out onto the balconies. People also came out of the neighboring buildings—a crowd of about 2,500 people had gathered. At the time, I was in the kitchen of number 3, which was located in the first part of the building facing the courtyard. I later learned that two of my girlfriends from the kitchen had run out to the tank and climbed up on top of it so as to ride into the courtyard in triumph. A lot of girls were walking behind the tank. At a certain moment, some military man called them away: 'Get away from the tank; it hasn't been checked out yet.' And he himself approached to look it over. I was standing in the kitchen. Suddenly… at such a close proximity, I didn't hear any roar. Everything went black, and I had the feeling that the building was collapsing on top of me. In the darkness, with my hands stretched out in front of me, I went forward through the ruins amidst moans—howling, actually. At a certain moment, a peaceful, steady voice penetrated the chaos: 'Keep calm. Don't panic. I'm here. Go help the wounded.' It was one of the commanders. He had been wounded in some earlier action and now had been buried in rubble, but he had extricated himself. I ran out into the street, and a horrible sight met my eyes. Heaps of dead bodies—tatters of bodies tossed around on the street; everything befouled to the height of the second floor. People were being burnt to death, alive. The fire from the time bomb set off the gasoline which had been stored in bottles in the entranceway to our building. I noticed a naked woman crawling along the street—on fire. I tried to put it out with a dishrag I happened to be gripping in my hand. Then I ran into nr 5 or nr 1, I don't remember which. I looked horrible: covered in soot from the stove and bleeding from being cut by glass—so the people there offered me help. After washing up, it turned out that I hadn't been gravely wounded. A while later, having come to myself some more, I went home. People were going along the street carrying body parts—tatters of skin—in their hands. Beneath my feet were corpses upon carbonized corpses. They looked horrible, but their death had been instantaneous. The wounded, the half-dead, the torn were worse off. Three of my friends had died, ripped to pieces. Two died on the tank, one in a room—she was a nurse on the first floor, in the front. Her arm had been torn from her shoulder—her intestines were splattered on the window among tatters of clothes and buttons. Those who had been on the balcony fell down onto the street."

Stanisław Komornicki, "Nałęcz," Lance Corporal of the 104th Company of the Union of Polish Syndicalists:

"Dusk is falling. The little square on Kiliński presents a shocking view: the streets and walls of the buildings are splashed with blood and white brain matter up to the height of the first floor. The carriageway is covered with a gigantic chaos of tangled body parts; everywhere—arms ripped from torsos, legs, bloody tatters of human meat and clothing, thick shards of armor, and other fragments of the exploded tank. Its wreck was thrown in the direction of Podwale, and there it lies. We are halted at the corner. Medics from the nearby hospital at Długa 7 are still searching for the living, piling the massacred bodies on stretchers."

Witold Sikorski, "Boruta," a soldier of the "Rudy" company of the "Zośka" Battalion:

"We passed Sapieżyńska, went through the ruins of Freta, in order to get onto Długa. When we arrived at the Ministry of Justice, we were hit by a horrible stench of corpses, such as we'd never smelled before. Chaos near the building. Crowds of people, numerous posts of the military police. We are stopped at the corner of Kiliński. At the foot of the walls, there lay innumerable tatters of human bodies, which special units were clearing away on wooden stretchers. A terrifying sight. Some sort of massacre had to have taken place. On the other side of the street, the walls of the buildings were splashed with blood, now congealed. The same with the sidewalks and the road itself. The walls were thickly pockmarked with shrapnel. We cover our noses and mouths with handkerchiefs—the odor is unbearable. We decide to try and find out something more and stop some military police walking past. It turns out that a captured tank had been passing by here, enthusiastically greeted by cheering crowds who had come out into the street. At a certain moment, it exploded."

Krystyna Wizówna-Łyczywkowa, a student and distributor of the underground press:

"Nothing remained but pieces of human bodies, massacred horribly: arms and legs had flown into the yard on Wąski Dunaj, impelled by the force of the blast. Not only those who were standing near the tank died—also those who were watching from the windows, balconies, and entranceways, and even some who had been sitting quietly in their own homes. It was impossible to identify people. After all, in the end, all those body parts were collected in bedsheets and buried in a common grave. With my heart hammering, I start running through the corridors and rooms. Chaos and ruin everywhere. I'm looking for Krysia—she's nowhere to be found. In the room where I had been sitting just half an hour before, everything is topsy-turvy, mixed up with rubble; an arm lies near a backpack—that's it, no body. My search is fruitless, and I have to get back. On the next day, I visit all the hospitals and sanitary points—people are lying on the floors in the cellars on stretchers. The list of names is incomplete. Some can't be identified because of their being unconscious, or on account of a lack of documents. Burnt faces, horribly disfigured. At one of the sanitary points, I'm shown Krysia—also from kitchen staff. I draw close; in the dim candlelight, I see a woman: legs bandaged, swollen face—one eye red and purple. I recognize the man's watch that Krysia used to wear on her left wrist and the bandage on her right (she had been scalded in the kitchen). I don't want to believe it. I touch her hair—it's not hers. The clothes, also, are different."

Tulewicz (first name unknown), a worker from the Issuing Bank on Bielańska St. She had been lying in the basement of a sanitary point on the corner of Franciszkańska and Bonifraterska since losing an eye:

"I couldn't sleep for hunger and thirst and fever. . . . Every now and then, we were visited by this madwoman from the St. John of God Hospital. She was thought to bring misfortune with her. A young, pretty girl with ash-blonde hair cut short like a man's, in a shirt that reached her knees, barefoot, wrapped in a gray mantle. It was probably just a regular blanket, but it was so tattered that her whole appearance was like that of a moth, a bat, or a specter. She'd run in completely silently on her soft feet and never say a word. She'd pause by each of us, bend down, peer carefully at us, deep into our eyes, one after another, as if she were searching for something or wanted to prove something to herself, after which she would immediately run off. She gave no answer to any question posed her; silently, she would run around the shelter and then hasten off to others. No one could restrain her, bullets whizzed by her—she was like some silent, gray shadow."

THE UPRISING AS AN ERUPTION OF INSANITY

FOR VARIOUS REASONS—chiefly reasons of propaganda—the Warsaw Uprising has been considered an eruption of insanity. Most often, this was indulged in by the Communists, but there's no reason to concern ourselves with their machinations, for it's obvious on whose behalf they were concocted. The Communists wished to present the Poles as people in need of someone's care (someone ought to put them in straitjackets). That's all that can and need be said on that topic. However, there have also been historians who—even though they had nothing in common with Communists and were even considered by the latter to be enemies of Communism—still, concerning the Uprising, and especially its outbreak, looked upon these matters in exactly the same way. That is, they saw in it the horrendous act of insane persons. To speak of such an evaluation formulated by people who were neither bribed by Russians or Germans but who worked up their evaluation in accord with their own free convictions, the most interesting example is found in that portion of the third volume of the *Najnowsza historia polityczna Polski* [*Most Recent Political History of Poland*], the masterwork of Władysław Pobóg-Malinowski, which is devoted to the Uprising. Pobóg-Malinowski was working abroad (his gigantic, nearly thousand-page third volume of the *Most Recent History* was published by the author himself on a subscription basis: London, 1960), and so he was not obliged, like in-country historians (subject to severe Communist censorship), to concern himself with anyone's opinions or any consequences—he could write whatever he

THE UPRISING AS AN ERUPTION OF INSANITY

wished. I do not want to involve myself here in any evaluation of the admirable work of this historian, the merits of which are obvious: the subsequent volumes of the *Most Recent History* smuggled into the conquered country played an important role in informing the Poles of their twentieth-century history, of which no one on hand intended to inform them—at least, not in a manner in accord with the truth. I have had my own London copy of the third volume at home for over forty years. It is in quite bad shape for being thumbed through so many times. So I will say only so much, cautiously: that Pobóg-Malinowski was a faithful soldier of the Marshal's, and this means that he had some clearly-defined political convictions, and from time to time, these induced him to set historical facts in order, in a manner consistent with them. If we are to speak of the Uprising, Pobóg, in line, after all, with the title of his work, considers, above all, its political causes and consequences, which one might also term spiritual, while the history of individual people and places interests him to a much lesser degree. Everyone who had anything to do with the Uprising—those who set it afoot and those who participated in it—Pobóg considers to have been out of their minds. It's not entirely clear (and rather cannot be definitively stated) what he had in mind in employing such words. Was he using them metaphorically (as a sort of metaphorical curse), or did he actually think that those two generals, Tadeusz Bór Komorowski and Tadeusz Pełczyński, "Grzegorz," were, as he saw it, authentic lunatics? It seems to me (although I can't prove it) that the words "lunatic" and "lunacy" (so often on his lips) appear in Pobóg's text in both senses: that he felt Bór, Pełczyński, and also Chruściel, and the cabinet of ministers of the Polish government in London were lunatics, maniacs sick in the head, possessed by a crazy idea, and at the same time he wished (unpleasantly and keenly) to vilify them. Such vilification had a very clear purpose (perhaps the only one, but quite sufficient all the same)—Pobóg-Malinowski understood the Warsaw Uprising to be "the greatest misfortune in the history of Poland." This is a consideration that cannot be batted away, nor perhaps even questioned. Neither the massacre that took place during the Confederation of the Bar (nor the Umań Massacre), nor the Massacre of Praga that rang down the curtain on the 1794 Uprising, nor the repressions following the November and January Uprisings, constitute such misfortunes as was the Warsaw Uprising—there can be no comparison here at all. The same thing can be said for all of the great battles fought and lost by the Poles in the past. Neither the Tatar victory (Legnica) nor that of the Turks (Cecora) nor that of the Russians (Maciejowice), along with all the consequences arising therefrom, allow for even the merest stalk of comparison (although all of them were great Polish misfortunes). Still and all, in treating of the Warsaw Uprising as our greatest historical misfortune, Pobóg-Malinowski is guilty of oversimplification (in qualifying all those who took part in it as lunatics). For he does not see that this greatest Polish misfortune is also the greatest event in all Polish history. And if we consider it thus, then of course, the significance of the "misfortune" is modified somewhat. The mighty fist of the AK battalions, the fist of "Zośka," "Chrobry," and "Łukasiński" pummeled the Germans, showing them who the Poles are and what they are capable of, even without tanks, cannons, armored trains and airplanes at their disposal—and the results of this are going to be visible (in our national psyche and therefore in world history) for centuries. It would also be good for the Germans to keep this in mind, forever. I wrote that the qualification made by the author of the *Most Recent History* encompasses all of the participants in the Uprising—commanding officers and common soldiers, but of course, according to him, there is a great difference between these two: he understands the first group, the commanders of the insurrectionists, as lunatics and cads, while the latter are lunatic-heroes. According to him, the soldiers were mad because they died senselessly or, in other words, in a frenzy of heroic sacrifice. As we read in this fragment describing the first day of the Uprising: "This all took place in the full light of day, often in open terrain, and thus the murderous fire of the Germans mowed down these mad heroes, scattering and pinning them down so that they could neither advance nor retreat." As is understandable given the fact that he was writing a political history, the author of the *Most Recent History* was, however, not so much interested in the frenzied heroes who, in the end, were merely carrying out the orders of their superior officers, as he was in those officers, the lunatic-cads, who insanely called forth the Uprising and, later, when it erupted, directed it insanely, and also in those politicians who not only did not restrain the officers but egged them on in their lunatic deeds, later to fall into raving themselves. The entire chapter in the *Most Recent History* devoted to the Uprising is, essentially, an attempt at describing (not even understanding, but perfectly describing) the activities of several or several dozen lunatics. The Uprising, as Pobóg-Malinowski states, was evoked by "the AK officers' blind rush to fight" (these words are directed at Tadeusz Pełczyński and Antoni Chruściel and their superiors), for it was their decisions that led to the misfortune. What is more, they turned out to be wretched cowards in the end. In his commentary on the later accounts of officers at headquarters, Pobóg writes: "the burden of responsibility for the crazy decision to take up arms is so horridly great, that it called forth not only mean-spirited attempts at escaping from that responsibility. . .but also attempts at distancing oneself entirely from any sort of association with said decision." Because the Uprising turned out to be a horrid misfortune, and this misfortune might easily have been avoided, the AK commanders and anyone else who by "this or any other coincidence" found themselves "in control of events, both within the government in London and in the underground at home," ought to have been severely punished (the author of the *Most Recent History* states)— "they are all deserving of the sentence of death, by firing squad, at least." They were to be punished for "being incapable of properly assessing both the situation and the sense of the coming events, despite which they had the conceited ambition. . .of taking upon their shoulders the burden of the decision." Pobóg lists the names of the lunatics who took the decision and, accordingly, should be shot. "The Uprising in Warsaw broke out because such was the decision taken by Mikołajczyk, Kwapiński, Bór-Komorowski, Pełczyński, Jankowski." Of course, the question arises whether the lunatics who desired to rise up against the Germans were only the higher officers in Warsaw and the ministers in London, and so, those who took the fatal (as

Pobóg sees it) decision—or was it perhaps all of the Poles? If we accept the proposition that the Uprising resulted from someone's mad decision, from madness, then the statement that the entire society was mad would likewise seem to rest on good foundations. It is not beyond the pale of reason that all Poles might fall into madness, might really lose their minds, their grip on reality, as the result of the German executions, the German tortures, the German displacements, as the result of all that German cruelty. Certainly some frenzy did occur once the Uprising had got well underway—a splendid frenzy that can be seen even in the deeds of the best, most disciplined Kedyw units. According to Pobóg, those who had the decision-making authority were raving mad, and they imposed their madness on all the others. For a "blind rush to fight" had possessed the AK leadership, while on the other hand, society as a whole acted, or at least wished to act, according to "common sense," as we read in the *Most Recent History*, for society was "both wiser and more prudent and more cautious than its underground directorate." In line with his political sympathies, Pobóg also maintains that the Warsaw Uprising would certainly not have erupted if the last word in the decision-making process had belonged to someone else—some other commanding officers or some other politicians. "The Piłsudskiites particularly always spoke to the point, arguing that. . .all insurrectionary activity can only be insanity, a mad twisting of the red noose already looped around the Polish throat ever tighter." Nor would the commander-in-chief of the time, Kazimierz Sosnkowski, ever have permitted the Uprising to break out, if only he could have prevented it: "he was most categorically against the Uprising, although in the conditions then prevailing he couldn't prevent. . .what the government demanded of the Underground." Obviously, at first glance, we are confronted here with a serious question, a serious historiosophical problem—does history itself begin to rave along with the raving of the mere few—those who set it in motion, give it direction? Or does it rave when everyone—whole nations—are raving? But we're not going to concern ourselves with this at the present moment, as such historiosophical questions do not concern the author of the *Most*

THE UPRISING AS AN ERUPTION OF INSANITY

Recent History—they're not his bailiwick. What are we to do with this idea of Pobóg-Malinowski's? How are we to deal with it? Even were we to acknowledge the Warsaw Uprising as having been evoked by lunatics, and, finally, in and of itself, in its content and its history, as a great explosion of insanity, in reading the *Most Recent History,* we would still be obliged to state that the medical diagnosis posed by its author is superficial, incomplete, fragmentary—for it is but the diagnosis of one side of the story, one of its aspects, and if only for that reason—not so much unjust, even, as insufficient. Pobóg-Malinowski (and here we have the serious mistake committed by this historian) considered the Uprising only from one point of view: his own Polish point of view. That is, from the point of view of Polish interests (postwar interests, as he imagined they would be) and the future of Poland (again, postwar, such as it might have been, had the Uprising not occurred). On the other hand (and what we are about to describe is the obligation of all historians writing of these events, if they wish to uncover their secrets and gaze into their depth), he did not consider them from another point of view, one just as important: namely, the German point of view. The Uprising, its sense at the time and its future (historical) significance, can only be understood in this way—by looking upon it with German, as well as Polish, eyes. By ignoring that second perspective (or better: by acknowledging, or pretending, that it didn't even exist), Pobóg, in his charges of Polish lunacy, overlooks something extraordinarily important. In addition to this: something obvious, something that it is impossible not to perceive when one is studying the history of the German war, when one comes into even fleeting contact with it, because, as a matter of fact, it is lying on the very surface, visible at first glance. The blindness—that's what we have to call it—of Pobóg-Malinowski is completely incomprehensible to me; I am unable to explain it; I cannot see its essential causes. The author of the *Most Recent History* does not see that the lunacy of the Poles, who decided on their lunatic Uprising, was merely a response to the lunacy they were faced with, with which they had to come to terms and deal with—and this was something that was horrendously difficult to deal with, something with which no other nation would be capable of dealing. The lunacy to which the Poles were responding with their own lunacy can be termed the lunacy of war, or the lunacy of the German war, but in such a case, we would be generalizing a bit—and this is something concrete, something we saw with our very own eyes, and whoever did see it will never forget it. The lunacy of the Poles was a response to the lunacy of the Germans. That is, the lunacy of murdering, into which, for some incomprehensible reason, the Germans fell. This was something inconceivable, inexplicable, mysterious—something indeed insane, and so it remains even decades later. "Hitler," Pobóg-Malinowski writes, "responded to the news of the Uprising with rabid fury. . . . So there can be no doubt that the unreasonable and fatal decision of insurrection unleashed the German fury and set Warsaw before it as its prey." No, of course, it was just the other way around. By August 1944, the rabid fury of the Germans and their Hitler was well-known to the Poles (they had had five years of it already), and that rabid activity of the Germans, their lunatic blindness and lunatic cruelty, are what evoked the fury of the Poles. Even if the natural mania of the Poles (such as appears from time to time over the course of Polish history) can be seen as something deep and enduring, something even genetic; even if we acknowledge that something of this sort exists, rooted firmly in the deepest depths of our history and national psyche—something that emerges thence, from some Slavic depths to overwhelm us in a Slavic or Proto-Slavic blizzard and make us rave—at the time, in 1944, this was merely a response and nothing more. And if we grasp it thus, we shall also be obliged to acknowledge that it was the only possible, inevitable response. The murdering carried out by the Germans had to be dealt with; its nonsense had to be answered; the Germans had to be told that their lunacy had now stumbled across something that they were going to have to take into account—forever since they choose to live next door to us. The Poles had to respond to the lunacy of murder with their own lunacy if they wished to remain in existence on the face of this earth.

CRAYFISH ON THE CORNER OF KOSZYKOWA AND ŚNIADECKI

MY INTEREST IN CRAYFISH (and all other submarine creatures) is of a theoretical rather than a practical nature. To put it another way, it is an interest based on the conviction, or rather the sense of an (eventual) community of being, perhaps even of essence. And if essence, then, on something just about metaphysical. Culinary questions have nothing to do with this, nor could they. It just so happened that never in all my long life had I eaten a crayfish, and as far as the little stub of life remaining to me is concerned, it's pretty certain that I never will. Now, it's not that I refused to eat crayfish because I thought them repulsive or disgusting creatures. On the contrary—I admire their sovereign and (completely independent of my aesthetic convictions) grayish-green beauty. I've never eaten crayfish because I had the feeling—probably—that they were deeply submerged in the cosmic darkness—more deeply than any other creatures around us. They are almost as deeply submerged in it as are the dragons of myth—those that once flew about over our settlements. Of course, you might say that all the creatures we deal with here (or whose presence we merely feel or allow for) are submerged in cosmic darkness and emerge therefrom before our very eyes—or that darkness gives them forth, wishing to present them to our gaze. And yet I have a sense, or a presentiment (that is, something of course beyond reason), that crayfish—perhaps because they live underwater, and even deeper, in the very mud at the bottom of our lakes, and therefore are not only underwater but under-bottom creatures, have been set lower than all other incarnations of life, and if there exists any sort of hierarchy there, in the cosmic darkness (and I bet there is), well, they can be found on a very low, low rung thereof. I'm thinking here of something like Lamarck's ladder (but one of spiritual gradations, which has nothing to do with the processes of evolution) and the grayish-green crayfish is twitching his whiskers on the very lowest, or one of the lowest, rungs. And so that's why I've never eaten crayfish—cosmic darkness is inedible. You can look at it, but you can't eat it. For that would be to take a huge risk, as you simply don't know what you might find on that deepest level—what is actually there. I feel that my conviction of its inedibility is well-founded. During the war and, of course, before the war too, Koszykowa St. ran a little differently than it does today. Everything changed in that fatal year when they put up those buildings on the Plac Konstytucji [Constitution Square], and the street of my childhood was brutally sliced into two separate portions having nothing in common with each other and meeting nowhere—one heading west and the other east of Marszałkowska. All you need do is glance at any map of prewar Warsaw to see what it looked like in the forties and earlier. You can also see it clearly on the map included in the little book *Führer durch Warschau* written by Karl Grundmann (a low-level academic at the University of Warsaw before the war and, during it, a high-level official in the Abteilung Propaganda beim Gouverneur des Distrikts Warschau) and published in Kraków in 1942. Koszykowa commenced near Tarczyńska and the EKD (Elektrische Eisenbahn) tracks, ran straight along the walls of Filtry, and transected Marszałkowska without bending wildly as it does today before breaking a little to the southeast, but much farther on, near Mokotowska, from which it headed, as it still does, towards the Aleje Ujazdowskie or Siegestrasse—Victory St. Of course, German Victory. In his book *Okupowanej Warszawy dzień powszedni* [*Daily Life in Occupied Warsaw*], Tomasz Szarota informs us that from the beginning of 1943 on, Koszykowa was named Lückstrasse. This is something that I don't remember, and I assume that the inhabitants of Koszykowa didn't take much cognizance of this at the time, either.

CRAYFISH ON THE CORNER OF KOSZYKOWA AND ŚNIADECKI

On Grundmann's map the name doesn't yet appear. SS-Obersturmbannführer Karl Lück, who before the war busied himself with research into the influence of German civilization on that of Poland, was killed near Orsha in March 1942—that's how scholarly research into dangerous topics ends up. But the Germans appreciated this SS man and offered him a street—mine, it so happened. So, running straight as an arrow from Tarczyńska and the EKD tracks to Mokotowska, at the place where it transected Marszałkowska, my street had to—there's no way around it—connect with Śniadecki St. to create a charming little corner. Now, as we know, the outlet of Śniadecki is divided from that of Koszykowa by several dozen, maybe even a hundred meters. Śniadecki St. has remained where it was, but Koszykowa shifted to the north, in the direction of Piękna or Pius IX, and Wilcza. "There is a carriageway, unsleeping cobbles," I wrote in one of my earliest poems, some fifty, even fifty-plus years ago—and that's still true. That life of mine is to be found there in the middle of the road, over which buses pass on their way to the Hala na Koszykach, in the building that disappeared in order to make room for the road. A building, unclearly existing, semi-transparent, rises above the road, still existing, somewhat (as long as someone can imagine it; even this phantom will vanish after my death). And there, where the charming little corner used to be, at the confluence of Marszałkowska, Koszykowa, and Śniadecki, stood a large block of flats. I remember, quite clearly, its ground floor. I can't recall its upper stories, but it seems to me that they had to resemble (on account of the location) the building that still stands at the meeting of Marszałkowska and Polna—the narrow façade of which gives out onto the Plac Unii Lubelskiej [Union of Lublin Square]. The narrow front of the building on the corner of Śniadecki and Koszykowa gave out, of course, onto Marszałkowska. A tram went along Śniadecki. During the war, it was "Eighteen." It then turned onto Marszałkowska; you could take it to the Plac Narutowicza [Narutowicz Square]. There were no tracks on Koszykowa. There was a large grocery store on the ground floor of the corner building. Its shop windows were facing Śniadecki and Koszykowa, while the entrance (though I can't be certain) was on Marszałkowska. I can't remember if this was one of the stores belonging to Meinl or one of those run by the Pakulski Brothers. In some memoir or other, I found a note that it belonged to the latter. And yet my memory tells me something else. There was a big difference between the two—which I'm about to explain. The Pakulski Brothers stores were open to everyone, while those of Julius Meinl were nur für Deutsche. My memory tells me—and I'm certain I'm not mistaken here—that I was never inside that store. On the other hand, I remember standing there (now on Śniadecki, now on Koszykowa) in front of the display windows, my nose pressed to the panes, trying to see what could be found inside there—what splendid things, what sort of chocolates and bananas a seven- or eight-year-old boy might buy. If only he could get inside and risk a purchase with his pennies. I also had some paper "Młynarki," for I did get an allowance—we lived modestly but weren't plagued by wartime poverty. If I never went inside (if I wasn't allowed inside?), well, that had to be a store nur für Deutsche, then. I don't know. Among the four Meinl stores mentioned in Grundmann's guidebook (*Lebensmittelgeschäfte für Deutsche in Warschau*), there are two on Marszałkowska but at different numbers (8 and 94). But of course, those numbers might have changed. It was very pleasant to gaze through the window into the mysterious depths of a store nur für Deutsche, but there, on the outside, in front of the store, some phenomenal things were going on, too. Because no tram went down Koszykowa and there were only a few dozen steps between our building and Meinl's (or the Pakulski Brothers') store, I was not forbidden such little excursions, even though the family fretted quite a bit over my safety. So I would stand in front of the Pakulski Brothers' store and gape, unable to tear my eyes away from the splendid show. More interesting, much more interesting than what was to be found inside—those eventual bananas or chocolates—was what was found outside. And outside the Pakulski Brothers' (or Meinl's, whatever) store, crates of crayfish were displayed. Have you ever seen crayfish in crates? Have you ever seen crayfish put up for sale, crayfish who have no idea that they are being sold? Have you ever seen crayfish in crates, crayfish who have no idea that they are in crates? Have you ever seen crayfish being transported, crayfish on the road, crayfish who don't know that they are being transported, that this is transport, and that somebody's transporting something? There, in those crates, is found all the knowledge concerning life that anyone can have—there is everything one can and ought to know about it. These crates were hammered together from light-colored, unplaned slats or slats planed in any old way. They were more or less the size of those white and green plastic bins used in supermarkets today to hold various items. And probably just as deep or maybe a little less so. They would be set out on both sides of the store, in front of the large displays, on the Śniadecki and Koszykowa St. sides, on trestles of exactly the perfect height to allow the upper edges of the crates to reach my chin, or maybe a little lower. Or maybe it was that crate was set upon crate and that the one that was stacked highest reached almost to my chin. How many crayfish there were there, I have no way of telling. I only remember that there were a lot of crates, and as for the crayfish (of course, my imagination might be exaggerating a bit here), they were countless: dozens, hundreds, maybe even thousands of crayfish. At present, their color gives me pause. I know from experience, for, in the early eighties, I hunted for them in the canals and ponds in the neighborhood of Wigry (this is described in my *Rozmowy polskie* [*Polish Conversations*])—so, I know from the nocturnal experiences of a crayfish hunter that, extracted from the depths of the mire, crayfish are greenish, grayish-green in color. At least, that's the way it is with crayfish from around Wigry. The crayfish at the corner of Śniadecki and Koszykowa were a different color: there wasn't the slightest bit of green to them. They were bright violet; some of them were grayish-violet. If my memory serves me correctly, you might also come across crates of grayish-blue ones. Maybe they were a different species of crayfish? Maybe they were transported to Warsaw from somewhere far away—imported maybe from Ostland, extracted from the depths of the rivers and lakes and forced out by the Germans on the road to Moscow? I grew dizzy at the sight; I kept closing and opening my eyes—it seems to me that I almost blacked out. Crayfish, crayfish, crayfish. What caused such a fluster in my head, so close to a fainting fit, was the movement inside the crates. The crayfish—and this is what surprises me most today, thinking back—were not trying to get out of the crates and scamper about Śniadecki and Koszykowa, although they could have if they wanted to, as the crates were unlidded—no cellophane, cloth, or paper covered them. You might deduce that life in the crates was completely sufficient unto them and that they counted on no other. The movement in the crates went from top to bottom and bottom to top; there was also diagonal and circular motion. The crayfish circled about, pushing in between one another and then pushing out again, walking over other crayfish and underneath them too, sticking out their claws and whiskers between the chinks in the boards before pulling them back inside again, shouldering their way in among the other crayfish—always down or up, diagonally, or in a circle. All of this was clumsy, chaotic, blind. Are crayfish blind out of water? Can they see only when they are submerged in water or mud? Maybe. I don't know. They moved about as if they were blind, so there's no reason to try and figure it out any further. I could stand there for hours in front of the store, observing their movements, which now as then I am unable to comprehend. At last, someone would come along, take me by the hand, and lead me home. This story of mine might suggest to the reader that the motion of these crayfish in the crates in front of Meinl's store was something like that of ants scrambling around an anthill, going away somewhere and returning again, that the movements of crayfish and that of ants (and that of other creatures too) are just different facets, different sides, different realizations of one and the same spiritual phenomenon that we call life. And so, in consequence, my fascination with the crates on Śniadecki might be compared to the fascination felt by people unable to tear themselves away from the sight of a large anthill—for, as is well known, not only children surrender themselves to the observation of anthills; not only they like (or need) to do so, adults do too. But I am firmly opposed to such an interpretation. The motion of ants—this is easy to prove: just poke a stick in any anthill—is always purposeful. It plays out according to some plan unknown to us; it is the realization of some kind of order incarnated in that very motion—even though that order be a hidden one. In the case of the crates in front of Meinl's (or the Pakulski Brothers') store—there was no plan there, no order, no aim. There wasn't even any reason for it. Don't try to talk to me about significance here—it meant nothing. Up and down, diagonally, and in a circle. Whiskers, thoraxes, claws, eyes appearing and disappearing in the chinks between the slats. My head would be spinning; I was about to faint; I had fallen into some sort of hole and just couldn't leave. I had to stand there like that until someone came to take me by the hand and lead me home to the other side of Koszykowa.

MASSACRE À LA GREIM

THE GREIM IN QUESTION is almost completely unknown in Poland these days. But a few dozen years ago, he might have had a decisive influence on the history of the Poles. In Germany, on the other hand, he has a place in the history of aircraft and that of Nazism. Now this mysterious Greim—mysterious, one might say, exactly because of the influence he might have had—this mysterious Greim of ours was, in 1944, the commander of the 6th Air Fleet (Luftflotte 6), active on the eastern front, and thus also in the vicinity of Warsaw. His first name was Robert. Near the end of the First World War, at twenty-six years of age (he was born in 1892), he was made a knight. From that time on, he appeared under the appellation Robert Ritter von Greim. His birthdate probably had something to do with his splendid career—Greim was almost exactly the same age as Hermann Göring—he was just one year older—and thus, he became the comrade-in-arms of the latter during the First World War. Was Greim a pilot of the famous 1st Fighter Squadron (Jagdgeschwader 1), commanded by Göring in 1918 and before him by that most renowned ace of the German skies the Red Baron Manfred von Richthofen? I'm not sure but it seems quite probable to me. Advancing swiftly through the ranks, as one might assume, thanks to the Field Marshal and creator of the Luftwaffe, but also, perhaps, on account of his own talents, Greim at last took over his comrade's position—but at the last moment, and thus, only on paper. When at last, in April 1945, Hitler acknowledged Göring to be a traitor and removed him from all of his posts, Greim was summoned to Berlin and there, in the

Führer's bunker, advanced to Field Marshal. In his political testament, Hitler also set him at the head of the Luftwaffe. Thus, Greim's career ended just as it should have—with panache. Just before his own death, Hitler decided to have Himmler put to death (for he, like Göring, turned out to be a traitor). This task he entrusted to his loyal flyboy. Greim emerged from the bunker and flew off from Berlin (as one of the last German pilots to do so, but he did not carry out the Führer's order. Most likely, the reason is obvious, but I'm not sure. Maybe Greim didn't want to kill Himmler, maybe he couldn't do it, or maybe he just didn't get to him in time as Himmler was already dead. A month later, Hitler's loyal flyboy found himself somewhere in the south of Germany, where he entered American captivity. He was transported to Salzburg, where he learned that he was to be handed over to the Russians. This was bitter news, which meant interrogation in the Lubyanka. Greim had to know something about this, for, quite prudently, he chose the lesser evil and committed suicide. Supposedly, he made use of the poison that Hitler slid into his pocket as he was leaving the Berlin bunker. None of these things are really necessary for us to know. I only mention them here because—as so frequently happens in such cases—in my search for information concerning Greim, I slowly and unintentionally became interested in his life story. You'll grant that it is very interesting. But the only thing of any importance to us is that in the summer of 1944, Greim, a Colonel General at the time, was commander of the 6th Air Fleet in support of the "Middle" Army Group (Heeresgruppe Mitte), and—being an important figure in the German military hierarchy—he had access to Hitler. In the first days of August, maybe even 1 or 2 August, at the very least, right after the outbreak of the Uprising, Greim made his way to Headquarters in East Prussia, where he presented Hitler with his plan of dealing with the rebellious Poles. It might also have been—this is unclear to me (and must ever remain so, as the details of Hitler's conversations with Greim are unknown)—that the Führer summoned Greim to his presence and ordered him to work up a plan, which he then accepted, or that he presented Greim with a plan of his own invention and ordered him to work out the details. The one and only source of information concerning Greim's plan is the so-called *Relation of von dem Bach Concerning the Warsaw Uprising*, a collection of answers to questions posed to von dem Bach by employees of the then Warsaw Institute of National Remembrance in 1947. SS-Obergruppenführer and Police General Erich von dem Bach, a prisoner of the Americans, was put into Polish hands (for a short while) and transported to Warsaw, where he was to appear as a witness in the trial of Governor Fischer and other high-ranking officials of the Warsaw District. Although Greim's plan was not executed (I'll get to this in a moment), von dem Bach devoted a lot of attention to him in his *Relation*. He takes up a lot of space there. Perhaps because, in presenting Greim's plan, the SS-Obergruppenführer could set himself in an advantageous light: as someone who did not wish to take part in the total extermination of the Poles. Von dem Bach's account of Greim's plan begins with some very interesting news. It seems that the commander of the 6th Air Fleet was (for some reasons which now we'll never learn) personally interested in what was going on at the time in Warsaw. "The air units that took part in the battle stations against Warsaw," writes von dem Bach, were led personally by the commander of the air fleet, Col. General Ritter von Greim. "He was always personally present at the mandatory conferences at battle stations in Warsaw." This seems a little strange, if we take into consideration the fact that the German air forces employed in the fight against the insurrectionists were made up of four Stukas. Each of these, taking off from Okęcie, carried out several dozen—or more—sorties per day. But still and all, we're not speaking of a large contingent, the commander of which was some Second Lieutenant of the Luftwaffe. But it turns out that the four Stukas were personally led by Greim. Was it that he didn't trust that Second Lieutenant? But let's get back to the plan. According to von dem Bach, the commander of the Air Fleet was acting under the direction of Hitler in working up his plan. He was fulfilling his wishes; he was incited by him. Von dem Bach uses the word "Anregung" here—"stimulation, incitement." "At the very beginning of my command, I rejected Greim's proposal, which, according to him, was worked up in accord with the incitement (Anregung) of Adolf Hitler." This statement also lets us know when Greim's plan came about—when it was formulated or discussed. After the war, von dem Bach stated (in response to the questions of Polish prosecutors) that he took command over all German units active in Warsaw as late as 12 August—but historians of the Uprising have proven beyond the shadow of a doubt that this actually occurred a week earlier—on 5 August. The words "at the very beginning of my command" thus indicate 5, maybe 6 August. What was Greim's plan? According to von dem Bach's *Relation*, Greim proposed to solve the problem of the Uprising in a manner as effective as it was simple. Namely, to "withdraw all troops from Warsaw beyond the city limits, and then, with the aid of all aircraft available on the middle portion of the eastern front, including communications planes, to level Warsaw to the ground and in so doing to stifle the Uprising." As von dem Bach noted, the realization of such a radical project would have presented no great difficulties. "Indeed, the plan was very simple in execution, because in the absence of any anti-aircraft defenses on the part of the Poles, even such sluggish craft as Ju 52s and transport planes might have been employed. What is more, by using all the landing strips in the area, setting the ships in pendulum-motion shifts would maximize fuel economy." Why then did Erich von dem Bach decide (Hitler's "Anregung" or no Hitler's "Anregung" and thus by his own personal engagement in the matter) to reject Greim's project—a serious plan, such as would certainly have defeated the insurrectionists in a few days, no longer than a week? There are three reasons that, most likely, were decisive here (or at least might have been), which caused the air massacre proposed by the commander of the 6th Air Fleet to remain unrealized. One of these is presented by von dem Bach in his *Relation*. Whether the other two were taken into consideration back then, in August 1944, we have no way of knowing; they are mere reconstructions, hypotheses wherewith our historians later attempted to clarify the behavior of the Germans. The reason given by von dem Bach looks like this: "I stated that such an attack would certainly accomplish the destruction of the civilian population but taking the national character of the Poles into consideration, this would not break the will of the insurrectionists. Those who survived would fight on even more fanatically, burrowing deeper into the ruins." Von dem Bach's argument, although very flattering to us, does not seem all that convincing. For it is easy to imagine such a bombardment, the results of which would be the complete annihilation, not only of the entire civilian population but the whole insurrectionist army as well. In the end, it would only have been a question of the number of aircraft used, the number of bombs dropped. If, on the other hand, despite the total carpet bombing, some insurrectionist units survived the destruction and, to use von dem Bach's terminology, "burrowed deeper into the ruins," all that would be needed to deprive them of any military capability would be to surround the devastated city, all its ruins and corpses, with something like a cordon sanitaire. The 9th Army of General von Vormann, holding the line at the Wisła, had some Cossack units of Vlasov's at its disposal. These were of little use at the front and would have been admirably suited to the task. But now let us consider the two remaining reasons, which might have inclined Hitler to cede to von dem Bach in the matter, resigning himself from Greim's plan (and, in consequence, accepting the less radical plan of the latter). As I see it, both of these reasons appear (if one accepts the military point of view, that is, if one keeps one's eye on the chances of the military success of the operation) a little more weighty than the first. According to Gen. Jerzy Kirchmayer (who speaks of this in his book *Powstanie warszawskie* [*The Warsaw Uprising*]), Greim's plan was rejected on account of supply problems on the eastern front. "To reduce Warsaw to rubble," Kirchmayer writes, "would mean the temporary paralysis of the Warsaw communications hub, via which the German command transported men and materiel east and west. Operationally speaking, this was certainly a serious problem and most likely decided in the end against the plan put forward by Greim." From the point of view of the experts, German experts, the commanders of the 9th Army, who had to worry about supplying their forces and keeping roads of communication open, this might indeed have been the decisive reason for the rejection of the plan. The only question is: did the commanders of the 9th Army have any say in the matter at all? Were their opinions taken into consideration by Hitler? It's also worth considering here the fact that the total destruction of Warsaw, along with its population, didn't necessarily have to result in an equally total rupture of communication routes; the aircraft of the 6th Air Fleet would be flying very low (taking into consideration the absence of anti-aircraft defenses), and the bombardment could therefore be well planned out and its results clearly foreseen, and both routes with bridges needed by the Germans (the Aleje Jerozolimskie with the Poniatowski Bridge and Chłodna with the Saxon Gardens, Nowy Zjazd and the Kierbedź Bridge) didn't need to be destroyed at all. Or they might have been damaged but in such a limited way that they could be repaired and returned to use quickly enough. And so, after a short break in the bombardment, they might still have served the Germans and supplied their fighting forces with materiel and reserves. The last argument that von dem Bach might have used to convince Hitler that there was a certain risk attached to Greim's plan would be the presence in Warsaw of several large German formations, which, following the outbreak of the Uprising, had been surrounded by the insurrectionists and could not get out of the city. German Kirchmayer also makes reference to this in his *Warsaw Uprising*. "Many of these [German points of resistance] would not be able to evacuate, and, that being the case, one had to take into account the fact that the ruins of Warsaw would bury not only Poles, but also a not inconsiderable number of Germans." Was the number of Germans who would perish along with the Poles very large? It's easy to count them up. In the so-called Police District (Szucha—Litewska and the area surrounding those streets) that would be units of the Security Police (Sicherheitspolizei)—"supported," according to von dem Bach's *Relation*, "by a few emergency Wehrmacht units and small motorized SS groups" (Reiter SS). These units were commanded by SS-Obersturmbannführer Paul Geibel. "The strength of Geibel's group," writes von dem Bach, "was not quite 4,000 men." Because of Greim, a (small) portion of the combat units of General Reiner Stahel would be killed—Stahel had been commandant of

Warsaw, and he was surrounded in the first days of August in the Brühl Palace. According to von dem Bach, "these were point-of-resistance crews, made up entirely of emergency units from the garrison, and at the time there were not quite 5,000 of them." If we still add to these some small German units surrounded by the insurrectionists and defending themselves in different parts of the city (units such as that holed up at the time in the so-called little PAST on Pius St.)—there were probably only a few dozen SS men there—Hitler and Greim would have to be willing to sacrifice some 10,000 Germans in order to realize their plans of complete annihilation. No more than 10,000, but probably less than that, which seems (in comparison to the possible advantages to be derived) a small enough number. As is well known, Hitler had no scruples in such cases. If earlier on he had been willing to sacrifice von Paulus's entire army surrounded in the cauldron of Stalingrad (anything but a shameful capitulation), then he certainly would have sacrificed the few SS men, infantry and cavalry, holed up in Warsaw. As can be seen, all these arguments, which back then, in the first days of August (potentially), spoke against Greim's project, could have been rejected just as easily as accepted. Hitler might have taken them into consideration (along with other arguments), but he might also have summoned von dem Bach, subordinated him to Greim, and ordered the concentration of the entire 6th Air Fleet to the landing strips around Warsaw. Two or three days later there wouldn't have been a single living being in Warsaw—Greim's air raids would have taken care of the dogs and cats as well. Not even the rats from the Hala na Koszykach would have been saved. And now we see with complete clarity that it is entirely unknown why this splendid project of total massacre—a project nearly one of a kind—was set aside. Let us take the essence of Greim's project under closer consideration. We know the premises upon which it was based, but it's also worth considering its significance. The massacre which actually took place—the one that von dem Bach's soldiers carried out in Warsaw—had (one might say, and not only one *might*, actually one *must* say) a human character, a human face, a human dimension. It was a deeply rooted humanistic massacre. It was composed of a thousand events, many thousands of events, and each one of these had its own character (each a little different from the rest), each with its own extent in time, its course, its tension, its individuality—its special coloration. Each of these was so unique, as unique as human things can be. Each of these events was also, in its own way, interesting; each had something of its own that set it apart from other similar events, and in this sense, each was interesting, curious. The reports of those who survived bear clear witness to this, the ones who found themselves in the very midst of the massacre, half-dead, not put out of their misery, who somehow escaped with their lives. One can say of each of these reports that it is interesting (for that which occurs in the midst of a massacre is interesting—how people perish and how some people survive), and what is interesting is human, and what is human is interesting. The massacre that actually occurred also had a human character because those who carried it out were human. Their faces were seen (everyone had a different face), as were their smiles (everybody has a different smile), and their fury (every fury is unique). One saw the sweat on their brows; one saw how greedily they drank their water after their toil. One saw their uniform sleeves rolled up above their elbows, their hairy, sweaty forearms. Later, they sat down on the pavement, took off their heavy helmets and, leaning against a fragment of a bullet-riddled wall—they rested. Like humans exhausted after hard labor, for all of this was very human. It would have been completely different with Greim's massacre—everything would have had a different appearance. Its inhuman character, its spiritual void, are—on account of that emptiness and inhumanity—indescribable. One might work up two or three sentences in reference to it—no more. Bombs, bombs, bombs. Darkness. That's it. The matter of participation in the massacre, and also the eventual responsibility for participation in the massacre of Warsaw, Greim-style, would also look completely different. In the massacre that took place in Wola, Ochota, the Old Town, thousands of soldiers participated: Wehrmacht, SS, Sicherheitspolizei, Luftwaffe, RONA, ROA. These thousands of soldiers were led by dozens if not hundreds of commanders, who gave the order to shoot or shot people to death themselves. These hundreds or dozens of officers were under the command of a few generals and a dozen or so colonels, who took no part, personally, in the massacre; perhaps they looked on, perhaps not. And so all the way up to Hitler and Himmler. This was no little killing spree; it was a large massacre and required the participation of many people. And in this sense too, that so many people were engaged in it, that such effort, such an outlay of labor and use of power was necessary to accomplish it, it was a human massacre. And what would have been the case had the massacre been carried out Greim-style? If it came about (then, at the beginning of August, in Warsaw), there would have been only two murderers to point the finger at. Adolf Hitler and Ritter von Greim. Well, maybe three, if we toss in von dem Bach as well. Because it would be difficult to speak of any direct participation in the massacre on the part of the airmen, who would be unseen, who would have been high above, enclosed in their boxes; they would see some fire, some smoke; calmly pressing the button to drop their bombs, they would have calmly flown over the massacre, flying away from it, leaving its territory behind, knowing nothing about it. Well, maybe they would know something, but only very unclearly—no details, nothing concrete. The airmen—in Greim's project—would be so far from the massacre, hardly concrete, as if they were not there at all. Rather, if there were anyone concretely there, any concretized culprit executing the massacre, that would be the aircraft. Or, to speak more generally, technology. So, in this sense, the massacre would have been dehumanized—it would have been a dehumanized massacre. Well, maybe not entirely but to a great extent. Taking all this into consideration, one might reckon that the future belongs to Greim. When the Europeans call to mind their old history and begin to murder again (and I can see no clear reasons why they should leave that occupation behind them for good), there will be no setting of people up against a wall, taking safeties off grenades and tossing them through basement windows; there will be no dousing with gasoline and setting people aflame. There will be no (to go a bit further back in time) skinning alive, breaking bones, cutting off heads, and hanging people upside down. But that's just how it seems, what it looks like—at first glance—that the Greim method is the method of the future. Massacre Greim-style has doubtless a lot of advantages over the classical style of massacre—it is more effective, more productive, and significantly easier to organize. All you need are a few dozen airfields, a few hundred aircraft, so many bombs, and two or three experts deep in thought, bent over a map, one map, one city map. But massacres à la Greim are lacking in one thing. Its advantage, essentially, lies in the use of technology—it is the advantage that perfect technology has over imperfect handicraft. But here is the Achilles' heel—here, in the eventual technological perfections lies the imperfection of the Greim style, one might say—its inadequacy in relation to its needs. For the use of technology, the employment of perfect instruments, leads to the vanishing of the perpetrators of the massacre (they are hidden) and the organizers and along with them disappear their faces, their feelings, their emotions, their thoughts, everything that they might have in their heads; their fury disappears, their anger, their hatred, their satisfaction; and, in the end, there also vanishes that something dark, which can't be named (we don't know how to name it; I don't). To put it another way, massacre Greim-style deprives the murderers of the pleasure they might otherwise experience from their murdering.

TURKISH ROMANCE

WOULD YOU LIKE TO change your nationality, chucking your Polishness in favor of Turkishness? Would it suit you—Turkish customs, Turkish dignity, Turkish power? In my boyhood, when I was six or seven, I thought that such a possibility existed, and I devoted a lot of thought to it, trying to imagine it from different angles, this eventual Turkish life of mine, all of its mysterious eventualities. Someone might say that these thoughts were completely nonsensical because the eventuality of such a change, from Polishness to Turkishness, even if it existed (it certainly didn't) was rather behind than ahead of me. Just listen, and then judge for yourselves—keeping in mind the fact that the great majority of ideas in the heads of small children are, in their childish nature, completely nonsensical. In 1942 or 1943, some spring or summer day—it was surely a spring or summer day, as my Mama was dressed in a light dress of navy blue, frilly silk, with little yellow, red, and white flowers, and white cork-heeled slippers, which I remember perfectly (in such dramatic, tension-filled situations—who knows why?—one remembers certain irrelevant details very well, which later, when the memory begins to get entangled in them, turn out to be completely unnecessary to anything)—I was dressed in white shorts, white socks, black lacquered shoes with lacquered straps fastened on one button, and a sailor's cap with "sailor" written on it, embroidered on its border in gold thread; it also seems to me, although I can't perfectly recall, that on that border too, above the inscription, there was also an anchor embroidered in gold thread—so, on some spring or summer day then, in the very middle of the war, I was walking with my mother along Koszykowa St., on that segment stretching from Marszałkowska towards the Aleje Ujazdowskie. So, we were walking from Marszałkowska in the direction of the Aleje; most likely, we were about to enter Pius or the Ujazdowski Park, but why, I don't know—perhaps (as indicated by the lacquered shoes and cap with the gold anchor) she'd made a date in a café with her girlfriends and was taking me along with her, to show off my cap and lacquered shoes. Or maybe she wanted to buy or sell some dollars or effect some other transaction of that sort. I liked going on these walks with my mother, so it was no matter to me where we were going and why, as long as she led me by the hand and talked to me. Somewhere in the area of Mokotowska or perhaps Natolińska it turned out, unexpectedly (and as far as I recall, such things always came about unexpectedly), we found ourselves in the middle of a roundup. Mokotowska was cut off at both ends. One cordon of gendarmes was set up past Szopena, a small distance from the little square bisected by Pius IX (today's Piękna St.), a second one blocked Mokotowska where it enters the Plac Zbawiciela [Savior Square]. Most likely, it was also impossible to retreat in the direction of Marszałkowska, so we could do nothing but continue on forward in the direction of the Aleje. But it was there, in fact, probably not far from the convergence with Aleje Przyjaciół [the Boulevard of Friends], or St. Teresa St., where the vans were standing, into which the first passersby were already being loaded. Here you can see what a person remembers from such situations and what, though it seems significantly more important (and more interesting), flies right out of one's head—and so radically that there's no way of recreating it later. I remember my mother's dress, my lacquered shoes with their one button, and some men being loaded onto vans. I even remember their bright shirts against the backdrop of the tarp or canvas that covered the vans (I think there were metal steps leading up in back, kind of like short ladders) but I don't remember what the gendarmes looked like, the ones standing on Mokotowska and the convergence with Aleje Przyjaciół—of course, they looked like Germans, that is, horrid, but were they wearing those steel helmets of theirs or just garrison

KINDERSZENEN

caps; were they armed in carbines or automatic guns? I don't know. When she caught sight of the German cordons, my mother immediately fell into a panic, and so I did too—I probably even began crying—this was all unnecessary, of course, as a young thirty-something woman leading a little boy by the hand, she most likely could have calmly passed right through the roundup; I bet they wouldn't even have demanded to see her Kennkarte or Ausweis. At the time, however, some unclear rumors were swirling around Warsaw to the effect that during roundups the Germans even took little children into the vans, and even that they organized specialized roundups of little children, to take them to the hospital and pump out their blood, which they then sent to the eastern front for use in transfusions for German soldiers somewhere beneath Moscow or Leningrad. These rumors had it that the bloodless corpses of these children were not returned to their parents, but after they had been drained of their blood, they were carted off somewhere else to be used for other purposes. I don't believe (now) these rumors to be true, but I can't discount the possibility that on that summer or spring day, there at the intersection of Koszykowa and Mokotowska, it was this that made my mother panic. She was a person, it seems to me, quite rational and able to evaluate the situation in which we found ourselves, but the screams, the gunshots, and the vans at the Boulevard of Friends may have caused her to lose her head. She imagined the Germans snatching me and draining me of my blood, which they would later pump into their living soldiers, and because she wanted to save me, she decided to run. Even though no one was chasing us, no one was shooting at us, nobody even shouted: Halt! Halt! It was an insane, hysterical, and for me now unforgettable race. It has so happened that I have been made to run later, too, for different reasons, but never have I run away from someone so passionately; no other escape has left such deep traces on my psyche. All of my later escapes from Germans in my dreams, dreams that have plagued me all my life long (and which, though much less frequently, plague me still)—escapes through courtyards, entryways and narrow alleys, escapes across roofs and up ladders, from balcony to balcony, escapes ending in corridors leading nowhere, or in attics with no way out: there is no door, but listen: here come the boots of the German gendarmes thumping up the stairs!—all of these frantic escapes, probably, have their origin in that springtime (or summertime) escape through the entranceways, courtyards, and offices on Koszykowa, Natolinska, and August Sixth Sts. And here we have the gloomy archetype, the ur-topos of my life, which exists in some dimension unknown to me, some certain time, becoming incarnate in my dreams at the behest of some power unknown to me. We raced to some entranceway, my mother pulling me by the hand; I'm tripping over my feet, maybe over hers—quicker, quicker, quicker. She wasn't pulling me as much as yanking and dragging me behind her with such determination and such strength that, sometimes, unable to keep up, I rose above the earth, my little feet windmilling the air, a bird pulled by his wing, a bird in lacquered shoes and a sailor's cap with a golden anchor. Or maybe it just seems to have been like this, later, that this escape was something like a real avian flight through entranceways, alleys, and yards in the vicinity of Koszykowa and Mokotowska. Now, so that my story should become comprehensible (we're still speaking here of a change of nationality, from Polish to Turkish), I have to go back in time a couple, even a couple dozen years. Somewhere towards the end of the 1920s, maybe a little later, around the year 1930, my mother (already engaged to my father, but I, of course, was not yet in this world) had a little romance with a certain Turkish officer whom she met during an excursion to Turkey. That officer, a man of extraordinary, one might say Turkish, good looks was a young military doctor in Atatürk's army, and the excursion there, in which my mother took part, was a trip organized for students of medicine about to finish their studies at the University of Warsaw, or perhaps for young doctors who had just completed medical school. This officer was entrusted with looking after his Polish peers and in this way, I suppose, the acquaintance I'm referring to, who had a certain influence on my life, came about. How long this Turkish romance of my mother's lasted, I can't say. Two, maybe three years. It came to an end, of course, before (or right after) her marriage to my father. It seems that this officer came to Warsaw a few times in the interests of romance, and my mother too, for the same reason, traveled now and again to Istanbul or Ankara. Both of us, my sister and I, were quite in the know concerning this Turkish romance, because my mother, who set great store by memorializing the important events of life and felt that each such event ought to be well documented, pasted a dozen or so photos of the beautiful Turk into one of our family photo albums. It seems to me—I have no other way of explaining it—that the Turkish photos pasted into the family album were a challenge of sorts (a risky one, granted) or even a warning directed at my father: Look! my mother said through them—I married you, a young Warsaw lawyer, but I had other, even more interesting opportunities. If only I so wished, I could be living in Istanbul with this Turkish officer. My father probably had to take these warnings or (secreted along with the photos in the album) confessions into consideration. He also, most likely (I never broached the subject with him, and I regret it), had to be prepared for my mother vanishing from the house someday, at which he would have to go searching for her in Istanbul. So, during the war we never gave it much thought—neither I, six or seven at the time, nor my sister, nine or ten—why my mother posted Razi's photos in the album (Razi was his name). No, we were interested in something quite different—not so much Razi and his romance with our mother as some unclear possibilities that might arise for a pair of children living on Koszykowa St. in Warsaw. We didn't so much as give a flip for Razi—probably not even half a flip; it was true that we admired his beautiful officer's uniform and stunning cap, his high stiff collar with the stars and his car, alongside which Mama took his picture—but how fascinating were the possibilities that circled round the green and red cardboard pages of the album! Was such a thing even possible? Was our living on Koszykowa St. something inevitable and irrevocable? Something that happened because it had to happen? Was it possible for us to be living, not on Koszykowa St., but in Istanbul, in some home that had been prepared for us, from which, when you went out onto the balcony, you saw—just like from our balcony—a tram, but not that one that went down Marszałkowska, but a completely different, Turkish tram that passed near the Hagia Sophia? Could we be Turkish children? Half-Turkish? Going to Turkish school or taking Turkish home lessons? And would we be the same children as those living on Koszykowa? Or would we be identical with those other half-Turkish or fully Turkish children? And those half-Turkish children of Razi's—would they be identical with us, the children from Koszykowa? Would we be a little different, somehow different—or completely different? Being someone who is somewhere, who is to be found in that place belonging to him, can he be someone else, who is in a different place, somewhere else? Razi in his officer's uniform with the high, stiff collar, and Razi in his white lab coat (bending over a microscope), Razi riding on a little donkey in a place that, as it said on the map—was known as Prinkipo (and next to him, on her own donkey, our mother riding in a striped bathing suit), and Razi lying on a lounge chair in some Turkish garden, Razi, Atatürk's soldier and the husband of our mother; from all of his photographic incarnations, Razi asked us—who are we? Are we really the children we think we are? And are there children somewhere in the world who are the same as us?—identically the same? Or somewhat like us and somewhat different? We were asked the same thing by the Hagia Sophia mosque and the Turkish tram rumbling past. The album lay before us on the round, poplar table covered with a lace doily; my sister turned the pages, taking care to keep me from writing on the photographs with my crayons or adding a moustache to Razi's face or two extra stars to that stiff collar. I remember that the very thought that I could make of Razi a Turkish general or even a field marshal with my crayons was very tempting. My sister was older, so she was smarter, too, but even she didn't know the answers to these strange questions posed by the Turkish officer. I suppose that our parents could have explained it to us, why we were Polish children and not Razi's Turkish children, why we were living in Warsaw on Koszykowa and not in Istanbul with a view of the mosque and the tram going past it (and whether we really lived only here and not here and there—that is also an important question), and why you could see Marszałkowska from our balcony and the Germans strolling there and not something else, but probably we lacked the boldness to ask them about something like that (something so unclear and mysterious). That album, among other family albums with photos, rests in my sister's armoire today—the photos are a little yellowed and faded, but Razi's questions have not lost any of their urgency and, just as then, some sixty-odd years ago, even now I don't have a good (satisfactory) answer to them. Near the Plac Zbawiciela, where there were no Germans, perhaps no passersby at all, my mother acknowledged that we were more or less safe (the gendarme cordons and their vans were now far behind us)—because she stopped dragging me. We kept on running a bit in the direction of the Plac Zbawiciela, now slowing into a quick stride. Now, all of this, that panicked escape through courtyards, all that horrid chase with no one chasing us—all of this lasted a rather short time—certainly only a few, at tops a few dozen minutes, but it was a real torment. When we got to the Plac Zbawiciela, I said that I wasn't going any further and sat myself down on the stone steps leading to the church, right next to where the armless and legless beggars to whom you'd toss some alms on your way to Sunday Mass, which I attended along with Genia, would sit. My mother bent down over me, probably trying to coax me, to convince me to get up and go somewhere with her, but it was all in vain—I had no intention of reacting at all. "Leave me here," I told her. "I'm not going anywhere. I don't want to be Polish. I want to live in Istanbul. I want us both to live there." My mother lifted her veil and looked at me, somewhat stunned, and then she employed her time-proven method, which (as both of us knew perfectly well) was always effective: she grabbed my ear and gave it a twist and set me back on my feet. "Stop talking stupid," she said. "Come on. We're going home." Today, years later, I'm obviously not capable of repeating exactly what she said or what I said precisely; this record of our short conversation in front of the Church of the Savior is a reconstruction. But it must have looked more or less just like that. This was (as I see it now) the only time in my life when my identity was seriously challenged, the one and only case when I was fed up to the gills with my Polishness and was in a mood to part ways with it; I didn't want to have to escape from Germans; I wanted my father to be a beautiful Turkish officer and there, in Istanbul, to be protected by his mighty and stately Turkish army. It wasn't far to our house from where we were, but we took a long way back, via Mokotowska, Jaworzyńska, Polna, and Lwowska—maybe my mother was afraid of us falling into a roundup again should we go by way of Marszałkowska. She had to pull and jerk me again, because I went along dragging my feet rather than walking, on wobbly legs, and probably crying a bit. There on the half-landing of our building on Koszykowa, beneath the golden-brown negresses who, in their fascinating half-nakedness (their breasts were bare, but their abdomens draped), held in their raised hands matte lampshades shaped like flowers. Beneath these brass or plaster figures, these mysterious witnesses to my childhood, my mother knelt before me and, pulling a lace handkerchief from her purse, she wiped my nose and my eyes. "Come on. Stop crying," she said. "Your face is all blubbery. You're dripping snot. And don't say a word to Daddy about us being in the middle of a roundup, 'cause he'd get upset. Don't say anything to Alinka or Genia either. And not another word about that Turk. You're to forget all about him!"

THE CAUSES
OF THE EXPLOSION

TODAY WE SEE THE Warsaw Uprising as a great burst of national enthusiasm, a grand explosion of national and civic emotion. And it is quite proper that we do. It was indeed such, and this is the way in which it ought to be presented in school to our children and grandchildren, so that they should recognize in this splendid explosion the best national traits of the Polish character. But in seeing it and evaluating it in this way, we must also remember that the Uprising was something else too (although we sometimes forget this)—the Uprising was also, technically speaking, a well-organized military undertaking executed by splendid experts—and these experts, career officers educated in prewar military academies, fought on both sides of the conflict, the Polish side and the German side. It was these men, these Polish and German military experts, who decided where and how to attack, as well as where and how to resist, to set up a defense. So the planning and execution of the battles was concentrated in the hands of men animated by their military expertise, not their emotions, patriotic, national, or others still. SS-Obergruppenführer Erich von dem Bach, to whom Hitler and Himmler entrusted the quashing of the Uprising, was no common murderer; nor was he, it seems, a man possessed by some wild ideas of German racial purity or German dominance in the East. He was, rather, the most renowned German specialist in the field of operations aimed at the destruction of partisan units and thus, the most renowned such specialist in all of Europe. And so, even if the thought of our wonderful Uprising brings

THE CAUSES OF THE EXPLOSION

tears to one's eyes, one must also think of it as a splendid, sometimes even stunning, military operation prepared by experts of no insignificant talent. Among the Germans there were also experts of a somewhat different stripe, such as SS-Obersturmbannführer Oskar Dirlewanger and SS-Gruppenführer Heinz Reinefarth, experts, above all, in murder, or rather men expert in nothing but murder. And yet, even those better military experts, Wehrmacht officers trained at prewar military academies, murdered with great expertise, and it seems that murdering and distributing coups-de-grace (to the wounded, and prisoners, and women as well as children) provided them, quite simply, with pleasure—less of the sort one derives from observing an electric lawnmower working over a neglected yard or the suction hose of a sump truck emptying a cesspool. If we look upon it from such a perspective—if we acknowledge that what was happening in Warsaw at the time was decided upon by experts and that, on the German side, there were two types of experts: the first possessed of military expertise in planning and executing military operations and the second possessed of expertise in murdering, then we are immediately confronted with a certain important question concerning that which occurred on Kiliński St., right near the entranceway to Nr 1, on 13 August. The question is as follows. What did the Germans wish to achieve by sending that armored ammunition carrier down Podwale—with the intent of exploding it at a certain moment, however that was to come about? What was their intention, and what were the advantages that might accrue to them from such an explosion? What were their calculations? The Germans never gave any clear answer to that question—on what that idea of theirs was founded. You can't count on them expressing themselves on it now because it seems very improbable that any of the officers who planned the operation and carried it out might still be among the living. If any one of them is still alive, he is certainly well past ninety by now. If such a person were asked about an exploding tank, he'd want to know if the tank in question exploded at Verdun, El Alamein, or Stalingrad. Learning that we're interested in a tank exploding in Warschau, he'd say that there is no such city, because the Führer was forced to give the order to completely raze it to the ground on account of Germans being slaughtered there. As I see it, to ask Germans about the events of that war now misses the mark entirely because, when grilled on that topic, they don't understand what you're saying to them. As far as the Poles are concerned, they've already expressed themselves on the question of German intentions but, at least at the beginning, they did so completely unambiguously. They had no doubts whatsoever because there could be no doubt about it. The Polish reading of German intentions, if one can put it that way, was that the Germans intended to murder as many Poles as possible, the greatest number possible. The explosion of the tank-trap (as it has often been called, and still is—already in the very term the evaluation of German intentions is concealed) was, therefore, a horrid crime, all the more terrible for having been cleverly planned, concealed, and treacherous. As Lucian Fajer (Captain "Ognisty") writes, this was "more evidence of Hitlerite barbarity and bestiality." The postwar conviction that the Germans brazenly dared carry out such a thing that in contemporary warfare (already only relatively civilized) was without precedent went hand in hand with the conviction that, in the explosion of the tank-trap, in that crime exceptionally hideous and treacherous, the timeless (timelessly monstrous) traits of the German nation were revealed. This conviction was best expressed in the account of a young woman, written down right after the war—a young woman who at the time worked in the Old Town at the editorial offices of one of the insurrectionary newspapers. As she saw it, it wasn't so much a crime of the Germans as it was of their mediaeval ancestors the German Knights of the Cross. "And so many perished in such a way, that no trace of them remained! That's how Krysia perished. She was jealous of the nurses because they were permitted to go out to the barricades. It never crossed her mind that she would die so suddenly, the victim of Teutonic treachery." Such an eventuality—that it was a subterfuge worthy of the Teutonic Knights, that the idea of sending a tank-trap onto Podwale arose from the gloomy depths of the Teutonic psyche—cannot be discounted out of hand, because it is something obvious that the Germans' intention at the time was murder: mass murder,

THE CAUSES OF THE EXPLOSION

quick and effective. However, another somewhat different interpretation of the cause of the explosion is also possible, a somewhat different reading of the Germans' intentions. The crime remains a crime, it's just that those who thought it up might have had something different in mind, and the murdering (if one might so comprehend it in such an unpleasant manner) was merely coincidental. It was, to put it differently, unintentional or, in this case, lacking an express, clear purpose. No subterfuge of any mediaeval Knights of the Cross; if there was anything Teutonic to it, it was a Teutonic blunder. Most clearly a blunder of Teutonic technology. Such an answer to the question posed by the explosion—what caused it—(doubtless worthy of being considered) arose much later on, as late as the 1980s. The journalist and historian Ryszard Bielecki presents it in his book on the "Gustaw" and "Harnaś" battalions, to which we have already made reference. It is his opinion that the explosion was caused by accident. So, what occurred at the entranceway to the building at 1 Kiliński (or, as Bielecki sees it, not right at the entranceway, but some distance from it) was decided by so-called blind chance. The Greek Moira so wished it. Now, Bielecki doesn't refer to it in such a radical way; the Greek Moira is my insertion here. According to Bielecki's version, the German intention was to destroy the barricade shutting off Podwale from the Plac Zamkowy, which would permit their tanks and infantry to clear a path for an effective attack in the direction of Kapitulna and Piekarska, and further, in the direction of the Rynek and Długa St., with the consequent division of the Old Town in two—and it was for this very reason, with the penetration of the depths of Old Town in mind, that they sent off that armored carrier or little tank of theirs. "What they [the Germans] were after was for the explosive charge carried by the little abandoned tank to explode at the barricade, destroying it." But the vehicle didn't explode at the barricade at the place where Podwale gives out onto the Plac Zamkowy because, as Bielecki would have it, the mechanism that was to cause the explosion either failed or was not engaged at the proper time. And so, the technological blunder of the Teutonic Knights—a poorly wound spring or a poorly paced hook—something of that sort. Then, at the intersection of Podwale and Kiliński St., some accidental movement of a lever led to the crate containing the explosive material (affixed, according to Bielecki, on the exterior of the vehicle) to fall to the roadway; the contact with the ground set the faulty timing mechanism in motion or depressed the fuse which had been caught on something earlier and then—what happened, happened. One can set up a whole range of rational arguments in opposition to Bielecki's version—why should the explosive charge be (so nonsensically) affixed to the outside of the vehicle; why should the Germans want to destroy the barricade on Podwale by using one vehicle operated by a driver, a vehicle that had to be escorted by a few Tiger tanks, if all one needed for the task was two or three or four remotely controlled Goliaths (which the Germans had in abundance); why did none of the earlier complicated maneuvering of the vehicle (during its course along Podwale and Wąski Dunaj) cause the crate with the explosives to fall and explode (rather clumsy manipulations of the levers were going on all that time)—but it's not worth quarreling over it all now, for nothing certain can be discovered anyway, and no definitive answers arrived at. Nor does it seem possible today to conduct any research experiments that might result in anything certain. So the version proposed by the author of the book on the "Gustaw" and "Harnaś" battalions is no better and no worse than any other. But I must say that it appeals to me, as it sets the explosion in the context where I'd like to place it, that is, in the context of the accidents of fate. Of course, fatal events on a grand scale—events with nothing petty about them. The white light of the explosion signifies Fate suddenly becoming manifest. As General Tadeusz Bór Komorowski was to write: "at that same moment I was blinded by a flash and a pillar of fire." This does not mean that I want to exclude a subterfuge of the Knights of the Cross—those who see it as a diabolical Teutonic plot are correct, of course. All that needs to be added to this is that, if the exploding ammunition carrier was a Teutonic subterfuge, such a subterfuge still fits perfectly into the inexplicable order of coincidental events. The ammunition carrier is not sent there, but here; not on this day, but that; it's heading not in this direction, but that; it stops here,

THE CAUSES OF THE EXPLOSION

not there; the hand that engages the fuse and sets off the explosion presses the lever or completes the circuit not at that moment, but at this one. It's him walking past there, not you. That's you exiting the building and turning right, although you intended to turn left, before you changed your mind. It's you entering through that entranceway, although you wanted to exit it instead. I'm thinking of the entranceway to the building in which the three of us lived, Ewa, me, and little Wawrzek—Kiliński 1. I know that if I put it this way, the whole story (the whole life) takes on the appearance of an order of things made up of various nonsensical (or sensical, but possessed of a sense mysterious) coincidences. The question (the age-old, timeless question of humanity) asks us: if such be the case, is it proper to speak of any sort of order at all?

THE DEATH OF THE TURTLE

MY ASSUMPTION THAT THERE had been thousands of turtles and that they might settle in the General Government, becoming in this way native turtles and ur-Slavic turtles (though from the German point of view, they would thus become some sort of Unter-turtles, having lost their European Uber-turtle rootedness and racial purity)—well, my assumption touching upon the number of turtles was confirmed by Zygmunt Zaremba, the well-known activist of the leftist underground. "There were so many of them," Zaremba writes in his memoirs entitled *Wojna i konspiracja* [*War and Conspiracy*], "that they were even crawling about the gardens in the suburbs of Warsaw." I don't know what side of Warsaw Zaremba has in mind here—the Otwock line or that of Piaseczno, but I can confirm his observation—I'll get to those suburban gardens in just a moment. Zaremba's book also explains how it came about that the turtles found themselves in Warsaw and its environs. "It was due to Polish speculators, who used to buy from the Germans on a shot in the dark basis freight cars intended for the army, regardless of what they contained, be it weapons, food, or clothing—and in this case they chanced upon turtles." This explanation of Zaremba's doesn't quite agree with my knowledge on the topic. For it seems to me that I recall a conversation about where the turtles came from that took place in our dining room on Koszykowa. Somebody who brought the turtles and offered them to my parents (having purchased them before, I reckon, on Koszyki or Kercelak) explained that the cars with the turtles (it might even have been a whole train) were on their way to Berlin when they had been taken in an armed ambush in the general area of Warsaw East station. But this version of mine (turtles garnered in an armed battle or turtles liberated from German enslavement by AK soldiers) is certainly a little mythic; it might have even arisen later in the head of a patriotic eight-year-old—for an attack carried out by some Kedyw unit on a train full of turtles standing off at a railroad siding seems highly unprovable. Also, a battle waged on behalf of turtles with STEN guns and VISes and bottles of gasoline (and thus a battle waged so that these turtles should not be transformed into turtle soup in Berlin) is probably something that could never happen. Too bad, really—it would have been a beautiful scene, and what's more, such a one as could rather never be repeated in this history of our nation. Unless perhaps a train full of Greek turtles should once more appear at the Warsaw East station, guarded by German gendarmes with submachine guns, heading from Athens to Berlin (everything's possible, after all). Zaremba's version, with speculators buying German freight cars "as a shot in the dark" is confirmed by evidence collected by Tomasz Szarota in his book *Daily Life in Occupied Warsaw*. There, the author writes that "the flooding of all the markets in Warsaw with turtles" took place in May 1943, when "persons occupied with blind purchases from German railway guards of portions of transports, made such a purchase of several cars. Upon opening them, they were discovered to contain thousands of turtles destined to be made into tinned meat for the army. The transport of the turtles was heading from Bulgaria or Greece in the direction of the Reich. . . . The turtles began appearing all over the city. They were being offered for sale at all of the markets for a certain time; they were also sold in the streets." The price of the turtles remains a mystery (there is no mention of this in Szarota's book). I've searched for this information through many a memoir but have come up empty. One can assume that the price was fairly high. Because to the value of such an attractive item must be added the price of the risk taken by the seller. For trading in turtles (just like all such petty crimes), one might be sentenced to death, and one might well assume that at least some of the street peddlers of the turtles were shot, their mouths gagged in plaster. We learn from

Tomasz Szarota's book that, in July 1943, the price of a kilogram of pork was 130 złoty. A kilo of butter cost 196 zł, a litre of vodka 170. Were the turtles sold by weight? I rather think by volume, and the price had to depend on their aesthetic value, perhaps also on the size and vitality of each individual turtle. Whatever the case may have been, I don't think that a turtle would have cost less than a kilo of meat. The turtles that made their appearance in our apartment on Koszykowa (I remind you: one of them was black, the other grayish-green) were shared out justly, that is, according to their size and the age of the children. The larger, grayish-green turtle fell to my sister, while I got the smaller, black turtle (with the yellow stripes). I wasn't very satisfied at this, because I wanted the larger turtle, the grayish-green one. But it soon turned out that (lucky me) I came out ahead on the deal. A month or two later, along with the turtles, we made our way to Piaseczno, where our parents rented one whole floor of a large villa for us for the entire summer, the owners of which were some White Russians. Behind the villa there was a large garden, which (as was the custom during the war) had been turned into a practical vegetable garden. There were beds of cabbage, carrots, lettuce, and still other greens. My sister's turtle, who was very spry and very quick (despite all common assumptions about the sluggishness of turtles) was deft in taking advantage of this vegetable garden and one day took himself off to the cabbage patch, never to return to us again. Long days of searching ended unsuccessfully, and the grayish-green turtle remained in Piaseczno (it's even possible that—if it was one of those turtles that can live a couple hundred years, even now he's living there somewhere, walking about the cabbage patches of Piaseczno in the summertime, sleeping in the compost during the winter). We returned to Warsaw in September—I with the black turtle, my sister turtle-less. There were no other pet animals at home at the time, no cats or dogs or anything of that sort (such as hamsters). So the black turtle was the only living creature (of course, I have in mind creatures of another species here), the only object upon which one might concentrate one's attention, toward which one might direct one's desire for coexistence (or cosmic co-presence). Was my little black turtle

THE DEATH OF THE TURTLE

aware of the feelings I had for him? I very much doubt it. It seems to me rather (and it probably seemed so to me at the time as well) that the black turtle formed a figure of strangeness, alienation, for me—a sort of symbol speaking to me of the impossibility of contact between different incarnations of life, that although their essence may be identical, that essence is not something that can unite them, permit some form of contact. This was no pleasant experience for me—even today I recall it with sadness and disappointment. Sometime toward the end of the fall or the beginning of the winter (a great year for the Poles, 1944, was in the offing, although I knew nothing of that), the black turtle went under the armoire and there fell asleep. I probably tried to get in there, or rather to crawl in under there, after him, but that was impossible; I was already too big to fit under the armoire. All I could do was to gape in underneath, trying to make out in the darkness what was going on with the turtle—was it sleeping with its head pulled in, hidden in its shell, or was it moving about, stretching forth its head, gazing back with its tiny black eyes into the eyes of that other creature—the one looking under the armoire? I figure that this looking of mine, this staring into the darkness beneath the armoire didn't last too long, because I'm sure they explained to me that it would be best not to disturb the turtle, to let him sleep through the winter in peace. A turtle asleep beneath the armoire was a good excuse to admonish me not to make a racket running all over the flat. "Stop screaming. You'll wake the turtle." When the spring of that year, so memorable to the Poles, rolled around, despite the fact that it ought to have woken up, the turtle didn't wake up, didn't crawl back out from underneath the chest of drawers. So someone decided to pull him out. And pull him out he did, probably (though I don't quite remember) with a broom or a rug beater such as was used to beat the dust out of carpets outside. But that which had been extracted from beneath the armoire was already no longer a turtle. It was just a shell, which had undergone no change—it was still beautiful, hard, and shiny, its black shell still decorated with yellow stripes. There were some remains still in the shell, remains such as would be difficult to classify and describe—it was something that dried up in the wintertime or broke down and decomposed. Such rotten or dried remains are very unpleasant, especially for children who are unused to dealing with such things, so (as I imagine it today) I preferred not to look at them, I didn't want to see them at all, and it is for this very reason that I remember them so unclearly. They were sort of gray and sort of green, sort of dry and sort of wet. I imagined that they must have been the sinews of the turtle, its guts, and its meat. I'd like to stress here that the little turtle was neither killed nor starved by me—on the contrary, some sort of greens were always waiting for him, all winter long, in the general vicinity of the chest of drawers, most likely (though I don't remember) somewhere near it there was a little bowl or saucer with water. The turtle was interested neither in lettuce nor water. It had no intention of doing any more eating or drinking. Did it wake up every few days or weeks, poke its head out of its shell, have a gander about the darkness that surrounded it, and then hide its head again and go back to sleep? Perhaps. But it might have been different, too—one gray winter day it fell asleep under the armoire, never to awaken again. At the time, I accepted the latter version of events because it seemed the best (that is, the most advantageous) to the turtle—in this way, it turned out that when the turtle fell into its hibernation beneath the armoire, it didn't suffer, it died in its sleep, unaware that it was dying. The fact that it could have suffered in its sleep too (that its dying dreams might have been filled with horrific visions and sufferings unknown to us) was something that I never took into consideration, as the possibility never even occurred to me. Only now, some sixty-odd years later (sixty-four to be precise, because just so much time has passed, is passing right now, since the death of my turtle), do I admit such a possibility. Sixty-four years since the death of a strange creature which, or rather who, came into the world unnecessarily. But maybe that conception of things is a bit too radical, too risky, and it would be better to say: who came into the world for reasons unknown to me, an element of an order unknown to me, and who vanished for a reason just as unknown. Whatever it was that sifted (or rather seeped) out of the black shell, those remains, those turtle-innards, were something undefined—and that was the trait of this, whatever it was, these remains, that was most important to me at the time: a corporality, but of such an indeterminate nature, having no certain affiliation and no exact purpose: it was impossible to know if this was legs, head, or something from the midriff. It might also have been something partially devoured by mice or rats—if there were rats in our house on Koszykowa; there might have been, for the Hala na Koszykach was close by, and there were hundreds, even thousands, of rats there, for sure. That stuff sifting or seeping out of the black shell must have stank a good bit, but this is just an assumption of mine in 2008, as that smell or rather stench from 1944 is not to be found in my memory. Nor can I recall where the great armoire stood, from beneath which the black shell and remains of the turtle were extracted in the spring, in the bedroom, from which a door led to the bathroom (in which a copper bathtub stood and where a large oval stove, copper as well, probably, heated from below by wood or briquettes, was placed), or in the central room, the dining room, where the windows were large, and there was also a balcony giving out onto Koszykowa St. If you stood in the door leading out onto the balcony, or on the balcony itself, to the right you had the end of Lwowska St. and beyond it the Hala na Koszykach, and to the left the trams going down Marszałkowska St. Those trams, clearly visible from the third floor, went in the direction of the church on the Plac Zbawiciela, but you couldn't see the church—it was blocked from view (from the view of the person standing at the balcony door) by the buildings on the other side of Koszykowa. At that time, I thought (and continue to think so even now) that it would have been much better for the little black turtle (his death would have been much more pleasant) if, instead of ensconcing himself for the winter beneath the chest of drawers in the dining room or bedroom, he had gone out onto the balcony and there, on the third floor, high above Koszykowa St., in the fresh air, mislaid himself and fallen asleep amidst the clay pots and flower boxes that stood out on the balcony. Other things were kept out there on the balcony as well—unneeded domestic implements, broken chairs, and old kitchen cupboards. The bells of the trams would have tinkled for him as they trundled past in the direction of the Plac Zbawiciela, the origin of which sounds, of course, would have been unknown to him but pleasant perhaps nonetheless—they would have made his final moments pleasant, his last dreams. A slow, quiet death by freezing in the winter of 1943–44 (the turtle would have frozen to death slowly, slowly), a death made pleasant by the mysterious, distant bells. Such a ringing from the trams on Marszałkowska, for the turtle, who had no idea where something like that was coming from (what's ringing, from where and why), such a tinkling, now louder, now softer, from a distance, a distance—would have been like a tolling from eternity, a cosmic peal—if a turtle is capable of forming in his turtle-brain a concept of the cosmos. These days the trams don't ring bells; back then, they did. In this way they warned the passersby entering Marszałkowska from Śniadecki St. or from Pius or Koszykowa to be careful because when they find themselves on the roadway, they might fall beneath the wheels. I can even say that I've lived out my long life in two civilizations—one civilization where trams have warning bells and one civilization where they don't.

GLOSSARY

AK—*Armia Krajowa*, Home Army. The most widespread and disciplined underground army in occupied Europe during the Second World War. The AK was directed by the Polish Government in Exile in London, the direct continuation of the independent government of the Second Polish Republic, which left the territory of the Republic at the dual invasion and occupation thereof by Germany and the Soviet Union, acting in concert in September 1939. The Warsaw Uprising of 1944 was the largest action undertaken by the AK. Following the war and the continued occupation of Poland by the Soviet Union and its Polish allies, a concerted campaign of disinformation and slander was directed at the AK by the Communists, and many AK soldiers faced severe repression at the hands of Communists, both Soviet and Polish.

ANHELLI—A pseudo-biblical prose poem concerning the Polish struggle for independence published in 1838 by the Romantic Poet Juliusz Słowacki (1809–49), the author of *Ojciec zadżumionych* [*The Father of the Plague-Stricken*], an Arabian-themed narrative poem in three parts also published in 1838 and also mentioned by Rymkiewicz. In the case of *Anhelli*, the earlier text to which it refers is Adam Mickiewicz's *Księgi narodu polskiego i pielgrzymstwa polskiego* [*The Books of the Polish Nation and Polish Pilgrimage*, 1832] and in the latter Job and perhaps the Koran.

AUGUSTOWSKA WILDS—See Puszcza Augustowska.

AZER SAPPERS—Although Azerbaijan forces mostly fought on the side of the USSR, there were Azerbaijani regiments in the Wehrmacht as well, made up mostly of prisoners of war. During the German occupation of Poland, at least one Azerbaijani military unit was stationed in Warsaw: the Aserbeidschanisches Feld Bataillon I./111, to which, perhaps, the Azer sappers referred to by Rymkiewicz were assigned.

BATORY AT PSKÓW—A reference to three victorious campaigns waged against Russia by Polish King Stefan Batory (1533, ruled 1576–86) during the years 1579–81. Batory laid siege to Psków (now Pskov, in Russia); the Polish victory was commemorated in an 1872 canvas by Jan Matejko, familiar to most Poles, which depicts the Russian Tsar Ivan the Terrible kneeling in tribute before Batory.

BATTLE OF WARSAW—From 13 to 25 August 1920, the Polish Army successfully defended Warsaw from the invading Soviet troops during the Polish-Soviet War. The victory, which has been ascribed to the miraculous intervention of the Virgin Mary, turned the tide of the war and prevented the spread of Communism into Central and Western Europe, which was the stated purpose of the Soviet invasion.

BELWEDER—A neoclassical palace in Warsaw. During the period of the Russian partition of Poland, it was the residence of Crown Prince Constantine, the viceroy of Poland under the Tsars. It was stormed on the night of 29 November 1830 by Polish cadets at the beginning of the November Uprising against Russian occupation.

BÓR-KOMOROWSKI (Tadeusz Marian Komorowski 1895–1966) —"Bór" (Pineforest) is a conspiratorial pseudonym. Career officer of the Polish Army, General, Commanding Officer of the Armia Krajowa (Home Army). Following the war, he emigrated to London.

GLOSSARY

BORMANN, Martin (1900–45)—Nazi, head of the Reich chancellery, Adolf Hitler's personal secretary. He committed suicide trying to escape capture by the Allies after Hitler's own suicide.

BRÜHL PALACE—A seventeenth-century palace in Warsaw, once occupying a portion of today's Piłsudski Square. Destroyed by the Germans along with the Pałac Saski [Saxon Palace], plans are being made in 2021 for rebuilding it, along with other structures in the area destroyed during the Uprising.

BRZEŚĆ—Brześć nad Bugiem, in English often Brest-Litovsk. A town in the former Eastern Marches of Poland since the redrawing of the borders by Stalin, Churchill, and Roosevelt located in Belarus.

CECORA—Located in modern Romania, the scene of two battles (1595 and 1620) in the long wars of the Polish Kingdom and the Turks. Most likely, Rymkiewicz has the 1620 battle in mind, which resulted in the loss of many soldiers and the captivity of various commanding officers by the Turks.

CHRUŚCIEL, Antoni (1895–1960). Career Polish officer, Brigadier General, one of the commanding officers in the Warsaw Uprising. After the war, he emigrated to Washington, DC.

CITADEL—The Cytadela Warszawska, which has played a significant role in the history of Warsaw from the November Uprising against the Russian Empire in the 1830s through the Warsaw Uprising of 1944 against the Nazi occupiers.

CONFEDERATION OF BAR (Konfederacja Barska) 1768–72. An uprising of the Polish nobility, in general, aimed at eliminating Russian influence over the weakening Polish republic. The name comes from a locale in the old Eastern Marches of Poland. The defeat of the Bar Confederates by the Russian army led to the First Partition of Poland and the death of many Poles exiled to Siberia by the Russians. One of the participants in the uprising was Kazimierz Pułaski, who later died in the

American rebellion against Great Britain during the American Revolutionary War.

DIRLEWANGER, Oskar Anton Paul (1895–1945). Sadistic German SS officer, infamous for his cruelty (such as burning people alive). Arrested in the French sector of occupation, he was beaten to death: some say by guards, others by fellow prisoners.

DUNAJ—"Danube" in Polish; a street in Old Town Warsaw named for a stream that used to flow there. Today, the street is apportioned into two "Dunajs," Wąski Dunaj (Narrow Dunaj) and Szeroki Dunaj (Broad Dunaj).

DYGASIŃSKI, Adolf (1839–1902)—Polish naturalist writer, journalist, and publisher. The animal fables mentioned here were composed shortly before his death.

FILTRY—A section of Warsaw in the Ochota region so named for the water filtration plants located there.

FIRST CADRE—An episode of the First World War associated with Józef Piłsudski. The First Cadre, made up of patriotic rifle associations active in the Austrian Partition of southern Poland, became the embryo of the independent Polish Army following the regaining of independence. On 6 August 1914, within the context of Austro-Hungarian mobilizations, they set out from the Oleandry region of Kraków as the first Polish unit to carry the war into Russian territory.

FISCHER, Ludwig (1905–47). Nazi, Governor of the Warsaw District of the General Government. He survived two AK assassination attempts and was wounded escaping from the Brühl Palace during the Warsaw Uprising. Known for his cruelty (among others, he was the creator of the Warsaw Ghetto and participated in its liquidation), he was sentenced to death and hung in 1947.

FRANK, Hans (1900–46). Nazi, a lawyer by education, Governor of the General Government (see below). Executed for war crimes at Nuremberg.

GLOSSARY

GAJCY, Tadeusz (1921–44). Polish poet, died in the Warsaw Uprising. Like Zdzisław Stroiński and Krzysztof Kamil Baczyński (1921–44), a modern poetic talent whose untimely death has given rise to the legend of a "lost generation" of poets.

GENERAL GOVERNMENT—Or *Generalgouvernement*. A buffer area governed from Kraków by the German occupiers during World War II. It contained all the lands of Poland to the west of the partition line with the Soviet area of occupation which had not been directly incorporated into the German Reich like the rest of western Poland.

GOLDEN SWINE—*Złote świnki*. Russian gold coins minted from 1897 until 1911 by Nicholas II. Their face value was 5 rubles, which in Poland at the time was the price of a pig, hence the name. A quick look at the collector's market today prices them between two hundred and four hundred dollars apiece.

GRUNWALD (also known in Germany as the Battle of Tannenberg)—An important battle waged on 15 July 1410 in which Polish troops, under the command of King Władysław Jagiełło, with aid from Lithuanian, Czech, and other Slavic nations, defeated the German Knights of the Cross (Teutonic Knights) who had occupied the Prussian seacoast.

HALA NA KOSZYKACH—Literally "Hall on the Baskets," a popular covered market in Warsaw.

HEYDRICH, Reinhardt (1904–42). Nazi Reichsprotektor of the occupied Protectorate of Bohemia and Moravia (hence a "pal from the neighborhood"). A successful assassination attempt was made in Prague on 27 May 1942; gravely wounded, Heydrich died on 4 June of that year.

HIMMLER, Heinrich (1900–45). Nazi, head of the SS; overseer of the death camps and one of the main planners of the extermination of the Jews. He committed suicide in British custody after the war.

IBL—Instytut Badań Literackich (Institute of Literary Research). A research institute of the Polska Akademia Nauk (PAN, Polish Academy of Sciences), located in Warsaw. This is a nonteaching institute of academics chiefly devoted to the study of Polish literature. Founded by the communist PRL in 1948, it continues its activity in free Poland.

JANKOWSKI, Jan Stanisław (1882–1953). Delegate of the Polish Government in Exile in Poland during the occupation. He authorized the Warsaw Uprising on behalf of the Government. Arrested by the Soviets after the war, he died in Soviet captivity.

JANUARY UPRISING—*Powstanie styczniowe*. A ten-month-long armed uprising, basically aimed at the Russian partitioning power, which broke out in January of 1863. This was the last widespread armed uprising of the Polish nation in the turbulent nineteenth century. After this, a period of "organic work" commenced, during which Polish organizations concentrated on cementing the cultural, linguistic, and economic bases of Polish nationhood, so that reunification of the three partitions of the country (Austria, Prussia, Russia) might be seamlessly effected once independence should be regained. Depending on the partition, these efforts were either open (Austria) or conspiratorial (Russia).

KAMIŃSKI, Mieczysław (actually Bronislav Vladislavovich Stroganof Kaminski, 1899–1944). Russian war criminal of Polish extraction (his actual name Bronisław and that of his father Władysław, as well as his last name Kamiński, testify to this), head of the Russian National Liberation Army fighting alongside the Nazis. His brigade is known more for cruelties perpetrated on civilians in Belarus and Poland than for any military acumen. He died in a car accident, which has variously been described as a successful Polish Home Army operation and an action carried out by the Germans themselves, who wished to rid themselves of him.

KAMPINOSKA WILDS—see Puszcza Kampinoska.

GLOSSARY

KING-SPIRIT—*Król-Duch* (1847). Mystical narrative poem by Juliusz Słowacki, in which the history of Poland is described as the reincarnation of the spirit of the nation through the ages. At the core of Poland's meta-historical significance is (redemptive) suffering.

KILIŃSKI, Jan (1760–1819). Polish patriot and insurrectionist during the 1794 Kościuszko Uprising against the partitioning powers of Austria, Russia, and Prussia. He commanded troops during the uprising in Warsaw and is commemorated by a statue and the street name.

KOMOROWSKI, Tadeusz (1895–1966). Code-named "Bór" [Pineforest]. General, career officer in the armies of Austria-Hungary and later Poland. During the Second World War he remained in Poland and took command of the Armia Krajowa [Home Army] subject to the Polish Government in Exile in London.

KRAKOWSKIE PRZEDMIEŚCIE—Literally, Cracovian Suburb—a main representative thoroughfare in Old Town Warsaw, along which many important buildings are located, for example, the Presidential Palace.

KRASIŃSKI, Zygmunt (1812–59)—Polish writer of the Romantic period, most famous for his monumental drama *Nie-Boska Komedia* [*The Undivine Comedy*, 1835], which takes a critical look at the dreaminess of Romanticism and the evil, practical consequences too much otherworldliness can have in real life. This and all his dramatic works are available in English translation; see: Zygmunt Krasiński, *Dramatic Works* (London: Glagoslav, 2018).

KWAPIŃSKI, Jan (Piotr Edmund Chałupka, 1885–1964), member of the Polish Socialist Party, Minister and Vice Premier in the Polish Government in Exile in London during the Second World War.

LEGNICA—Town in Silesia, site of the Battle of Legnica (1241) during which Christian forces (Poles, Moravians, Germans) were routed by the Mongol horde.

MACIEJOWICE—Site of a decisive battle (10 October 1794) of the Kościuszko Uprising, the result of which was the capture of Kościuszko by the Russians and the eventual defeat of the independence uprising as a whole.

MARIENSZTAT—A residential area of Warsaw on the left bank of the Wisła. It derives its name, "City of Maria," from Maria Potocka, who, along with her husband Eustachy, once owned the land. The main thoroughfare of the quarter has the same name.

MARKET SQUARE—The Rynek Starego Miasta in Warsaw. Completely devastated by the Germans during the Warsaw Uprising, it has been completely rebuilt.

MARSHAL—See Piłsudski, Józef.

MICKIEWICZ, Adam (1798–1855). Romantic poet; Poland's national bard. He introduced Romanticism to Poland in 1822 with his *Ballady i Romanse* [*Ballads and Romances*], which had the same significance for Polish literature as Wordsworth and Coleridge's *Lyrical Ballads* for the English. Chief among his works is the idyllic national epic *Pan Tadeusz* (1834) and the Dantean-Goethean play in four parts *Dziady* [*Forefathers' Eve* (begun 1822)], his masterpiece, which initiated the genre of Polish Monumental Drama. For an English translation of the entirety of this work, see Adam Mickiewicz, *Forefathers' Eve* (London: Glagoslav, 2016). *Pan Tadeusz* has been translated into English several times. See, for example: Adam Mickiewicz, *Pan Tadeusz* (New York: Hippocrene, 1992).

MIKOŁAJCZYK, Stanisław (1901–66). Polish politician of the People's Party, Prime Minister of the Polish Government in Exile during the Second World War. At Churchill's insistence, he participated in the Communist-controlled Provisional Government of National Unity created by the Soviets on Polish territory in 1945, which shortly proved to be entirely under Communist control. Threatened by arrest and repression, he fled the country, emigrating to the United States.

MŁYNARKI—Banknotes used in occupied Poland. Their name derives from that of bank director Feliks Młynarski (1884–1972), economist and director of the Bank of Poland as well as the Emissioning Bank of the General Government (with the permission of the Polish Government in Exile).

MO—*Milicja obywatelska* (Citizens' Militia). This is what the police were called in the PRL from 1944–90. The use of "militia" rather than "police" was common practice in communist states in Europe.

MORZELANY—In Adolf Dygasiński's book *The Hare*, this common living space of the great "community of life" is a compound noun that combines in it both sea (*morze*) and grain fields (*lany*).

NAŁĘCZ—A Polish heraldic coat of arms.

NOVEMBER UPRISING—*Powstanie Listopadowe*. A year-long uprising, aimed primarily at the Russian partitioners, which broke out in November 1830. After its defeat, many noteworthy Poles emigrated or remained abroad—a group known as the "Great Emigration" (*Wielka Emigracja*).

OCHOTA—A residential district in Warsaw. Its name ("Desire," "Hankering") derives from a tavern that was located in the area in the early nineteenth century.

OLD TOWN—*Stare Miasto*. The old, central portion of Warsaw, where the Royal Castle and Cathedral of St. John, among other things, are located. Completely destroyed by the Germans during and following the Warsaw Uprising, it was completely rebuilt, often using eighteenth-century cityscapes by Canaletto to resurrect the original appearance of the historical buildings.

KINDERSZENEN

OLSZYNKA GROCHOWSKA—A region of Warsaw in Praga. It was the site of the largest battle of the November Uprising on 25 February 1831, as well as during the Nazi invasion of 1939.

PALACE SQUARE—*Plac Zamkowy* (hence, sometimes translated as "Castle Square")—the central square of Warsaw's Old Town, where the Renaissance palace of the Polish kings was built after the capital was moved from Kraków to Warsaw. Razed by the Germans following the Warsaw Uprising 1944, it has been rebuilt with historical accuracy.

PANCER VIADUCT—*Wiadukt Pancera*. A viaduct in central Warsaw, built in 1844–46 by Feliks Pancer (1798–1851), a Polish civil engineer, hence the name. It was destroyed one hundred years later by the Germans during the Warsaw Uprising.

PAST—"Little PAST" [*mała PAST-a*]. A building belonging to the Warsaw telephone company. The acronym stands for Polska Akcyjna Spółka Telefoniczna [Polish Joint-Stock Telephone Corporation]. This particular building was found on 19 Pius XI St. (which during the Nazi occupation was renamed "Strasse der SA" by the Germans).

PEŁCZYŃSKI, Tadeusz Walenty (1892–1985), Brigadier General, Deputy Commander of the Armia Krajowa (Home Army). After the war, he emigrated to London.

PIAT—An anti-tank weapon of British production (Projector, Infantry, Anti-Tank).

PIŁSUDSKI, Marshal Józef Klemens (1867–1935). Polish soldier, man of state, creator of the Polish Legions during the First World War, architect of the resurrected Second Republic of Poland following the war. Though positively looked upon by the majority of Poles, he is a polarizing figure. His merits in the regaining of independence after a century of Partitions between Russia, Prussia, and Austria are obvious and unquestioned. However, he can also be seen as one of the "strong men" who appeared in the political constellation of Europe during the first half of the twentieth century, staging a successful coup d'état in May 1926, following which he was de facto head of state until his death. He is buried among the Kings of Poland in the royal necropolis in the crypts of Wawel Cathedral in Kraków. Although arising himself from Polish Socialist traditions, he was *persona non grata* to the Communist régime imposed on the country by the USSR following the Second World War.

PLAC ZBAWICIELA—Savior Square, the Square of the Savior. A circular square in the Śródmieście [City Centre] quarter of Warsaw. Its name derives from the Church of the Most Sacred Savior [Kościół Najświętszego Zbawiciela] that fronts a portion of it.

PLATER, Emilia (1806–31). Legendary female soldier in the November 1830 Insurrection against the Russians. A national hero, she is often depicted in Romantic art.

PRAGA MASSACRE—An episode during the closing days of the Kościuszko Uprising. Following the Russian pressure against the defenses of Warsaw, a massacre of civilian residents of the suburb of Praga was carried out, during which from five to twenty thousand civilians were slaughtered. The capitulation of Warsaw occurred soon after.

PRL—Polska Rzeczpospolita Ludowa (the Polish People's Republic). The official name of Communist-led Poland from 1952–89.

PUSZCZA AUGUSTOWSKA—The Augustowska Wilds. A national park far away from the capital city of Warsaw in the northeastern corner of Poland, where it spills over into Lithuania and Belarus. It is some 160,000 hectares (1600 square kilometers / 618 square miles) in size, of which 114,000 hectares (1,140 square kilometers; 440+ square miles) lie within Poland.

PUSZCZA KAMPINOSKA—The Kampinoska Wilds. A national park northwest of Warsaw comprising some 670 square kilometers (260 square miles) of wilderness, both forest and wetlands. The national park was established in 1959.

RAJZA—From the German *Reise*, an ironic reference to the anguished clogging of the roads by Polish civilians seeking safety during the first weeks of the German invasion of their country in September 1939 (complicated all the more on 17 September, when Hitler's ally Stalin invaded Poland from the East, in accord with the secret clause of the Ribbentrop-Molotov Pact).

REINEFARTH, Heinz Friedrich (1903–79). Nazi war criminal, responsible for the mass execution of at least 50,000 people in the Wola section of Warsaw. Protected from prosecution by the Western Allies, who wished to use him as a witness against other defendants at the Nuremberg War Trials, he never answered for his crimes, becoming after the war a successful politician in West Germany.

ROSTWOROWSKI, Fr. Tomasz (1904–1974). Jesuit priest, chaplain of the "Wigry" and "Gustaw" battalions during the Warsaw Uprising. He witnessed the mass murder of the wounded in the hospital on Długa St., carried out by the Germans after the fall of the Uprising. Imprisoned by the Polish Communists as well, he later became head of the Polish section of Vatican Radio.

SAVIOR SQUARE—*Plac Zbawiciela*. A public square in Warsaw named after the church that stands there.

SENTENCES AND COMMENTS—*Zdania i uwagi* (1833–1835). A cycle of mystical couplets and aphoristic short poems by Adam Mickiewicz, many of them translations from mystics such as Jakob Böhme, written during the poet's particularly mystical period.

SIEBERT, Friedrich (1888–1950). Nazi general, who served for a time as head of the Department of the Interior of the General Government.

SIMONS PASSAGE—Pasaż Simonsa. A two-building commercial complex near the Old Town in Warsaw, named after Albert Simons, a German entrepreneur from Berlin, who built it in 1903. It was destroyed during the war.

GLOSSARY

SŁOWACKI, Juliusz (1809–49). Polish romantic poet, second only to Mickiewicz in the minds of most Poles as the greatest poet of the nineteenth century. His great significance is in poetic drama—fascinated by Shakespeare, he introduced Shakespearean drama to Polish literature. Some of these works are available in English translation: see Juliusz Słowacki: *Four Plays: Mary Stuart, Kordian, Balladyna, Horsztyński* (London: Glagoslav, 2018).

SOSNKOWSKI, Kazimierz (1885–1969). Polish General, Commander in Chief of the Polish Armed Forces following the death of General Władysław Sikorski in 1943. After the war, he emigrated to Canada.

STAHEL, Reiner (1892–1955). Nazi general, in charge of the Warsaw garrison during the Uprising. A war criminal, he ordered all Polish men of military age captured by the Germans to be summarily executed; he ordered the liquidation of a prison on Rakowicka St., the burning of a large number of buildings, and the use of captured Poles as human shields for German troops advancing on insurrectionary barricades. He died in a Soviet gulag.

STAWKI—A street in Warsaw that, as the name suggests, is located on terrain where ponds once stood.

STROIŃSKI, Leon Zdzisław (1921–44). Polish poet, died in the Warsaw Uprising.

SUKIENNICE—The Cloth Hall, a public building with market stalls on the Main Market Square in Kraków, originally founded at the turn of the fourteenth century.

SZUCH BOULEVARD (Aleja Szucha)—A boulevard in the central portion of Warsaw that during the occupation was reserved for Germans. At the former Ministry of Religious Confessions and Public Education, the Nazis installed their police headquarters (SD, Gestapo). The street is named for Johann Christian Schuch (Jan Christian Such, 1752–1813), a German emigrant from Dresden, who practiced architecture in Warsaw.

ŚNIADECKI STREET (Ulica Śniadeckich or, more properly, Ulica Jana i Jędrzeja Śniadeckich)—A street in central Warsaw named after the brothers Jan Śniadecki and Jędrzej Śniadecki, professors at the University of Wilno (Vilnius). Jan has entered into the Polish consciousness as the "wise-man" in Adam Mickiewicz's poem *Romantyczność* [*Romanticism*, 1822], who seeks to disprove the existence of ghosts and love lasting beyond the grave by way of a magnifying glass.

ŚRÓDMIEŚCIE—The heart of Warsaw, comprising the Old Town and the New.

UMAŃ MASSACRE—Rzeź Humańska. A massacre of Poles and Jews in the city of Umań (presently in Ukraine) that occurred during an uprising of Cossacks and Russian (Ukrainian) peasants, which took place on 20–21 June 1768.

UPRISING OF 1794—A seven-month-long Uprising of the Polish nation under the leadership of Tadeusz Kościuszko, following the Russian occupation of the country in 1792 and the quashing of the Constitution of May 3 by the Russians. Its defeat marks the Third Partition of Poland between Russia, Prussia, and Austria and the disappearance of Polish statehood until 1918.

VLASOVITES—Troops of the Russian Army of Liberation, Russians soldiers under the command of General Andriej Vlasov (hence the name) fighting alongside the Nazis.

VOLKSDEUTSCH—A term applied to persons not being citizens of the German Reich (including Austria after the Anschluss) resident outside the borders of the Reich but acknowledging themselves to be ethnically German (often to avoid the repressions facing the citizens of Nazi-occupied countries). A similar category, Reichsdeutsch, applied to citizens of the German Reich living beyond its historical borders.

VON DEM BACH, Erich (Erich Julius Eberhard von dem Bach-Zalewski, 1899–1972), German general, responsible for the stifling of the Warsaw Uprising, ironically of Polish extraction (although, as an adult and a Nazi, he did his best to distance himself from that fact). Although his hands are not free of blood (troops under his command committed war crimes against the Poles in Warsaw and elsewhere), he is said to have striven to soften the harshness of repressions ordered by Hitler and it has been suggested that it was he who convinced Hitler to acknowledge the soldiers of the Home Army as combatants.

WARSAW UPRISING—A popular uprising against the Nazi Occupiers of the Home Army and citizenry of Warsaw as the war in Europe was starting to turn against the Germans. It erupted on 1 August 1944 and lasted until 2 October of the same year. The plan was for the Poles themselves to liberate their capital city as the Soviet Red Army was advancing so as to "greet" the Russians as hosts in their own home and not to allow the Soviets the political capital of having "liberated" the city. On Stalin's orders, the Red Army halted their advance on the eastern shore of the Wisła River, in the suburb of Praga—which allowed the Nazis to decimate the population and subsequently, vindictively, to destroy what remained of the city (on the orders of a furious Hitler). The shameful decision was politically motivated, as Russia had eyes on making Poland its satellite following the war (having already received the tacit approval of Poland's "allies" Churchill and Roosevelt at the Teheran and Yalta conferences), which also handed over to the Soviet Union half of the territory of the pre-war Polish Republic (which the Soviets had invaded on 17 September 1939, in line with a previous agreement with Stalin's original allies, Nazi Germany).

WAWEL—The royal castle and cathedral complex in Kraków, set upon the hill of the same name, which has been occupied since time immemorial. It is the traditional center of government not only in Kraków but throughout Poland ever since the early Middle Ages. The cathedral itself contains the graves of many Polish kings and queens, important statesmen, and poets. During the Nazi occupation of Poland, Hans Frank installed himself in the castle, renamed Krakauer Burg, from which he ruled the General Government.

WILSON SQUARE—Plac Wilsona. A public square in Warsaw. Rymkiewicz is possibly referring here to the events of 3 May 1943 (the Polish national holiday) when, at 18:00, the underground Directorate of Civil Resistance (Kierownictwo Walki Cywilnej) managed to take over the Nazi loudspeakers on the square and deliver a patriotic program concluding with the Polish National Anthem.

DIE WELT ALS WILLE UND VORSTELLUNG—*The World as Will and Representation* (1819), a work by the German pessimistic philosopher Arthur Schopenhauer (1788–1860).

ZALESZCZYKI—A resort town on the Dniester, near the border of the Polish Republic of the time, since the re-drawing of the borders by Stalin, Churchill, and Roosevelt located in the Ukraine.

ZYGMUNT'S COLUMN—One of the central features of Palace Square; on a high column, the figure of King Zygmunt III Vasa stands, cross in hand. It was originally built in 1634–35 and restored after the war.

ŻEROMSKI, Stefan (1864–1925)—Polish novelist and playwright, a Nobel nominee. His daughter Monika (1913–2001) was an artist and illustrator.

ŻOLIBORZ—A northern district of Warsaw, on the left bank of the Wisła. The name derives from the French *joli bord,* or "pretty bank," used as early as the eighteenth century. The church of St. Ann in Warsaw is located on the Krakowskie Przedmieście—and so the suggestion is that, according to this account, the Liberator in question would be flying up from the south—or any other direction than from the north. The bell tower is separate from the main corpus of the church. The Krasiński Square (Plac Krasińskich) is to the north-west of St Ann's.

This book was set in Plantin, designed by Frank Hinman Pierpont and Fritz Stelzer and published in 1913. It is based on the "Gros Cicero" type created by Robert Granjon in the sixteenth-century which the modern designers found in the Plantin-Moretus Musuem—an institution devoted to the history of printing— in Antwerp, Belgium.

This book was designed by Shannon Carter, Ian Creeger, and Gregory Wolfe. It was published in hardcover, paperback, and electronic formats by Slant Books, Seattle, Washington.

Cover photograph: *Polish boy in the ruins of Warsaw September 1939* by Julien Bryan.

www.ingramcontent.com/pod-product-compliance
Lightning Source LLC
Chambersburg PA
CBHW030854170426
43193CB00009BA/602